# SOCIAL DREAMING
# IN THE 21ST CENTURY

# SOCIAL DREAMING IN THE 21ST CENTURY
## The world we are losing

*John Clare and Ali Zarbafi*

Foreword by W. Gordon Lawrence

**KARNAC**

First published in 2009 by
Karnac Books Ltd
118 Finchley Road
London NW3 5HT

British Library Cataloguing in Publication Data

A C.I.P. for this book is available from the British Library

ISBN-13: 978-1-85575-554-3

Typeset by Vikatan Publishing Solutions (P) Ltd., Chennai, India


www.karnacbooks.com

# CONTENTS

# ACKNOWLEDGEMENTS

We are very grateful to all the dreamers in each of the matrices without whose dream telling and associations this book would not have been possible.

In particular we want to show our appreciation to the hundreds of people at the Hay Festival who contributed their dreams by letter, email and in person. This includes the people of the town of Hay on Wye many of whom took part. Their interest and enthusiasm (and their dreaming) was inspiring. We apologise to those many contributors whose dreams were ultimately not included in the text. They nevertheless played a vital part in the whole project and we read and reflected on every dream.

We would also like to thank Clare Purcell and Peter Florence at the Hay Literary Festival without whose help our study would have been much more difficult.

Also many thanks to Jane Storr for her personal reflection of the End of the Dance.

Last but not least our gratitude to Dr. Karen Baistow Clare whose support, editing and sense of humour have been invaluable.

# FOREWORD

## 'DREAMING THE SOCIAL'

John Clare and Ali Zarbafi came to the project of 'dreaming the social' from backgrounds in sociology and psychoanalysis and have pursued it with different groupings from heterogeneous backgrounds, as varied as writers at the Hay-on-Wye literary festival and the staff of a community centre for young people in North London. Both are psychotherapists, but they successfully have made the mental transition from an ego-centric orientation in their private practices to the socio-centric one demanded by 'dreaming the social'. They have written a book of dream research that is, probably, unrivalled because of the profundity of the detail of dreaming and their discussions of each dreaming event. They have made a major contribution to 'dreaming the social', joining others in the international community who pursue the same objective.

What is meant by 'dreaming the social'? Human beings have been doing it for millennia, certainly from the time of *The Epic of Gilgamesh* dating from the third millennium BC which makes it the oldest oral, epic poem describing Gilgamesh's futile search for immortality. 'Dreaming the social' demands a different mind set, and a different method from that used in personal psychotherapy. The two approaches to dreaming can be seen as complementary, both adding to knowledge.

The authors consistently used the same method of research throughout their dreaming projects. Because the idea of 'dreaming and the social' may be unfamiliar an attempt will be made to clarify its meaning to provide a context for the book.

Dreaming has been associated with individuals and the analysis of their psychopathology, since the time of Freud. While this century-old project has added substantially to the knowledge about the psychic life of individuals, it could not directly inform the social context and culture in which individuals live. One major difference between individual and 'dreaming the social' is that in the former the perspective is on the individual dreamers and their personal problems, but in the latter it is the knowledge contained in the dream that is the focus.

Taking this different vertex resulted in a number of other key ideas. 'Dreaming and the social' is done simultaneously with a number of people (the number can be as small as six and as much as a hundred). This is a major shift from therapeutic encounter with its dyad.

As founder of social dreaming I had been preoccupied with dreaming because it was felt that it could make a contribution, as a tool of cultural enquiry, to the quality of human living because it always seems to illumine the current problems of existence. This hypothesis came to mind in the late 1970s. While on the scientific staff of the Tavistock Institute of Human Relations, London, a personal psychoanalysis was deemed to be the essential element of professional training to be a consultant who used psychoanalytic insights for social research. (Indeed, it then was written into the contract of employment.) But psychoanalysis is designed for the education of individuals into the nature of their psyche and the quality of their psychic existence; it cannot be used directly in action-research to understand the social life of schools, hospitals and industrial organizations. The idea of using the dream in social and cultural contexts was heretic for senior colleagues as psychoanalysis was seen to be the private project of individuals.

A number of experiences led to the idea of social dreaming. There was the anthropological literature which made use of psychoanalysis in cultural research. More immediately, there were experiences derived from interviews with role-holders in industry, e.g. the senior manager who dreamt of coming to work each day through a grave-yard, resulting in the insight that the company was in financial jeopardy. The most important experience was the work on Group Relations done at the Tavistock to understand the place and effect of the unconscious on group life. This tradition had started with the pioneering work of Wilfred Bion who discovered the importance of the basic assumptions that could unconsciously inform the life of working groups.

In the introduction to his classic *Experiences in Groups* he made a critical distinction as to how psychoanalysis could order the phenom-ena being encountered. First, there was the Oedipus vertex which looked at the pairing relationships of the individual participant. This was to match psychoanalytic insights to the individual. Second, there was the sphinx vertex which examined the knowledge and the scien-tific understanding that the *group as a whole* were using to make sense of the life of the group. This is to make psychoanalysis relevant to the systemic dimensions of the group by understanding the unconscious culture on which the group as a totality is proceeding to perform, or not, the purpose, or primary task of the entity (Bion, 1961).

The question became: how could the sphinx perspective be used in the study of dreams, how could dreaming be used for the cultural exploration of systems and society? The Oedipal vertex is highly regarded in psychoanalytic practice as analysands and practicing psychoanalysts pursue the project of understanding the psyche of the individual. Freud had made this a central, indeed a defining, feature of his life-work. Although I had valued the benefits of my own psychoanalysis, there was still the puzzle of how this dream thinking could inform the social.

Every human culture, society, civilization, and the social group-ings they generate, or rely on, owe their existence to the human mind. But as George Frankl, the philosopher and psychoanalyst, observes this social reality is not determined by 'objective reality', it arises from human beings unconscious minds. He writes, '...any study of man's social reality, the external conditions as well as our responses to them must acknowledge that it is humanity which creates its con-ditions and, what is more, does so largely unconsciously, and then depends on the conditions it has created' (Frankl, 1989, p. xvii).

If dreaming has long been recognized as an unrivalled entry to the unconscious minds of humans, how could dreams be used to understand the conditions of social reality? To cut a long story short, social dreaming was re-discovered at the Tavistock Institute in 1982 by devising the Social Dreaming Matrix.

Why was matrix chosen as the container for Social Dreaming? Group was the obvious choice. However, in devising Social Dreaming the organizing idea was to focus on the dream exclusively with its embedded knowledge and scientific method. If it had been a group as a container the chances are that group phenomena could have become the focus, to the detriment of discovering the knowledge of the dreams.

'Group' could be used as a system of defence against the discomforting challenge of grappling with the unknown of matrix, i.e. the awesomeness of the unconscious. What was already known of groups could interfere with the unknown. Individual and group phenomena are held in suspension by the matrix. Although this was originally an intuitive decision, it has proven to be the correct one in the long run, for a matrix exists to explore what only a matrix can discover. Matrix can be likened to a mental Faraday Cage excluding extraneous processes which would interfere with the act of dreaming and its related exploration.

A pure matrix is when a diversity of people are gathered together, having had no previous contact. In actuality, members may come from the same institutional background, e.g. a counselling centre, or a firm. Matrix represents the 'matrix of the undifferentiated unconscious' (Ehrenzweig, 1964). Even though the dreamers come from the same institution the possibility of mentally attaining the configuration of the matrix, allows the free-flow of the unconscious, undifferentiated thinking which is present in every group, every social relation, all social reality, but rarely voiced.

Although the idea of dreaming socially is not new, the invention of the Social Dreaming Matrix is. It provided a method for discovering new dimensions of the dream experience. Free association and amplification are recognised ways of working with dreams. These take on different meanings in Social Dreaming, as opposed to individual psychotherapy. The former eschews the certainty of the 'interpretation', often spurious, but uses the dreams and the associations to make working hypotheses on the dreams and themes that connect, to develop thinking on what the dreams are telling the matrix, and the larger systems represented by the matrix. Interpretation narrows the meanings of the dreaming, whereas working hypothesis (sketches of what the reality might be) enlarges the thinking of the dreaming.

The Social Dreaming Matrix only lasts for a limited time, and always begins with a statement of purpose provided by the hosts, which is the name given to the consultants, or takers. The participants have an image of what, and how, they are to explore in the Social Dreaming Matrix, to play in it, but also know that it is a temporary arrangement which will end.

Very often there is a thinking group, or Dream Reflection Dialogue, for a short period after the Social Dreaming Matrix ends. While Social Dreaming is a liberating experience, it can become an entertainment exclusively but from the beginning Social Dreaming was seen in the context of work. The Dream Reflection Dialogue is an attempt to make a bridge from the dream-time to the world of reality, work and consciousness, making use of any insights and findings derived from the Matrix.

Social Dreaming is not an abstract venture for the knowledge of the dreams comes from the lived, night-time, experience of the dream. It is personal knowledge to differentiate it from knowledge of the inanimate world, i.e. mathematics, physics, mechanics, with their associated metaphors and formal logic. Personal knowledge is also different from knowledge of the organic world, i.e. biology with its organic and evolutionary metaphors. Both inanimate and biological knowledge are *knowledge about*, acquired intellectually through concepts and theory, as opposed to personal knowledge which is *knowledge of*, derived from sense experience and is understanding based on what two, or more, people agree to be real. Personal knowledge is the highest form of knowledge, containing the other two. To be fully aware of the world through the senses means paying attention to emotions which often will be hidden from conscious awareness, i.e. will be motivated by the unconscious. As MacMurray, the Scottish philosopher who first adumbrated these forms of knowledge, writes, 'Emotion stands directly behind activity determining its substance and direction' (MacMurray, 1935, p. 26).

With this heuristic perspective, Clare and Zarbafi proceed to unpack, deconstruct, the dreams in a variety of matrices. What may surprise is the wealth of thinking expressed through free association in the matrices and the symbolic links made. The free association leads to expansion of thinking, indeed to the infinite, as the range of possible meanings are explored in the matrix.

Clare and Zarbafi have contributed to the study of Social Dreaming by joining the international community of practitioners. Since its re-discovery in 1982 Social Dreaming is pursued in the UK, Ireland, the USA, Australia, India, Israel, Rwanda, Spain, Italy, Switzerland, France, Germany, Poland, Hungary, Holland and Sweden. Most of this is done by Social Dreaming Limited, London, but other practitioners have taken on the idea of dreaming the social, e.g. The Jungians, the American Group Psychotherapy Association, the Systems Centred Therapy conference, followers of Transactional Analysis, and others not known.

In choosing the name Social Dreaming, the basic idea was to define the sphere of enquiry while being parsimonious and unpretentious. Inevitably, others have taken the method to 're-badge' it for their own purposes claiming it as their own. So cultural dreaming comes into existence and organizational dreaming, but these special applications were anticipated in the original, generic idea.

Clare and Zarbafi have stuck with the original formulation to produce a very rich text through working at the free associations in the Matrix, thus extending the thinking of the participants and themselves with their *apercus*, insights and literary references throughout the text, coupled with their very substantial discussions of the findings of the Matrix as evinced by the dream thinking of the participants. As such, as has been indicated, they have made a major contribution to the social dreaming project.

What is exciting about the matrices is that the extraordinary characteristics of the unconscious are made ordinary and tractable to people without any specialized knowledge. At the beginning of the twentieth century the unconscious was seen as belonging to the individual, 'inside' the person and, consequently, it became gagged and bound by this narrow, narcissistic perspective. As people began to discover how groups worked dynamically, there grew the realization that an individual unconscious was related to others with their unconscious. This move from an egocentric position to a socio-centric one, led, on the basis of the evidence, to the construct of the 'social unconscious', i.e. that the unconscious was also 'outside' of people. The Social Dreaming Matrix acknowledges this which makes the unconscious less about human beings' personal repressed sexual desires or aggressive motivations but more directed to social reality where the unconscious pervades all social relations influencing life in work organization, the family, social configurations. politics and economics.

In an age when Reason is treated as an ideology, even as a god, leading to a near totalitarian state-of-mind, much of thinking which is non-rational is dismissed from daily discourse. Social Dreaming had to be discovered to make this lateral and divergent thinking and thought accessible through the dreaming of the unconscious. The paradox is that the more reason is venerated and used exclusively, the more the unconscious will influence life, even though it is constantly denied. (Chapter One) Furthermore, reason comes through science and technology to be instrumental in the domination of nature, comes to be used as a means to power and for manipulation of others, frequently serving goals that are contrary to reasonable thinking (Frankl, 1989, p. 31). Human ends and spontaneities are thus negated.

There are two exceptions to all the other reported matrices. One is the chapter entitled 'Counselling for Adolescents—Dreaming in the Inner City'. This is singled out as it could be a model for action-research. The staff of the centre which provided a service for young people in a run-down area of London was invited to participate in a Social Dreaming Matrix. Although it was only for a day, and some were ambivalent to talk about their dreams, the matrix discerned the feelings, thoughts, and opinions of the staff in a direct, vivid way. The personal knowledge was used in a way that would have eluded conventional, qualitative research using interviews, group discussions and questionnaires. The Matrix achieved in one day what conventional research would have taken months, possibly, to complete. They were able to identify the difficulties of work 'as a fence' around the counsellors, be aware of the need to think together as they dreamt of their practice with its issues of growth, autonomy and the contemporary, social life of very under-privileged adolescents.

The other is Chapter Six, which is the report of a mass dreaming experiment conducted at the Hay-on-Wye festival of 2005. The authors collected a few thousand dreams by post and personally during the festival. This innovative approach to social dreaming mirrors Mass-Observation but relies on pure dreaming in contrast to interviewing. No matrix was held, but the matrix existed in the minds of the dreamers. As ever they write a riveting account of this experiment which taps the dreaming mind of the respondents, offering a new slant on contemporary pre-occupations.

Among all the conclusions that can be drawn from this text, one is pre-eminent. The Social Dreaming Matrix has shown that the unconscious is not all bad experiences, to be avoided and dismissed as so much junk, but is also a source of creativity, the source of the bright idea. It can be benign and good. All the participants in the matrices reported were drawn unwittingly into this creative milieu as they voiced their dreams and associations and, most importantly, were able to express new thoughts and thinking to be heard by others.

The last word is to be left to the authors. In the final chapter they write: 'There is a purity to social dreaming as a method, or a form, because it is like a clear window onto a vast landscape, helping to pinpoint the whole and parts of the landscape, as well as seeing what is missed, and how much more there is. In this way it creates possibilities of creative thinking on many levels from the human to the cultural, to the organizational and to the family. Every social dreaming matrix taps into deep collective possibilities, which can be discovered in that moment with that group of people on many levels' (Chapter Eight).

Gordon Lawrence

# The world we are losing

"No one knows who will live in this cage in the future ... specialists without spirit, sensualists without heart, this nullity imagines that it has attained a level of civilisation never before achieved".

—Max Weber, 1880

We are running out of ideas in Western society. Faced with global warming, Third World devastation, nuclear proliferation and the threat posed by religious conflict, we need new ways of thinking. After the loss and carnage of the Twentieth Century there is a prevailing mood of uncertainty and paranoia, yet at the same time a denial of tragedy, a salvation fantasy, an illusion that we will be saved. The decline in social solidarity, the fragmentation of communal values and a growing sense of 'I' as opposed to 'we', are all signs of an inversion of moral certitudes, a disconnection from reality. This book asks what methods do we have at our disposal to understand and reverse this breakdown of communication within and between communities. In an age overshadowed by the memory of Auschwitz and the fear of nuclear annihilation, there has been a deadening of the soul, a weakening of our

inner being and of our intuitive connection to the universe. This book
is about the world that we are in danger of losing.

> *"The capacity to be amazed and surprised may be a faculty that man-*
> *kind in the West is in danger of losing. Despite the growth of psy-*
> *chology and the social sciences in general, man may already have lost*
> *the faculty of imaginative awareness and consciousness that takes*
> *him beyond his immediate, narcissistic preoccupations with survival*
> *in contemporary mass industrial society to link him with what may*
> *underlie existence."*

(Lawrence, 2000, p. 182)

This world that is fast disappearing—the interior world of the
novel, the capacity for play, the imagination, the dream, the unconscious, a sense of collective solidarity—is crucial to what makes life
feel worthwhile. In this book we suggest that, in losing touch with
the unconscious, we are losing a vital link to an essential part of our
nature without which we may not survive. This self reflexive faculty,
the spirit of an intuitive moral sensibility, would, in the past, have
been referred to as the 'soul'. It is a vital inner awareness of ourselves
which has been overlaid and dislocated by the logic of Western capitalism, especially since the Second World War. In this late capitalist
world our lives have changed radically. Soap operas and reality television are treated as if part of real life. In fashion magazines, vacuity
is promoted as a desirable motif celebrating anorexia and narcissism.
The cult of celebrity reduces the human figure to commodity and mere
image. Photography and advertising strip everything away leaving
only appearance, with no feelings or inner depth. Young people now
go to music concerts to photograph themselves, to watch themselves
being watched. In Frederick Jameson's phrase, there has been a 'waning of affect', emotion is dissipated, with apparently nothing inside
and nothing to express (Jameson, 1996).

As psychotherapists we have noticed that, in addition to the
paranoid and narcissistic configurations of the Twentieth Century,
we now encounter people with lives so busy and complex that they
don't have time to think: people with unliveable lives of relent-
less acting out. There is a kind of chaos where the unconscious
has been ejected, evacuating our 'otherness' into a shallow world
of gloss and fragmentation. We meet patients who demand quick
solutions for highly complex life problems just as they would order

fast-food from McDonalds. As a response to unprecedented levels of 'depression' in British society, the present government intends to set up counselling services to treat people with a meagre six sessions of cognitive behavioural therapy. These have already been called 'happiness centres.' The quick-fix mentality is pervasive. People have lives where there is not enough time to talk to their children, read a book or make love. Interminable consumer activity stymies the possibility of internal reflection. Shopping, eating, overworking, or fanatical jogging may all, in part, be used as displacement activities to avoid finding out how we actually feel, who we really are. Parents are over-protective, surveillance is ever-present, any element of risk is legislated into oblivion.

Intimacy is problematic. There is an atmosphere of hysteria which is especially associated with sex and this has led to political correctness and a phobia of molestation. It can now be perceived as dangerous for a man to show genuine affection for little children. Parenting for some has become a wary and self-conscious role. Many parents dare not touch their children and are fearful of actually telling them what to do. In recent research at Kent University, *most* men said, when asked, that they would not pick-up a distressed child that was crying (Furedi, 2001). Despite unprecedented affluence, Britain and the USA have the most depressed children in the western world. This is not to imply that previous circumstances were without faults but rather that something vital to our being is now disappearing.

## The ethos of the book

In a society in which individuality and autonomy have been marginalized by organizational bureaucracy and technological mass reproduction, perhaps it is not surprising that there is little space for the dream. This book is a challenge to the orthodoxy which insists that science and rationality are the only solutions to the problems we face. In the Eighteenth Century the Enlightenment promised justice, liberty and happiness within societies of coherent political order. This has not come about. Fascism and Soviet Communism were two results of this idea. Mass poverty co-exists with space-travel; affluent capitalist societies have high rates of mental illness. This is not to reject science and reason—both of which play an essential part in shaping and understanding the world—but we do share Max Weber's scepticism of the Enlightenment's faith in progressive scientific reason as a means to control nature and ourselves. In the 19th Century he predicted that the increasing rationalisation of human life in capitalist societies would trap individuals in an iron cage of rules and bureaucratic control. Rationality would supplant the soul in a social order which he referred to as the "polar night of icy darkness." (Weber, 1905) The age of reason, despite its undoubted benefits, has had a dehumanizing effect. Rationality has replaced meaning. Bureaucracy and controlled planning for a "better society" has resulted in the deaths of millions of people. Descartes' 'I think therefore I am' encapsulates only one particular view of what it is to be human—of rationality, consciousness and reason, contained within a discrete body; a self which is aware of itself. This book suggests there is more to us than this unified controlled concept of a human being. It invites the reader to take seriously the idea that we are often ruled by forces and ideas of which we are not conscious and that this applies to societies as well as individuals. The present research suggests that we could discover much more about ourselves and the world we inhabit and that this is made possible by taking our dream life seriously and taking the trouble to share it with others. It is a subversive idea. Social Dreaming has been banned in many totalitarian societies. This project is not about order or control but about shared meaning and the power of thinking together; rather than leaving it to 'experts' who know what is best for us. Instead of 'I think therefore I am' we might substitute 'I dream therefore I am able to think thoughts which I did not know I had.' It is the things we *don't* know we know, which give us strength and make the world more interesting, coherent and surprising. Aboriginal people, the Native American Indians, the Senoi tribe of Malaya are examples of societies where a sophisticated understanding of unconscious knowledge, through taking dreams seriously, once helped these so-called primitive people to survive, living relatively peaceful lives in harmony with nature. The practice of social dreaming, rediscovered by W. Gordon Lawrence in the 1980's, offers a different path towards communication and understanding, a form of self-expression to gain access to things we know but are unable to think.

## The experience of social dreaming

Social Dreaming means the coming together of individuals to share their dreams and associate to them in a gathering called a matrix.

This book is about several such meetings, each in very different circumstances. It describes and reflects on the sense that people make of their shared dreaming in the context of the social environment. It also examines the *process* of Social Dreaming: in other words the experience itself, what it feels like, how and why it constitutes a unique way of human relating. At the core of this phenomenon is the inaccessible truth of social reality, the gap, the thing which is always missing when we meet one another. What Lacan calls the 'excluded interior', or The Real. This absence can only be represented by something else. Crucially this something else may often be the dream itself. There is a sense of disconnection, absence and separation in most of our adult encounters. We never seem to 'know' or 'reach' the other person entirely, or them us. This impossibility of relationship opens up something new—the contingency of the encounter. Social dreaming has this quality of The Real, a confluence of the inaccessible and the intimate. There is an impossibility between what is said and the thing itself. The dreaming discourse stands for this gap. Dreams frequently reveal the unthinkability of certain thoughts.

The fact that the social dreaming matrix is such a fitting configuration for working with a dream is because the process itself matches dreaming. This enables a sense of freedom in the social encounter. Many people have reported a feeling of lightness or liberation during the dreaming discourse. Using the language of psychoanalysis, this rarefied, intense sense of relating has been described in various ways. For Winnicott, it is the playful use of an object, for Wilfred Bion 'reverie', or, for Christopher Bollas, the of dissemination of the self's aesthetic. These ideas are explored further in the chapter on Social Dreaming and the Self.

## The research

The book is based on the following social dreaming research since September 2000:

- A three year dreaming and thinking matrix in London, including dreams before and after the 9/11 attacks on the World Trade Centre.
- Social dreaming with writers and visitors at the literary festival of Hay-on-Wye in 2003 and 2004.

- Social dreaming conferences in Southern France with dreamers from different countries.
- Dream research with counsellors and health workers on a deprived, multi-cultural housing estate in North London.
- A mass dreaming experiment in which several hundred dreams were collected and analysed during a ten day period.
- Various dreaming matrixes with refugee workers, psychotherapists, children and academics.

## The effect of 9/11

All the material described in the book came after the al Quaida suicide attack on New York in September 2001. This event has engendered an atmosphere of instability and vigilance. People are trying to decipher the future, not hopefully but guided by dread. As chapter 4 will show, dreams changed after the attack on the twin Towers. For a short time people seemed unable to dream. The vista of terrorism and a breakdown in mutual perceptions of reality had been a feature of dream-work throughout the 1990s. In many ways after 9/11 the night thoughts had a more intense edge– firstly in recovering from the shock which dreamers registered and then in contemplating future fears and past failures. The sense that the world had changed appeared repeatedly in many dreams and conversations.

## How it was written

This book is collaboration. We are two psychotherapists, a Freudian and a Jungian, who trained together. Together we have listened to and discussed literally thousands of dreams. Our interest in Social Dreaming developed out of a post graduate reading group, led by Dr. Judit Szekacs, in the early nineties. After this we worked with Gordon Lawrence in various dreaming matrixes in London, France and Wales. Originally we had both studied sociology which, when complemented by psychotherapy, has found expression in the amalgam of 'dreaming and the social' which is the territory of this book. Thus the work is collaboration between two different analytic traditions, produced in the spirit of shared ideas, acknowledged differences and a mutual belief in free association and the primacy of the dream. In addition to Freud and Jung, we are influenced by thinkers such as Donald Winnicott, Wilfred Bion, Christopher Bollas and readers will find an exposition of some of their ideas in the Chapter on Social Dreaming and the Self. The work of Gordon Lawrence has been an overarching influence since we first worked with him in 1994.

## How to read it

The heart of this book is made up of six chapters which give examples of social dreaming in different settings. We start with two chapters of a more theoretical nature which we hope readers will find useful as references to explain and expand some of the concepts used in the later chapters. They are personal statements of our two different approaches to the work. The essence of social dreaming is experiential. We felt it important to explore aspects of this praxis and process to demonstrate what is unique about the shared experience of the matrix. Thus chapter 8 presents a detailed, almost verbatim, day to day account of an intense 5 day matrix in the south of France. It should be useful for anyone who wants to understand the ricochet of the dreams and associations, re-called and echoed in the spontaneity of the dream-telling. We have also included a brief glossary of the less familiar terms.

* * * *

# CHAPTER ONE

# Social dreaming and the self

*John Clare*

"Freud democratised genius by giving everyone a creative unconscious."

—Philip Rieff, 1987

The shared experience of Social Dreaming is quite unlike most other ways of having a conversation. This chapter is an attempt to describe the phenomenology of the matrix in order to understand what happens to the self in Social Dreaming. First I want to look at the connection between self experience and free association and to ask what we mean when we talk about being real or 'true to ourselves'. Then I will use the work of four psychoanalytical writers to elucidate the freedom and aliveness of mind, and its relation to the social, which is typical of the social dreaming matrix.

## The night train

People often dream about trains and train journeys. Freud invited his patients, when they were embarking on psychoanalysis, to tell him whatever came into their heads, no matter how trivial or embarrassing. He suggested they imagined a train journey where they looked out of the window and reported to their analyst every-thing they saw as the world flew past, even the smallest things.

> 'Act as though, for instance, you were a traveller sitting next to the window of a railway carriage and describing to someone inside the carriage the changing views which you see outside.' (Freud, 1913, p. 135)

Here Freud was introducing them to the process of free association, the basic rule of analysis, that most subversive idea that they should just speak clearly everything that came into their minds. This is some-thing ordinary which we all do internally every day, thinking to our-selves, one idea following another. Freud's innovation was to suggest that in the analytic session these meandering thoughts were spoken out loud, so that even the most irrelevant ideas could be heard.

> "It is uniformly found that precisely those ideas (the irrel-evant) … are of particular value in discovering the forgotten material" (Bollas, 2002, pp. 7–8).*

Freud introduced a train journey to illustrate how free association creates a 'train of thought'. Most of us probably have memories of being on a train. My own experience of a journey in France evokes the following vignette. Imagine you are on the night train from Paris to Geneva. As the train moves through the night, you walk slowly down the coach observing the sleeping passengers. Just as one thought leads to another, you pass from one coach to another and observe the next night-time interior. By the time you arrive in Geneva, you have reached the last coach and come to the end of the train. Similarly a train of thought starts in one place and leads from one thought to another, and then another, until it reaches its destina-tion. Looking back, through all the connecting coaches, you can then see how you arrived at this latest thought. A dream is like the night train from Paris to Geneva. As you wake up you begin to recollect all the different, inter-connected night thoughts which have trav-elled through your mind but remain intact and undisturbed in the dream. In the social dreaming matrix, one dream leads to another.

---

* This brief book is an excellent resume of the concept of free association.

This dream sparks off a new train of thought, which further elicits someone else's dream and then more thoughts and more dreams and so on. The following week another stream of ideas from our nocturnal travels is recounted and the journey continues. There is no destination: just the next dream.

Trains of thought can lead to thoughts of trains. At a matrix in the South of France, one dreamer noted that the subject of trains reminded him of a sign which stood by the roadside near many French railway crossings. It read, "*Un train peut se cacher un autre*" (one train may hide another) and this in turn suggested that an unknown thought may be hidden behind an object in one of the dreams. Similarly, one dream may hide another. This leads us to Christopher Bollas's idea of the *unthought known*, (Bollas, 1987) a concept which is central to the social dreaming matrix—that we know things which we are unable to think, thoughts which remain unknown until we are able to dream them. Such 'thoughts' are easily discarded. Sadly, in a society where people demand the quick fix, the hard fact, the measurable result most people discard their dreams as surplus junk, even though they may then be haunted by them throughout the day. And yet a dream may hide a train of thought which could radically alter our lives, change the journey we take, bring us to a different destination. Social dreaming is about the social—what concerns us in the world and yet evades our waking mind—but it is also about the self. The self which is hidden behind another self, behind the constructed shape of our being which has developed over time with a logic and coherence which we are expected to live up to and yet which evades something real inside us; the thing that is missing which makes us what we are. Of course psychotherapy is also concerned with this hidden self but social dreaming entails its public discovery, its gradual flickering emergence into a train of thought, taken on by others and given back to the individual in the form of new ideas, other dreams, fresh metaphors.

The matrix is not a hermeneutic group of interpreters or organisational analysts; it is a body of dreamers on the night train to Geneva with their own nocturnal baggage, sleep thoughts, passing glimpses of towns and stations and their own dream-like destinations, hopes and desires. As dreamers, they are all on the same train and on their own different trains. None of them knows where s/he'll arrive. The destination, if there is one, is to arrive at our subliminal, shared knowledge about the social world. At the same time it is a venue for the unknowable, inchoate but potential self. Through our dreams, as we encounter the vitality of objects, we explore the mystery of the world and our being in it. The train of thought—this free flowing caravanserai of associations which come in response to a dream— creates new thoughts. It extends who we are. Treating dreams as living objects of creativity, provides insight and this, in turn, invokes further dreams. Thus the world, and our self in it, becomes the dream work of our life. At night, while asleep, we allow ourselves to dissolve. We deconstruct who we are into strange and various identities. We dream ourselves into being. 'We are a dream that dreams.' (Unamuno, 1954, p. 39)

Within this apparently impossible aphorism lies a metaphorical truth: everything that exists does so because of our capacity to think—from the wilderness to the wheel, from French cuisine to jumbo jets. These things are only possible because of our capacity for thought: and our thinking originates in the dream. Dreams are our first access to thought in the hallucinatory state of infancy when we dream close to the mother's body. Thus the dream always has a trace of the maternal. We conjure up a reality upon which we can then reflect, introducing the paternal symbolic order of thought. Hence Bollas's term 'Mother Dream, Father Thought'. (Bollas, 1987, p. 73) We dream ourselves into being, we are a dream that dreams.

*New ways of seeing*

Little has been written about the contingency of the dream and yet a chance encounter with an idea or an image in our own dream, or in the dreaming of another, may have a profound effect on our life. This change will not necessarily be conscious. We can be moved by fragments. Something glimpsed at the margins may have the most significance. We may think that reason rules our lives but we are not discrete, consistent, unified entities. The mind constantly contradicts itself. As Freud discovered, our lives are ruled by irrational forces. Conscious perception is only a fraction of what we know through our senses. Most of what we perceive is through subliminal perception and most of our mental life takes place unknown to us.

*"Our lives are more like fragmentary dreams than the enactments of our conscious selves. We control very little of what we most care about; many of our most fateful decisions are made unbeknown to ourselves. Yet we insist that mankind can achieve what we cannot: conscious mastery of its existence."* (Gray, 2002, p. 38)

Unconscious and 'other' ways of seeing the world have largely been expunged by Western perception. We live in a world which in many ways devalue any form of expression outside the rational, positivist ideal of late capitalism. And yet we clearly need new ways of thinking and have to look to artists, musicians, poets and playwrights for alternatives to the cultural norm. All of these forms are closer to the dream; closer to the imaginative order of maternal reverie than to the paternal language of the social order which has faltered so drastically in recent history. Science, logic and measured control serve only to give us one truth, one version of the human condition, one way of treating one another. Like a dream, a work of art provides another version of reality. Van Gogh presents a universal image of suffering in his 'Peasants Shoes'. The Expressionists painted intense emotional landscapes: Edvard Munch portrays the abject anxiety and sickness of modernity; the Fauves created their own emotional language of colour; the Surrealists took images directly from dreams; de Kooning's primitive women emerge from abstract daubes which tell of some ineffable reality, some pre-verbal haunting, unavailable to ordinary consciousness. Picasso's fragmented portraits break up the image, revealing something in its entirety and thus creating an object which can then be used by the viewer for self-realization. Something real is expressed which does not pertain to the given accepted world. Perhaps we could say, with Kafka, that art is the axe for the frozen sea within us. Early Paleolithic cave paintings described a vision without the hindsight of history and civilization, a view free of self-surveillance. Here is one representation of the sense-world we risk losing, with its lack of propriety, its subliminal sensitivity, its intuitive understanding of nature and its receptiveness to the dream.

The way we see and understand reality has changed and with that something vital has disappeared. It is this intuitive, numinous way of seeing which can, in some ways, be revived in the social dreaming process. Our perception is largely culture-bound and our basic assumptions are repeatedly reflected in the world around us. We continually find out what we already know. In modern consumerist societies there is increasingly less agency of free thinking to act as a catalyst and challenge these implicit ideas and thus create a space for new ideas to be tested. Even art has become part and parcel of the market mentality with the post-modern irony of work produced as a critique of a capitalist world, which it simultaneously embraces with very high price tags.

Social dreaming is an antidote to this conformist world of ready-made ideas and taken for granted truth. It creates a space in which to think without having to fit in or conform. The matrix enables an unmediated form of perception with less need for self-scrutiny or justification. It can thus help to soften the internal saboteur of the psyche: to suspend the habitual dialogue of critical self-surveillance by letting us use our dreams to elaborate unconscious aspects of the world we know. As one social dreamer put it, "It gives us permission to be who we are." The hypothesis here is that, in this way, it can even enable us to identify with the extremes suffered by distant oppressed people who we may never meet. I have illustrated this elsewhere with reference to dreams of the crisis in Third-World countries in the months before 9/11. (Clare, 2002, p. 57) These were dreams which delineated the experiences of people at the margins of human existence. This 'identifying-with-others-through-dreams' is comparable to the profound apperception engendered by contact with the art or music of people who sing or paint about loss and rejection, sadness and joy. Jazz musicians from Harlem, the gypsy groups of Romania, the Township musicians of South Africa, Aboriginal artists, Flamenco, American blues singers of the Deep South are examples of this 'dreaming' identification.

## Dada and Expressionism: when Kurt Schwitters met George Grosz

'Being a person' is a continually moving, fluid experience. The self which acts and reacts to this perception is also not a fixed, absolute, finite entity. Paradoxically, this self can come into being only if we abandon the attempt to know it. It is only if we can stop being who we are, that we can 'be' ourselves. Only when we stop trying to compose ourselves, can we get a glimpse of who we might be behind our self-conscious attempt to be somebody we construct.

When we look in the mirror who is it we see? Although the conventional notion of reality tells us that we *do* have a self which is fixed and definable, an identity pinned to a name or category: although we can talk of a public and a private self as if it is self-evident who we are: although we may seem predictable, obvious, knowable— what do we actually mean when we talk about our *self*?

*One day in pre-war Germany, the Dadaist painter Kurt Schwitters decided he wanted to meet George Grosz, the outspoken German Expressionist.*

*George Grosz was decidedly surly; the hatred in his pictures often overflowed into his private life. But Schwitters was not one to be put off. He wanted to meet Grosz so Mehring (a friend) took him up to Grosz's flat. Schwitters rang the bell and Grosz opened the door.*

*"Good morning Herr Grosz my name is Schwitters,"*

*"I am not Grosz," answered the other and slammed the door. There was nothing to be done.*

*Halfway down the stairs Schwitters stopped and said "Just a moment". Up the stairs he went and once more rang Grosz's bell. Grosz, enraged by the continual jangling, opened the door, but before he could say a word, Schwitters said, "I am not Schwitters, either". And went down stairs again. Finis. They never met again.* (Richter, 1965, p. 145)

In addition to Schwitters' spontaneity and wit, there is a serious idea here. In a sense, perhaps both men were right. Grosz was not Grosz and Schwitters was not Schwitters. We are never who we seem to be. The name of a man suggests a unified entity, a coherent discrete personality with a fixed set of traits, temperament, attributes and appearance. But does a self experience itself in this consistent and logical way? If someone mentions Margaret Thatcher, or the name of your best friend, you probably know exactly who they are talking about. A character springs to life and you see someone in your mind's eye, you have an emotional sense of who they are, a coherent solid image of a person, an internal memory of their being. Emotion returns before memory. You remember how you feel about that person. But if you suddenly hear your *own* name spoken you may have no idea who that person is. We do not experience our own self as a coherent character. We are not logical or consistent, we change from moment to moment, we are endlessly contradictory and who we are could not possibly be summed up in a name. We do not add up. We are many different things. We are a dream that dreams.

### The self as invention

Our existence as a person is an invention. We are not an observable concrete fact but a complex set of ideas. Of course we have a body which we can see in the mirror but that is not who we are. We are not born with a fully-formed, character or personality, rather this is made and negotiated gradually over time in relation to our environment as we discover and elaborate experience. The formatives stage of development in infancy, childhood and adolescence is crucial but who we are is continually developing and changing throughout the rest of life.

In the given context of a family, society and culture (over which we have little choice), we then 'make' ourselves with our thoughts and feelings, expressed in words and music, work and play, tragedy and comedy, fears and desires. Dreaming is part of this process of becoming. Dreams and day-dreams in infancy are our first forms of thinking. We dream about being and becoming, about 'me' and 'not me', and this creates a sense of an inside, an interior world in which to think and feel. This in turn extends and changes what we find. In a sense our dreams create who we are. This is what Shakespeare poignantly alludes to when he says,

> We are such stuff as dreams are made on
> And our little life is rounded with a sleep

> (Shakespeare, The Tempest)

As Gordon Lawrence has shown, this poetic truth highlights the first forms of thinking which we experience (Lawrence, 2000, p. 218–9). We dream ourselves into being when we remember and reflect on our dreams. We do not exist as an entirely knowable, unified self, a logical person with a fixed conceptual existence. But as we dream and imagine ourselves into being, most of what we know is unconscious. Anton Ehrenzweig, with his theory of 'unconscious scanning', has laid bare the vast daily round of unconscious observation, the scrutinising and selecting of objects which we all do:

> 'Unconscious vision ... [has] proved to be capable ... of gathering more information than a conscious scrutiny lasting a hundred times longer ... the undifferentiated structure of unconscious vision ... displays scanning powers that is superior to conscious vision.' (Ehrenzweig, 2000, p. 14)

The process of dreaming and thinking leads us into awareness. As we experience the effect of our actions we gradually discover that other people have thoughts and feelings independent of our own, separate and exterior to us. Other people, we come to know, also have an inner world. They too dream and have an unconscious being which shows itself fleetingly and unexpectedly, making us laugh, frightened, aroused, curious—surprising us with a glimpse of the other which we may recognize as just like us or as totally alien. We find out about *ourselves* in similar ways especially when we dream. We are surprised to discover that we are not always who we thought we were. But if a large part of us is hidden and unknown, what sense can we make of our lives? As John Gray has said, we think we are different from other animals. We are conscious and believe we have choices and that consciousness raises us above all other creatures. We like to think that reason guides our lives but this is not the case. We are not unified beings.

> Conscious perception is only a tiny part of what we know through our senses. By far the greater part we receive through subliminal perception. What surfaces in consciousness are fading shadows of things we know already. (Gray ibid p. 60)

There is nothing uniquely human in conscious awareness, except that animals lack a sense of selfhood. We are often at our most skilful when least self aware. As Gray points out, selfhood is not altogether a benefit and many societies have developed techniques of avoiding self awareness. Buddhism is one such attempt. We just cannot take in everything that we perceive and have to censor ourselves to make life bearable. What we *know* is very different from what we are *conscious* of.

"The life of the mind is like that of the body. If it depended on conscious awareness or control it would fail entirely" (ibid p. 64).

The sense of 'I' which develops with language is an illusion, a necessary construction to justify our actions, to make ourselves harmonious, avoid self-contradiction and convince ourselves we are rational. It is this sense of self which is dissolved during dreaming. Similarly it is in abeyance when we are absorbed in action. Children at play are not thinking what convincing cowboys and Indians they are. Fleetingly, they *are* cowboys and Indians. We cannot drive a car and simultaneously think of ourselves as drivers, for if we do so we are suddenly de-skilled. If we go to the theatre to see Macbeth we have to believe in the play in order to *really* experience it. If we stop and remind ourselves we are just watching a play then the experience breaks down. Our self is no longer absorbed in the action. It is no longer real. We have become a self watching itself. This self-consciousness prevents us from being who we are. Each time we try to grasp this concept of self it disappears. We are never who we think we are. Paradoxically, we can be ourselves only when we abandon the attempt to be someone. The exemplar of this abandonment is when we dream. Perhaps in the unconsciousness of the night we get closest to who we really are, a subjectivity made up of myriad characters, images, sensations, colours, animals, fragments—a kaleidoscope of the self and of the world we inhabit. In dreams the self is not mediated by a conscious waking ego. We cannot will it, a dream just comes.

The point I am trying to make here is that if we can give up the idea that we are a fixed, known and finite self, then we are free to find out what else is possible without being confined to a rigid definition of self. Dreams, both therapeutic and social, are a path to these new possibilities, a manifestation of that hidden being. This is the essence of social dreaming. It enables the dissemination of the self for further elaboration and awareness, while simultaneously entering the public sphere to provide dream material for others to ruminate on or adapt in the next dream. A social dream can extend the self and create new ideas about the world: ideas which can then be reflected on and dreamed about. Of course something similar happens in the kind of 'therapeutic' dreaming which takes place in the seclusion of psychoanalysis but that is the domain of private troubles rooted in the past. In social dreaming the focus is on the dream not the dreamer, on the infinite possibilities concealed in layered images of the world, images shared with others who can then associate to the dream—not to the person who dreamt—and who, in turn, can dream in response to these original images.

Psychoanalysis and social dreaming have one thing in common: that is the use of *free association*, highlighted by Freud as the essence and goal of psychoanalysis. The setting of the analytic situation is designed to facilitate free speaking, underpinned by the silence of the analyst and the invitation to say whatever comes to mind. Here the focus is on the personal. In social dreaming the setting is also arranged to encourage spontaneity but the key factor which enables free speaking is the dream itself. We concentrate on the dream not the person. It is not a forum for competing egos. When listeners respond they tend not to talk of the dreamer but rather to give their immediate thoughts, no matter what, to the content of the dream. They may have nothing to say. They may introduce a dream of their own. They may go off at a tangent. But the crucial factor, which makes this a unique conversation, is that no one is talking about a known, definitive self, a conscious fact. This is a conversation about the *unconscious*, the part of ourselves, which is, like a distant country, unexplored; the part of ourselves, which is other. The unconscious has no conception of time or place. Its relationship with consciousness is "Won from the void and formless infinite". (Lawrence, 2000, p. 24)

## The 'Jazz' of the matrix

What is it about the *process* of the matrix which is different to any other form of group interaction? Since the purpose of this book is to highlight the danger of losing touch with our humanity in postmodern society, we need to ascertain how the process engenders relatedness: how the matrix itself enhances each person's access to something mysterious and connecting.

- The starting point is always the dream and not the dreamer.
- The creative act of telling the dream in itself produces further creativity.
- We immerse ourselves in the other's dream which tells us something known but hitherto unthinkable.

Thus the essence of social dreaming is its conjunction with a different quality of communication. Typically when a group of people sit in a room discussing anything, an atmosphere develops which is over-shadowed by competing personalities, an insistence on 'I' and 'my', a fear of exposure, an overly-calculated use of disclosure, a vigilance behind self-presentation, a dread of humiliation. But when conversations begin with the dream, there is a sense of 'otherness' which tends to be less mediated by group values or the ego's defences. A dream just emerges; you cannot prepare it in advance. Telling a dream opens up the potential for spontaneity. It is an unpredictable presentation of uncontrollable forces, social and psychic. Like music or poetry, it introduces us to the ineffable. In normal everyday life there is often a self-scrutiny behind our public persona, an observing self-invigilator who checks and mediates our performance while simultaneously trying to second guess the response of others. Participants in the matrix are noticeably less calculating as they speak their dreams and respond to those of others. There is a less contrived presentation of the dreaming self. A dream is just a dream. We know not where it came from, nor where it will lead. Like musicians in a jazz ensemble, dream tellers play together and improvise. After the statement of the theme, the tune is broken up into spontaneous solos which are unrehearsed and unexpected. An atmosphere ensues in which fresh ideas emerge and new themes—new dreams—blow in. It is a group improvisation. Individual notes and harmonies cry out and an atmosphere develops in which new melodies emerge. Stemming from the 'otherness' of the nocturnal images, the collectivity of the dream orchestra now holds and contains the players. The matrix develops its own tempo. The message is in the medium. As Duke Ellington put it, "Of course we love chords but rhythm is our business." Just as in jazz, when we stop worrying about who we are and just play, we come alive, we connect and this makes it possible for others to join in.

Thus an essential factor in the social dreaming encounter is the spontaneity of the moment with a partial evaporation of the conscious self. This creates a different level of social reality. Several psychoanalysts have written extensively on this other dimension of being and relating. For Winnicott this comes close to idea of the 'true self', for Lacan it is the 'real', for Bion 'O' or the unknowable and for Bollas it is the self's idiom. I want now to explore the meaning of these ideas to understand the intense reality of communication intrinsic to the matrix.

## Winnicott: the true self

Winnicott's overarching concern was with relatedness; that is between the baby and its mother, between the ego and the self and between the individual and external reality. He saw the True Self as the essential kernel of a subject's being, as opposed to the politeness, compliance and subterfuge of the False self which we inevitably present to the world as a defence and protection. It is a quality very much connected to the sense of aliveness, spontaneity and feeling real. He distinguishes between the polite or socialized self on the one hand and the personal private self that is not available except in intimacy. However, by True Self he means something more profound than this customary distinction. He is describing a core part of us which is apparently absent and beyond everyday communication. It is an inherited potential, the totality of sensory motor aliveness.

> "At the earliest stage the True Self is the theoretical position from which comes the spontaneous gesture and the personal idea. The spontaneous gesture is the True Self in action. Only the True Self can be creative and only the True Self can feel real. Whereas a True Self feels real, the existence of a False Self results in feeling unreal or a sense of futility," (Abram, 1996, p. 280).

Winnicott's idea of inner reality is an extension of the baby's fantasy, which is so primitive that, although never lost, is not available to consciousness. This primary 'core self' becomes isolated and never communicates with the world of objects. We only experience a real self when we experience separateness but paradoxically this sense of an integrated separateness comes primarily from the experience of being alone with another person. The mother is present and available but allows the baby to stay in its own world, separate and discrete. Thus the essence of his idea of the True Self is difference. This is the keystone of mental health, epitomising the unique and separate individualised nature of life. This is a self which is pre-verbal, *in* the world but not *of* it, inseparable from physiology and bodily tissue but with a transcendent quality. It is unamenable to scrutiny and unavailable in the therapeutic transference, says Winnicott, but nevertheless intuitively 'there' and encountered in the spontaneous gesture.

## Transitional objects

For Winnicott creative play is the essence of healthy, integrated development in infancy. This requires a potential space—a safe, calm, facilitating environment—where illusion is possible and objects can be encountered as if created by the baby. Objects such as a teddy bear, a sheet, a thumb, a pillow, a sound, a lullaby can be used for comfort when mother is not there. Winnicott called these 'transitional objects'. In the absence of the mother these can be used to evoke her presence as a comfort and a memory. Although provided by mother, they are the baby's creations and as such they are the first 'not-me' objects. In combining mother's image and baby's sense of self they symbolize something which represents both but which is neither. Here we see, the creation of an incipient other, a separate object which can be used,—i.e. loved, hated, played with, sucked, bitten or destroyed. It can be imagined, forgotten, remembered, re-discovered. It is an object which stands for self, other and, most importantly, for the space between self and other. The baby begins to gain a sense of me and not me, of separateness. Thus the transitional object symbolizes difference and separateness and the possibility of relating to an external object—in a reliable situation of trust, where creative mental activity manifested in play is possible. Then the child can come together and exist as a unit: not as a defence against anxiety but as an expression of 'I am', I am myself, I am alive. This safe environment, where something happens in the space between the child and the mother, Winnicott called *the potential space*.

In Winnicott's description of healthy infant development, we can find key elements of the social dreaming experience:

- the *potential space* of the matrix
- *transitional objects* (dreams) which can be used
- the capacity for *play* emanating from the dream telling
- glimpses of the *true self* in the spontaneous gesture of free association
- articulation of the *relationship between self and culture* as the dreams are both internal and external, personal and social.

In the dream matrix, with this combination of spontaneity and playfulness in the service of the dream, a heightened sense of relatedness and connection becomes possible. This 'safe' environment of non-compliance and non-competition, enables the expression of just whatever comes to mind in response to a dream. The freedom to speak unselfconsciously is the *sine qua non* of the matrix. Free association is the presence of the true self in play. The matrix engenders the possibility to be real, alive, and present. The dream is an object which can be used, played with, ignored or dreamed again. There is much more to most dreams than first thoughts or preliminary interpretations. The train of associations is endless and may take us to places we never imagined, both crazy and constructive., amusing and tragic. It is immediate and non-compliant. Winnicott's notion involves a paradox, in that the true self is out of reach, incommunicado, yet fleetingly available in the spontaneous gesture of the moment.

## Lacan: the real

For Lacan, the core of our being is an absence, the thing which is missing which makes us what we are. He called this part of experience the 'Real', the thing which is impossible to say, impossible to imagine because it constitutes a key part of us which has been hidden from memory. So what Lacan called the Real, means the lived awareness which has been repressed. The Real is the primordial wound we incurred by our fall from the pre-Oedipal Eden. The baby's original world of spontaneously lived experience undergoes repression, covering up the 'before and after' of the separation from mother, from her nursing, suckling and all the intimacies of infancy. This is the cut or the trauma of rupture. It is the necessary gap in the psyche left by lost satisfaction, the lack which constitutes the individual's desire. This process begins with the advent of language and introduction to the social order, the Oedipus complex, the father, the law, the external culture. This leaves us with a sense of incompleteness or dissatisfaction—the gap as Lacan terms it. We do not remember the actual event but we do retain the moment something happened that was real—not imaginary or symbolic—and which deeply affected us. This could be the birth of a sibling, the loss of the maternal breast, a mother crying in the street, a father falling downstairs.

Something happened. (In the social dreaming matrix we similarly recall world events—wars, bombings, hurricanes, famines—happening usually to other people in far off places. When it 'comes home to us', when we dream it with affect, or experience it face to face, this has an element of the Real.)

At the 'mirror stage', when the child first glimpses its image, it has to construct a picture of the self as whole, although this does not pertain to the complex mass of fragments and sensations which constitute its actual lived experience. Through this exterior self-image, he creates an imitation of himself but this increasingly alienates him from his profound inner sense of feeling. The self here is a concoction, an illusion of whole identity, trapped in projective mirroring processes. What Lacan calls the Symbolic order—language, music, art, dreams—offers a way out of this self entrapment through the acknowledgement of the gap, revealing what is hidden and missing. While language always entails loss, it also offers the possibility of expression. Now the gap can be worked with rather than filled in, especially through the interplay of language and the unconscious. Despite the impossibility of perfect communication, the subject can be gradually recreated through the fluidity of language by revealing unconscious meaning and contact with that 'other' part of ourselves. Thus, in psychoanalysis, the subject discovers his own voice—the Real—revealed through slips of the tongue and idiosyncratic wording.

Dreams are a vital part of this symbolic work, the gap in our being from which our desire flows unstaunchably. The Real always escapes and so this gap can only be represented by something else. The dream discourse in the matrix stands for this gap. In psychoanalysis the interpretation of resistance, may reveal the existence of this gap which has been hidden by symptoms and defences. In social dreaming, the matrix/process is the gap. The session will begin quite simply with the question, 'What is the first dream?' We go straight to the potential space of 'otherness'. Thus the dreams put us closer to that which is missing, the absence that, according to Lacan, essentially defines our being. Whatever can then be put into this new-found empty space is allowed to spring forth from the infinity of the unconscious via the parapraxes, free associations and subsequent dreams. This can only come about through the disruption of the constructed omnipotent self, which hitherto has maintained an illusion of self sufficiency. This illusory self is dismantled when we dream. In social dreaming we regain contact with the void and experience the gaps through which authentic meaning flows. The absurd, irrational, enigmatic content of the dream tells us more about this interior and exterior reality then any scientific attempt to measure and define. Ordinary speech is invariably a sort of camouflage, a disguise for what really moves us.

*And here lies the key to the authenticity of the social dreaming process.* The illusory self dissolves in the presence of the dream. As we get closer to the other space—inside us and between us—there is a capacity for contact with the real. As Harold Pinter has noted, when two people are talking to one another there is always something important which is not being said. The drama lives in the unspoken. Thus the dream discourse holds the promise of contact with the Real—the thing we constantly desire which is impossible to say. This may be a statement of a sexual wish or a refusal to obey orders. Surprisingly, it may also be a wish for catastrophe—contact with the rupture of destructive forces which has been put somewhere else. Thus we avoid confrontation with that which unconsciously we know is bound to destroy us. The widely reported dreaming in the U.S. and elsewhere of a terrorist attack in the months preceding 9/11 is a case in point. (Lawrence, 2005, pp. 81–2) In 'Welcome to the Desert of the Real' (Zizek, 2001) it is suggested that in the catastrophic Twin Tower attacks, America got what it had been dreaming of for decades, a future that is glimpsed but deemed unthinkable and therefore quickly banished from consciousness. In the Interpretation of Dreams, Freud stated that "A dream is a (disguised) fulfilment of a (suppressed or repressed) wish" (Freud, 1900). Lacan's notion of the Real is absolutely central to social dreaming. It may be only in dreams that we have access to the split-off vision of reality which is out of sight and out of mind. Behind the American "Dream" of the unreal, perhaps, was hidden the psychotic Third World nightmare of the real.

## Bion: 'O' or ultimate reality

The English psychoanalyst, Wilfred Bion used the symbol 'O' to stand for ultimate reality, absolute truth, the infinite, the thing-in-itself.

In psychoanalysis it is used to refer to the ultimate emotional truth of a session, even though this truth may be unknowable. It is not the same as knowledge. One cannot know 'O', you must *be* it. This is a paradox—we give our attention to something which we cannot know. Something—emotional reality—can be recognized and felt but it cannot be known. For Bion the good therapist does not try to help, otherwise this may infiltrate the space in which 'O' can evolve. If we try and control the emotional reality of a session then we may prevent perceptive listening. Trying to know gets in the way. This paradox applies in social dreaming. We need to trust the dream whatever it brings and not set out to consciously try and pin point the direction. The dream takes us to the edge and we are left pondering its infinite depths behind the camouflage and deceptions of dream imagery. Uncertainty is a constant part of this process. It involves an act of faith that something is being expressed which is ineffable. Bion picks up Freud's idea of free floating attention (on the part of the analyst), or as he calls it, 'reverie', where a state of relaxation enables the mind to flow from the sensual to mental. This requires the absence of memory or desire. If we consciously try to keep something in mind, or to hope for a result, then our wishing for an end-product intrudes. He suggests a mind-state similar to Buddhist meditation: the capacity to stay with uncertainty, to be able to bear not-knowing. Bion uses the term 'negative capability', an idea he quotes from a letter which Keats wrote to his brothers: "I mean negative capability when a man is capable of being in uncertainties, mysteries doubts, without any irritable reaching after fact and reason." (Bion, 1970, p. 125) Bion even suggests that this is how psychoanalytic papers should be read. That is "they should be read in the same conditions as those in which a psychoanalysis should be conducted—without memory or desire. And then forgotten. They can be re-read; but not remembered." (Bion, 1967, p. 163)

What he illuminates here is a central tenet of our findings in social dreaming. That in order to reach a state of intuitive insight—of shared emotional experience, indefinable yet close to the absolute truth of the matrix—individuals need to dispense with memory (previous sessions) and desire (hoped for future achievements). As Samuel Beckett shows in his essay on Proust, the integral purity of an experience is only retained *because* it has been forgotten and then is retrieved by accident. As with Proust's famous Madeleine, involuntary memory suddenly evokes a past experience and triggers the world of lost time. Now the original sensation itself returns to engulf the subject.

> "... then the total past sensation, not its echo nor its copy, the sensation itself, annihilating every spatial and temporal restriction, comes in a rush to engulf the subject in all the beauty of its infallible proportion."
> (Beckett, 1989)

Here Beckett encompasses Freud's revolutionary idea of free association, which makes way for the possibility of the return of the repressed. Thus we breathe in the true pure air of the Paradise—or the trauma—that has been lost. Our research in Social Dreaming suggests that this 'open' state of mind is facilitated by the *source* of the material—the dream. We do not start from the person but from the dream. Thus intuition springs from emotional experience but this is something that is never defined—a web of thoughts, feelings and bodily sensations that create a matrix of unspoken and unconscious experience. There is no attempt to solve or cure, we are not purposively trying to 'get somewhere'. Doubts, uncertainty, not knowing are essential. As Christopher Bollas has said of the analytic encounter, by abandoning the attempt to find truth we arrive at it. Moreover notions of cure,

> "however intriguing and worthy, oversimplify a fact that will not vanish with the ideology of progression towards a curative point whether depressive or linguistic" (Bollas, 1995, p. 40)

We are not trying to make anybody 'better'. In social dreaming there need be no purpose, nothing on offer. Indeed we have noticed the difficulties encountered in matrixes where members have felt they should be trying to reach a particular destination, or that someone needed rescuing, or protecting from a dream's idea. An example comes to mind of a matrix of highly intellectual dreamers, where one member felt the need to 'protect' another from the spontaneous but vulgar statement made by another. This not only broke the train of thought but sabotaged a comment which had touched upon the emotional core of the session. (The still radical idea of free association, espoused by Freud at the start of the last century, is difficult for most people to trust—including some psychotherapists.) There is no need for a moral compass, or promise of benefit to be derived. Indeed, one young man who attended the

Hay on-Wye matrix, said that the very thing which attracted him to the event was the fact that we promised nothing re: health, wealth or intelligence. Interestingly he dreamed of a greenhouse where different plants could just grow. The matrix is a place with a dream-like quality, a reverie where new ideas and new dreams can just be allowed to grow through unconscious communication. It is a place for waiting and listening. The matrix acts as a container, a receptacle for the emotional experiences produced by the dreams and the responses to them. It is a process of fertilisation and nurturing, in which perception and attention are the best tools rather than remembering and knowing. It is inaccessible yet intimate, closer to the gap, to that which is always absent, infinite', formless and incommunicado. For Bion this is 'O', the unknowable, for Lacan the real and for Winnicott the True Self. It refers to a level of reality, an emotional truth, which is normally overshadowed by our insistent search for the absolute, our desire to measure and control, our need to grasp an ultimate fixed identity frozen in time.

## Bollas: idiom

This idea of an unconscious force inside us, a unique potentiality for defining our experience, has been developed in the work of Christopher Bollas. This self potentiality Bollas calls *idiom*. From birth each person has a defining essence. Parents and environment play a role in this but we are not merely the sum of those who brought us up. Idiom refers to "the unique nucleus of each individual, a figuration of being that can, under favourable circumstances, evolve and articulate" (Bollas, 1989, p. 212). For Bollas each person is like a foreign country with its own language and landscape.

His writing emphasises the uniqueness of each individual, the essential enigma of the true self. For Bollas the 'we' or the 'I' is too near to experience to become its own signifier, whereas the 'me' is close to the experience of self but cannot speak. This is the preverbal self "saturated with residues of vast unconscious experiences". This 'me', is an internal object that is sensible and can be felt even though it has no voice. This he calls the self's idiom, a core part of us which is an absent presence rather than an articulate active subject. Here he refers to the unconscious ego which evinces a desire to give unique shape to what it experiences. It is a kind of "thinking desire", as Joel Beck puts it. ( Scalia, 2002, p. 18)

*"Each individual is unique and the true self is an idiom of organi-*
*zation that seeks its personal world through the use of an object ...*
*the fashioning of life is something like an aesthetic: a form revealed*
*through one's way of being"*. (Bollas, 1989, pp. 109–10)

This idiom is expressed through our character, an aesthetic of being
which is transitional, in that it is formed in the area between the self
and the outside world, within the overlap between inner and outer
reality. We each have a precise way of forming our world, both internally and in relation to others, so that each of us is a kind of artist
with our own sensibility. Christopher Bollas is the writer par excel-
lence who helps us celebrate the good things in our being, awaken-
ing our curiosity to the ordinary and everyday. A memorable theme
described in his writing is the 'capacity to be the dream work of
one's life' (Bollas, 1992, p. 53) where who we are is disseminated in
unconscious forms, moving and growing in the free articulation of
the self. This is about how we deploy our aesthetic in the world, how
we make sense of our unique potential, our unthought sense of self,
our unconscious intelligence. As we walk down the street, listen to a
friend, make love, experience a piece of music, cook a meal, play with
a dream, how do we take in, and respond to, the sensations, physical
and emotional, of our being in the world? How do we create ourselves? It is also about how we allow *others* to 'use' *us*, in order to discover and articulate their own enigmatic sense of self. It is a fluid idea
of personality perhaps nearer to music than the physical, the visual
or the linguistic. It is about the mystery of how we make our lives and
our selves as we interact with the world of people and things.

*"Our idiom is an aesthetic of being, driven by an urge to articulate its*
*theory of form by selecting and using objects so as to give them form"*
(Bollas, 1995, p. 150)

In social dreaming this process is in the transitional space between
the self and the social. Here life becomes an object while the social
world is the dream work of the dreamer. In childhood, the need to
think forces us to develop a mind—of memories, emotional experiences, desires—and this enables us to develop and elaborate a sense
of self. For example, through our choice of music, way of speaking,
relating, dressing, job, sport—as an expression of our own personal

aesthetic or idiom. A dream is an example of this inner presence, "a puzzling illumination of one's unconscious interests, a manifestation of intangible interests seeking presentation." (Bollas, 1999, p. 171)

## Psychic genera and the matrix

Being aware of what moves us changes who we are. Our interest in this internal aesthetic and those external objects enriches psychic textures, which are able to grow and take shape, a process Bollas terms *Psychic Genera*. By this he means an internal gestation of unconscious communication from others. We *affect one another in mysterious forms which develop and grow inside us*. Similarly in the facilitating environment of the matrix, a non-intrusive attention to the dreams—through free association, listening, silence, and then further dreaming—engenders new thoughts and ideas about aspects of the social world; ideas hitherto unavailable to consciousness. Slowly new links and meanings emerge which suggest causes, outcomes, patterns and conflicts which we 'knew' but were unable to think. An illuminating example is the evidence of Charlotte Beradt's work on dreams in pre-war Germany, where many people were dreaming of the catastrophe to come and of their future part in it as victims or perpetrators. (Beradt, 1966) In a totalitarian society they were dreaming of what they could not talk about. Similarly there is evidence that in the months preceding the 9/11 disaster, many people were dreaming in detail of such an event without realizing its significance (Clare, 2003). Furthermore people sharing the same situation—at work, in a sports team or within a group of friends—may discover they have all had the same or similar dreams, though none had been aware of what was on their minds. Members of a tribe have been shown to dream together of when and where to hunt, or about the meaning of a problem or conflict. An example from our own work may throw more light on the relevance of Bollas's concept to social dreaming.

## An example of psychic genera—eight therapists in search of an idea

A group of psychotherapists (of which the authors were members) had trained together and then maintained a weekly post-graduate reading group, throughout the 1990s. After six years, they felt stuck and in need of a new direction and decided to undertake a social dreaming programme with Gordon Lawrence. From the start they dreamed of their past and their future. In the first dreaming matrix, to their surprise, several members reported a similar dream of a house with many rooms, which was being priced to go on the market. In it were people of different nations—black, Iranian, Chinese, Spanish, men with spears, mysterious dark women, children playing. Something was being examined and evaluated. An object was emerging which seemed interesting. What was it for? In the weeks to come they began to recall and realize their history as a group, their regrets, disappointments, hopes and desires. The task seemed to be, 'What can be done with this house (the group)? how can we use it creatively?' Their shared sense of difference carried hidden significance. They now realized that most members of the group came from a foreign country, spoke two or more languages, had trained in a 'second' language, worked as therapists in this 'foreign' language and were all in some sense outsiders, émigrés, newcomers, foreigners. Perhaps the house of diversity could have great value.

Out of these dreams a new idea gradually developed—of the need in London for a multi-lingual psychotherapy centre. They began to build up a clinical network for foreigners who wanted psychotherapy in their mother-tongue. The dream-thought became a reality. The group had dreamed themselves into existence and the Multi-lingual psychotherapy Centre was conceived. As the project unfolded the therapists held meetings open to the public. Now other émigré psychotherapists emerged to talk about their experiences. Thus the dialogue developed from a story of immigrant and refugee *patients*, to one of immigrant and refugee *therapists*. Out of this continuing 'dream space', of free association and open discussion, a place for émigré psychotherapists was born. Thus otherness—difference, foreignness, emigration—became an object which could be used, internalized, dreamt about and spoken. The matrix nurtures the unformed object. When an idea can be taken in—thought about, played with, found in film, music, poetry, in dreams and in dialogue—then it can be discovered afresh to surprise us. It can be used. Not theoretically or in an instrumental, calculated way but playfully in pursuit of the unknown; discovering aspects of self and society which were lying dormant, waiting to be found. This echoes

Bion's idea that often in a room there may be a thought floating around, waiting for a thinker. This conjunction cannot be achieved through the usual channels of theorising or logic.

When people take time to communicate with one another through dreams, something begins to grow unconsciously which, with patience and detachment, may emerge as a new thought. This involves what Bollas meant by psychic genera. An aimless kind of listening, with the invitation to say whatever comes to mind, creates a subliminal connection between individuals. In the matrix, after a dream, there may be silence, or the arrival of something completely different. Unconscious dialogue ensues. Thus, silently, the matrix is an incubator for ideas. Frequently, these new perspectives take life in our dreams. Bollas's conception authentically represents lived experience through its aesthetic idea of psychic structure as fluid and self elaborating. He sites the example of artists who experience germinal ideas as only semi-autonomous—coming from within but without their consciously willing it. Thus it is not uncommon to hear, "I don't know where that painting came from", or "the book just seemed to write itself." A thing is brought forth which we didn't know we had in us. He suggests that this surprise at the inexplicability of creativity may be why so many writers and philosophers are disenchanted with the notion of a unified self. As Bollas implies, there is a simple self who dreams and an organizing intelligence that gives it meaning. We just don't know how the dream arrived or from where.

* * * *

With each of these four thinkers there is a tension between spontaneous and self-monitored aspects of the mind. Our dreams are discrete personal creations unmediated by conformity or compliance. The adventure of social dreaming is not dependent on mastery or control but develops through the spontaneity and playfulness of telling, listening and responding. It is a subversive idea—that free association creates access to something 'other', something which is real for us and touches on the emotional truth of our being in the social world. Certainty is not possible but communication via dreams makes for dialogue and relationship in which new ideas of the social emerge and hitherto unknown aspects of the self can be articulated.

# CHAPTER TWO

# The night train of social dreams

*Ali Zarbafi*

This book emerged from a discussion we had in a particular social dreaming matrix (SDM) in the South of France. The discussion was about how we started observing that the matrix was somehow bringing up the idea of 'being misused'. Various ideas occurred to us. At first it felt as though the SDM was a thing in itself, directing us like a deeper consciousness.

A few weeks before this matrix I had a dream where I was in a room with John Clare and Gordon Lawrence. In the dream I was sitting in the doorway and there was a discussion going on. In the dark corner of the room there was an old man who was not part of our meeting or consciousness, who was listening to our discussions. Later it felt to me that this dream was linked to the idea of 'O' as described by Bion—a greater consciousness which remains unconscious but is there, watchful, acting as a guide but which cannot be known. It described social dreaming, as this was what the three of us were doing together. It also meant instead of 'three' there were 'four' in the room; the possibility of completeness like the square or the circle. The four in symbolic language represents the 'collective self as well as a transcendent possibility' (Chevalier & Cheerbrant, 1996, pp. 402–7).

In this particular matrix there was a series of dreams, which emphasised this feeling of 'misuse' and pointed to ways in which the matrix may be a space, which is ultimately a 'symbolic' space with meaning, which grows and moves. This was particularly represented by two dreams about an alligator in a violin case. How do you keep an alligator in a violin case if it is growing? Another dream was about a shoal of fish with letters on them. As soon as you tried to read the letters they changed into another configuration. A marvellous spectacle—wonder with no set meaning—always expanding and changing. This seemed to reflect the question as to whether one can 'box' dreams and pin them down so easily? To misuse social dreaming is to think you can somehow pin it down to mean one thing, whereas it's meaning has infinite possibilities. The weekend was concerned with the use of dreams in organisations but how do you introduce a 'moving thinking' or a 'moving meaning' into an organisation or a box?

This led to the idea of social dream as a form. Social dreaming has a pure form rather like the platonic idea of forms—'pure' social dreaming. This social dreaming matrix was pointing to its own nature. The form is a symbol which is not known but has infinite possibilities. The Theory of Forms typically refers to Plato's belief that the material world as it seems to us is not the real world, but only a shadow of the real world.

The form though, is pure because it has a clear structure like a train which is a mode of transport which offers a journey. What one makes of the form or journey depends entirely on the contents, which are not determined by the form. Plato's theory of forms is illustrated by the 'Myth of the Cave' which is a suite in five movements for clarinet/bass clarinet, double bass and piano, composed by Yitzhak Yedid in Jerusalam in 2002. This composition was inspired by Plato's philosophic metaphor The Allegory of the Cave.

A group of human beings sit in a cave, in chains, their backs to the entrance. The shadows of things moving outside are projected by the light onto an inner wall of the cave. As the prisoners have never been outside the cave since birth, they believe these shadows are reality. One of them succeeds in freeing himself and walks outside into the light. He realizes that he has lived his whole life in the shadow of an illusion. Delighted by his discovery, he returns to the cave to communicate it to the others. Violence erupts between the one who ventured outside and those who do not want to understand. The story ends with the death of the person that had gained insight into reality.

This allegory is an appropriate metaphor for the difficult reality of our times, a delusional reality, and ignorance of the truth and of suffering in the world. The music expresses feelings of criticism, pity, prayer, mercy and a keen desire to recognize the truth.

Lawrence has referred to social dreaming introducing thinking to the infinite (Lawrence, 1998, pp. 9–41). The infinite has many 'moments' where something can be suddenly understood and then one moves on. Social dreaming in this sense has many moments, that is, it can elaborate what a family, an organisation, a culture or a community may be preoccupied with and at the same time focus on the nature of meaning in existence. The layers go on and on and we can stop at the moment we are concerned with or go on to as many possibilities as our minds can fathom or try to link all the possibilities, layers or levels as we find them. The symbol encapsulates all of these but is not any one of them. Discussing symbols Jung says, 'The concept of a symbol should in my view be strictly distinguished from that of a sign ... Every view which interprets the symbolic expression as an analogue of a known thing is semiotic. A view which interprets the symbolic expression as the best possible formulation of a relatively unknown thing which for that reason cannot be more clearly or characteristically represented, is symbolic. A view which interprets the symbolic expression as an intentional paraphrase of a known thing is allegoric.' (Jung, 1989, p. 475).

This book therefore aims to illustrate these 'moments' as they occur in the context of the organisation, our concerns about the current and future state of western society and the planet and, our more profound preoccupations with myth and religion.

## Freud and Jung

In some ways the book traverses the territory between Jung and Freud. Freud was concerned with how the dream elaborated a symptom in the individual patient, whereas Jung, though interested in this, concentrated on the ways in which the dream opened up the possibility of discovering a lived 'meaning' in the individual's collective experience.

For Jung meaning was a lifelong experience full of lived moments. The unconscious for Freud was linked to desire whereas for Jung it was linked to energy. For Freud it was important to incorporate unconscious desires into a knowing ego with perspective which was the individual project in the analytic situation. For Jung the unconscious informed the ego and was teleological—had a purpose greater than the ego could know because of its ultimately collective nature. The ego emerged from the collective unconscious rather than being there to repress undesirable thoughts. These issues also lead to questions about the Unconscious. For Freud the unconscious was something which belonged to the individual and where libido or sexual energy was present. However Freud was also interested in the collective in his writings on Moses and Monotheism and Totem and Taboo. It was clear that Freud was trying to grapple with a collective unconscious even though he never specifically used these terms. For Jung the unconscious was personal and collective. The personal unconscious was the first stage of analysis in most cases where the patient, pre-occupied with his or her personal histories, needed to become conscious of repressed feelings and memories linked largely to parental figures and siblings. As Jung put it, to develop a relationship to their personal shadow. The personal shadow, simply, was where all the hidden shameful thoughts and feelings lived.

However Jung, through his work with schizophrenics, came to believe that the individual also shared a collective unconscious with all of humanity. The origins of this idea lay in his experience of patients who brought material, which was clearly not 'individual' but belonged to a myth or to different historical era. Jung saw the collective unconscious being present in the individual as a backdrop to discovering meaning beyond his individual confines. The experiences with patients which led him to his notion of the Collective Unconscious were sealed when he had the following dream:

> 'I was in a house I did not know, which had two storeys. It was 'my house'. I found myself in the upper storey where there was a kind of salon furnished with fine pieces in rococo style. On the walls hung a number of precious paintings. I wondered that this should be my house, and thought, 'Not bad'. But then it occurred to me that I did not know what the lower floor looked like. Descending the stairs, I reached the ground floor. There

everything was much older, and I realised that this part of the house must date from the 15th or 16th century. The furnishings were medieval: the floors were of red brick. Everywhere it was rather dark. I went from one room to another, thinking, 'Now I really must explore the whole house'. I came upon a heavy door, and opened it. Beyond it I discovered a stone stairway that led down into the cellar. Descending again I found myself in a beautifully vaulted room which looked exceedingly ancient. Examining the walls, I discovered layers of brick among ordinary stone blocks and chips of brick in the mortar. As soon as I saw this I knew that the walls dated from Roman times. My interest by now was intense. I looked more closely at the floor. It was of stone slabs and in one of these I discovered a ring. When I pulled it, the stone slab lifted; again I saw a stairway of narrow stone steps leading down into the depths. There, too, I descended and entered a low cave cut into the rock. Thick dust lay on the floor and in the dust were scattered bones and broken pottery, like remains of a primitive culture. I discovered two human skulls obviously very old and half disintegrated. Then I awoke.' (Jung, 1995, p. 155)

A Freudian approach may go straight to the skulls, for example how deeply buried are Jung's murderous fantasies about the parents etc. This is what Freud was particularly interested in when Jung told him the dream. Jung's comments were:

'It was plain to me that the house represented a kind of image of the psyche—that is to say of my then state of consciousness, with hitherto unconscious additions. Consciousness was represented by the salon. It had an inhabited atmosphere, in spite of its antiquated style. The ground floor stood for the first level of the unconscious. The deeper I went, the more alien and the darker the scene became. In the cave, I discovered remains of a primitive culture, this is the world of primitive man within myself—a world that can scarcely reached or illuminated by consciousness. The primitive consciousness of the man borders on the life of the animal soul, just as the caves of prehistoric times were usually inhabited by animals before men laid claim to them.' (Jung, 1995, p. 156)

As a psychotherapist myself I would be interested in both aspects of the dream which are to do with depth and the hidden and the significance of this. For Jung the interest was in the form of the dream, where the structure of the psyche of 'man' is clearly being described in a collective way. This house exists in all of us, so the collective in this sense is of a psyche with all of human history, consciousness and possibility in it. A form is being described. I sit in this 'we', which I will always be in the presence of and never know entirely, but know that somehow I am part of the 'we' which is a collective journey in which I can find my individual 'lived' meaning or purpose. However it is clear that this 'collective psyche' that Jung describes, is social in the broadest sense, that is, of species: man as a social animal with, the need for the other, and this represents itself in various social arrangements throughout history.

So the implication of this is that social dreaming first touches on the 'eternal' issues that the species is concerned with and throws this 'light' on a particular context, that is, the moment in which we may be involved, whether it be family, group, culture and so forth. As Jung puts it 'I term *collective* all psychic contents that belong not to one individual but to many i.e. to a society, to a people or to mankind in general … It is not only concepts and ways of looking at things, that must be termed collective, but also *feelings.*' (Jung, 1989, p. 417). Citing Levy-Bruhl he describes these collective feelings as 'feeling values' which are not merely intellectual but emotional. These feeling values affect thinking, feeling, intuition and sensation in individuals (ibid p. 418).

The Social Dreaming project assumes that the dreams in a matrix belong to the collective. The first rule is that the dream introduced into the matrix does not belong to the individual dreamer. The author of the dream however is the individual and this is not in question. The dream points to something truly other and in that way represents the true self, the idiom or aesthetic of the dreamer, who then chooses to share it with the collective. However the act of willingly sharing one's dreams with the collective as happens in social dreaming has two consequences. Firstly it seems that the shared dreams and associations seem to be following certain themes. People are dreaming of similar things, for example similar images are appearing. So the question then is what is happening? This leads to the second hypothesis which is that something 'already known but not thought' is becoming apparent 'between individuals'. This is 'the social' but it also suggests that the idea of the true self, as described by Winnicott, when explored in this way leads to the idea of the Collective Self as described by Jung. It is the discovery of the need of the social and community *in* the individual. This need predates the personal mother. The dreams therefore when willingly shared, open the door to a complex collective which is *created and found*.

This idea, developed by Lawrence (1998) has been born out of practice. He realized that dreams introduced in group therapy or group relations were somehow not worked with, even though it seemed clear that the dreams had potential to describe something beyond the individual dreamer's personal inner world and the group process. The introduction of a dream in a collective context means something for the collective because it is random, unconscious, and is tearing at a cosy concrete and rational consciousness which has emerged in the collective. It is a 'spanner in the works' so to speak. Suddenly a door is found which was not there before. The idea that the dream has a collective meaning is not acceptable to many practicing analysts. But things have different meanings in different contexts. A dream in psychoanalysis will have meaning within that particular piece of work to do with the individual's inner life, whereas the same dream introduced randomly into a social context may lead to all sorts of other possibilities for those present. Many people do not necessarily think of dreams as individual. Some think of it as a form of prediction, as a message for the dreamer, as an omen or as the work of the devil. Many people believe that dreams have 'objective' meanings and consult the readily available books on dreaming to find out what their dreams 'mean'. So individually somewhere we know that dreams are subject to collective possibilities and meanings.

Jung, who was very interested in Freud's use of free association, developed a further concept called amplification. 'By way of association he (Jung) tried to establish the personal context of a dream; by way of amplification he connected it with universal imagery. Amplification involves use of mythic, historical and cultural parallels in order to clarify and make ample the metaphorical content of dream symbolism. Jung stated its aim was to make both explicit and ample what is revealed by the unconscious of the dreamer. This then enables the dreamer to see it as unique *but of universal significance, a synthesis of personal and collective patterns.'* (My italics) (Samuels et al, 1987, p. 16).

## The Night Train: the gallery of dreams

An example of the importance of the objective possibilities of a personal dream in a social context is the painting 'The Night Train' on the front cover of this book. In 2003 when we were returning by train from a Social Dreaming Matrix in France I jotted down some thoughts and these went as follows. The Night Train is composed of a motley crew of people being taken through the great night where they experience something about being together as humans and something about the polyverse (First Hay Matrix) or the infinite they are journeying through which expands their wonder and consciousness. This happens because everybody allows themselves to 'look out from within' in order to discover their human predicament rather than their individual lives.

A year later I was standing in front of this painting,' The Night Train' by John Clare. The painting took me back to this experience. John and I had both been to this matrix and it seems that he had painted an experience which we had maybe shared but not discussed. This painting is a symbolic painting as it captures something eternal to do with the human predicament. You could put it in a nursery or a gallery and both audiences would be able to relate to its playfulness and its importance in a dense darkness full of subtle colour all around. The image and title captured a general shape or place of discovery where a group of people together go on a journey into darkness where they share what they discover 'in the night' when we dream. The train is also a train of thought discovered in a haphazard fashion by people looking 'out' the windows and then maybe talking to each other. Inside and outside are intimately working together. Everybody has a different view but they all share the same communal space in the carriage where they can discover thoughts and feelings. The darkness somehow is essential for there to be light or enlightenment in the carriage.

The painting also enables us to see the train clearly as the darkness defines it. Somehow the train and the people in it with their little light define a place or context, which is being 'in-formed' and illuminated by what they share. Consciousness is emerging. The darkness 'points to them' very clearly and so enables them to face what they share in this moment or this place and eternally. This 'pointing' though is also a 'bearing down' where one is awash with images and free associations and feelings. They are a gathering of people who share a culture, a history, maybe a workplace or a task and a planet. All these things can be 'pointed to' by the darkness. All we have to do is to allow it happen, to open ourselves up to our imagination and our free association through our dreams or our darkness. The darkness enables them to discover their 'human' predicament in terms of a group and individuals on an individual and communal journey through a short life span.

A great deal could be made psychoanalytically from this painting in terms of its individual possibilities. This is relevant for the individual journey but the painting is also a metaphor for a dream, which is hung on a wall for observers to make something of, to discuss in terms of associations and other images. Social dreaming in this sense is like a gallery where people sit and discuss their paintings with each other and then paint other paintings. Here, the 'individual' and the 'collective' are present together and working together. The individual feels expanded while the collective is being discovered. The collective is of course always there as a sense of 'human belonging' rather than geographic belonging and it can feel wondrous to allow it to just be there, rather than to fight over the anxieties of feeling that one does not somehow belong geographically or racially or linguistically.

In this way social dreaming, like this painting, points to a yearning for a moving discovery where more thoughts are discovered. These thoughts though, are generally based on the need to say something, be it a dream or a thought as there is an 'emotional basis' to the utterance. It has meaning in this context. All 'meaning' comes from an internal engagement of feeling and thinking. It is not just cerebral. The 'need' to say something comes from a 'waiting' for a thought or dream to emerge from within. There is an urgency and sometimes there are so many thoughts and feelings that participants spend a great deal of time struggling with themselves until they 'have to speak'. It is the right moment as many of the thoughts and feelings are shared in the room. What you are thinking somebody else may say (a common experience in many situations) and sometimes there is an uncanny resemblance between dreams. How can somebody be dreaming about a similar thing to you? Some of the matrices in this book show an uncanny similarity of dreams by participants in the same matrix; this is partly the point of the book, that we are all dreaming similar things.

## The importance of wonder

When one embarks on a social dreaming matrix one is invited to be in the presence of wonder. There is a story told in Winnie the Pooh of Pooh Bear, who is walking around a tree and as he walks he discovers two footprints and he thinks 'Umm' there is somebody ahead of me. Soon he comes across more footprints and thinks that there are many people ahead of him. He is enchanted and excited by these discoveries as he walks around the tree. At this point Eyore, his companion, who is sitting on top of the tree says to Pooh 'Oh Pooh those are your footprints that you are following' and they both laugh at this marvellous discovery and play they have enjoyed together. Pooh was in Wonder and Eyore offered him perspective. They were both in the experience until a thought arrived. Social Dreaming is like this play and discovery followed by perspective and then play and discovery and so on. In this sense it is 'alive' and 'present'. So I would invite you, the reader, to allow yourself be present to your own wonder when reading through some of the matrices we offer you in this book. This is also thinking space as Eyore clearly shows but it is a 'moving thinking', which comes out of being open to the darkness within and sharing our thoughts and dreams with each other in order to discover our human community.

## The numinous

Ultimately however our experience in all social dreaming matrices has been one of being close to something larger and vaster than ourselves. Perhaps this is the collective within us all which becomes active in this creative way when we sit and allow dreams to come forward. This felt very important. The matrix in the South of France suggested that once the process was underway, the collective could start to guide us. Our deeper, shared, unthought human experience was profound. This relates to the idea of the 'numinous', a guiding principle or force which is not generated by individual will power but is a collective experience which can change consciousness. In Roman times it was seen as divine and Jung felt it was linked to the God Image (Samuels et al, 1987). However this type of experience is present in a particular way in social dreaming, as participants feel part of something larger within themselves, which is being created in the process. There is a sense of something intensely significant and very alive.

Through this method, we have available to us profoundly meaningful, possibilities of relating, connecting and creating which are at odds with our often disconnected, individualistic lives. The experience can demonstrate our importance to one another and the potential for a deep, knowing respect amongst humans, which is there to be discovered but feels lost. This is why this book was written.

# CHAPTER THREE

# Dreaming after 9/11

"In every calm and reasonable person there is a
hidden second person scared witless about death."

—Philip Roth, 2002, p. 153

## Dreams before 9/11/01

A social dreaming project began in London in October 2000 meeting
once monthly and consisting usually of ten to fifteen people of
various nationalities. It was to run for just over three years, with
two-month breaks in summer. Most participants had never met
before and did not belong to the same institution or occupation. The
group included teachers, organizational consultants, social workers,
writers, psychotherapists, a student, an advertising executive and
a poet. There were Hindus, Muslims, Christians, Jews and non-
believers. It was a disparate matrix in that dreamers came from different walks of life and did not share a common activity that could
become a focus for their dreams. Perhaps because of this, people

tended to dream more of the world 'out there' rather than of a shared community with insular themes. Each dream-telling matrix lasted ninety minutes and was followed by a thinking session of one hour. It was enjoyable but hard work. This began in the year leading up to the al-Qaida bombing of the Twin Towers in New York. During that year people dreamed of floods, of plague and quite specifically and tangibly of the disaster to come. Critical themes of the first year's dreams included:

• mass murder and a sense of impending danger which could not be contained
• a war of racist persecution
• the difficulty of constructing a container, a boat, a ferry, an ark, a place of refuge
• fear of descent into an underworld of chaos
• the possibility that dreaming might be a portent, a Cassandra - like prophecy
• how to find new ways of thinking, lateral, indirect and creative rather than the positivism, rationality and logic of conventional discourse

Not surprisingly, there was an eerie sense of déjà vu when the terrorist attack on New York happened. I have written elsewhere about the matrix of this first year, in the months leading up to September 11th 2001, (Clare, 2003, pp 36–60). It seemed that people had been dreaming about this disaster for most of the previous year. In their dreams they had been "thinking", and when the dreams were scrutinized it appeared they had all along known something that was unavailable to waking thought. One member of the matrix, watching television in an airport on 11 September, believed he was watching a Hollywood film of a twin towers attack until someone told him it was real and happening live, there and then. The disaster movie had become reality. America had been "dreaming" this for years. As I noted then, this is not a reference to magic, or clairvoyance; nor is it about the chosen few, the new age beings of a sci-fi world in which people with special powers can foretell the future [The work of Charlotte Beradt in pre-war Germany shows that people were dreaming of their fate a long time before the "final solution" (Beradt, 1966)].

The suggestion is not that dreams were magical predictions of future events of which people had no prior knowledge. Of course they were dreaming about the future but it was a future that lay dormant in the present. Lawrence Wright has given ample testimony to the wealth of evidence available long before 9/11 as to the intentions of Islamist Revolutionaries. (Wright, 2006)

The specificity of the imagery in the dreams before 9/11 was remarkable but the wider context of a growing crisis was also being dreamed. The escalation of politico-religious and economic difficulties was clear. We dreamed and talked regularly of the Middle East crisis; The dangers of cultural relativism, terrorism, fundamentalism, American foreign policy, the mass murder of both humans and animals (It was during the foot and mouth disease crisis). The particularity of objects and place is also similarly no mere coincidence. People knew that the World Trade Centre had been attacked before. The American embassy in Nigeria had been bombed with heavy casualties. The threat of Islamist suicide bombers was common knowledge (Wright, op cit). The dreams named things. The detail of thing and place was impressive. In retrospect it may be surprising that dream imagery included an attack on a market place, a high-rise building threatened from the sky. People dreamt of attackers who had no fear and were impervious to dialogue, a wounded centre, an attack by terrorists from the country on cosmopolitan city-dwellers: the psychosis of being torn apart in a third world country, the phrase, "Your time is coming". *Of course this was dreaming about the future, but it was a future that lay dormant in the present.*

Dreams may announce certain situations long before they happen but this is not necessarily a form of precognition. Many crises have a long unconscious history. Step by step we move towards disaster but we fail to see consciously what is visible in our dreams. This is as true of nations as it is of individuals. In the aftermath of 9/11 there was a deep sense of shock and depression. This was powerfully manifested in the content of the dreams, with perverse and psychotic features, leading to disconnection and fragmentation in the subsequent dialogue. This matrix—with some changes in membership—continued to meet monthly for a further two years. It is the development of dreams and ideas following 9/11, which I want to look at in the present chapter.

*Dreams after 9/11/01*

Initially, after the Twin Towers attack, there was a mood of excitement and anticipation in the matrix. Snippets of dreams and associations reveal both vulnerability and attempts at re-enactment:

> *I was part of a bombing group*
> *I went on hunger strike till death in support of the Palestinians*
> *There was a mushroom bomb—I panicked too soon*
> *I feared the Taliban—a society where no dancing is allowed*

How do people respond when they are the subject of other people's psychotic fantasy? 9/11 made everyone insecure about the future. This catastrophe might change the way we think and act for unknown years to come. Parts of our world had crumbled into the terrorist's nightmare, which meant we were living in a place of danger and rage. People felt pushed to the edge—presumably as had the suicide bombers. There was confusion as to how to think, how to construct meaning in the aftermath of disaster: how to guess the future when guided only by dread. In the words of Don DeLillo, "The narrative ends in the rubble and it is left to us to create the counterculture." (DeLillo, 2001, p. 1) The social dreaming process demonstrated this struggle for understanding, this grasping at structure. As one member of the matrix put it, "It seems we have to be almost about to be killed, in order to realize we can save our lives." And another, "Doris Lessing said, after the world is blown up, the young children will communicate through thought from the corners of the earth."

In the next matrix there was a dearth of dreams, a silence after the trauma. One man even dreamed "of no dream". The sense of uncertainty and incoherence in the ensuing jumble of thoughts incorporated images of unprotected sex, of castration and circumcision. There was an idea that we were in uncharted territory with people who did not speak the same language. There was a desire for sanctuary, ordinariness, the great need for women. There were also noticeable misunderstandings and disagreements between participants, of a kind not typical in social dreaming. Something had happened that we knew was going to happen. Fate and tragedy had been generated by suicide. Anyone could be a suicide bomber, no one could be trusted. We were the recipients of someone else's frenzy. We had become the realization of someone else's dream. Was this our destiny? But perhaps not everything is pre-determined. Think of the person who did not go to the office in New York on September 11th. Life is also about contingency. Encounters in dreams, for example, seem to be completely open to chance. The question is, when we meet something new in a dream, what might we do with it?

Thus dreamers conversing in the matrix searched for meaning and hope in the wake of New York's devastation. The Flood and Noah's ark appeared in several dreams. There was too much water in the world, the ark was a useful boat but this could be the end of an era. In one such dream a benign female Indian bus driver had a calming influence, telling her passengers, "It's okay, we're going to make it but we'll be late." Water, too, had benign connotations in relation to creativity and the maternal. People were looking for ways to survive the storm with sound companions. As with Noah's ark, there was a desire for sanctuary in the face of disaster, a need for ordinary competence and simplicity. Someone recalled the biblical slave song reference at the start of "The Fire Next Time" quoted by James Baldwin—

> "God gave Noah the rainbow sign,
> No more water, the fire next time".

> (Baldwin, 1964)

(Baldwin believed that black people's suffering was redemptive and their example had curative powers for the whole nation. If the efforts to redeem whites, in their innocence and ignorance, failed, then he believed the words of the slave song would come true—it would be the fire next time).

Associations came in bits and pieces. People feared a matrix with no dreams. It was felt that events were overtaking us inexorably, this would bring about a catastrophe of the imagination. The name of Beckett's minimalist play, *Imagination Dead, Imagine*, emerged with the chilling idea that we had become a figment of somebody else's imagination, a symbol in *someone else's* dream. Imagine if you had no imagination. The dreams were apocalyptic and disjointed, as if we were sifting through the rubble in this post mortem of disaster. There were many dense and chaotic dreams. Just a few will serve to describe this atmosphere of trauma and incoherence.

> At work the managers are throwing up black bile; something's coming, there's a change, worlds are changing, they can't keep it down, something's going to shift. Then a baby appears. I pick it up and it says, "Look how twisted they are". I fly across the room, everything morphs and I shoot out of this tunnel shouting, "save me".
>
> I was rifling through scripts looking for Woody Allen but only found Tarkovsky.
>
> I am on top of a building and it's dark. I'm with three others and we have light in our palms in order to communicate but the fourth corner isn't in the right place.
>
> I am in an L-shaped room. People are partially sighted. A woman says people are not really alive. I go down from the circle to the stalls. There is nothing of note to write down. How do we see Bin Laden? A Chilean analyst is bored. He reads 'Breakfast with Frost'.
>
> A Jewish colleague went on hunger strike in support of the Palestinians. He looked hazy and said, "You want to know how long it'll be before I die? It'll be Thursday or Friday. I'm leaving some money in my will for Turkish people."

Amongst dreamers there was a sense that the dreams were confused and hopeless, as if it was our fate, we had no choice over what happened to us.

> A man found me a house, which I did not want, as if I had no choice, as if it was fate. I wrote, 'Karma', meaning it is not just my fate. Karma means you live the consequences of your choice.

As people tried to make sense of the feeling of impotence, a philosophical stance developed. Nothing new was happening. We had been here before in history. We had survived the blitz. Yes, it's just business as usual, we must not give in to terrorism. It was seen to be heroic to try and remain calm, to not throw things away, to bear the fragments and hold them together; to be able to look at the trauma and not flinch. A thought arose that the dreams were helping to survive a conflict and regain our balance.

*"We're searching for our inner strength to get out of the way of things that fly at us.*

*We're like the alchemist. The world is in rubble and we look for what substance will rebuild it. The most grotty, shitty stuff we can find may change the world."*

But all that emerged were fragments; dreams and associations in bits and pieces. Although there was now an explosion of dreams— fourteen in the next matrix—it was difficult to put anything together, to connect and elaborate the themes. When communication is generated via the self rather than through the dream, the narrative becomes self-conscious, competitive, uneasy, even paranoid. The spell is broken, reverie evaporates. (This disconnection was symptomatic of a developing 'ego—versus—dream' split amongst dreamers, which we will come to later).

## The perverse matrix

This period of disorientation continued over the coming months as people dreamed of the fear in society of both individualism and of the collectivity, of narcissism and totalitarianism. It seemed the extreme 21st Century individualism of Western society had isolated us from one another, while a religious fanaticism wanted to kill us. Nobody voiced the thought that perhaps this referred to *us* and our experience in the matrix, too. There was a growing idea that the very existence of dreams as containers for knowledge—of dread and trauma—might be in jeopardy. Images of death and destruction emerged in the night thoughts. This included the eating of the father (the destruction of the phallus, the symbol of potency and knowledge) and the killing off of mother, with dreams of mummification (the maternal container with no internal space for reverie). Participants in the matrix appeared to be grappling to connect with lost memories as they dreamed, with marked psychotic anxiety, of disconnection and avoidance. This rejection of the unpalatable was vividly demonstrated in what could be termed *the perverse matrix*, where the dreams seemed to obfuscate terrifying thoughts at all costs. By perverse I mean an avoidance of truth, where something unbearable had to be covered up and denied, so that no thinking was possible. Something could not be named. Rather than shedding light, these dreams hid the trauma. The unbearable was split off. It could be glimpsed but only in little pieces, one bit at a time. Briefly the matrix became a sort of dead, stuffed maternal entity, unavailable for nourishment or play, a muse with out reverie or inspiration, a catastrophe of the imagination. A verbatim excerpt from such a matrix in January 2002 conveys the sense of depression:

*"We could be reborn."*

*"There's a sleepiness here, we're not connected. There's no spontaneity.*

*"This anxiety is like that of psychotics. It's undifferentiated material, there's a lack of connection.*

*"Yes, there seems to be a suppression of thinking, too much material."*

*"We've lost our way with these dreams. We seem to be trying to grapple with something which is not there."*

*"Maybe it's what's going on in the matrix. It's like a dormant matrix. It's gone to sleep on us."*

*"Dreams spark off in all directions to hide what we're traumatized by."*

*"Through talking about films we're trying to get back to the 9/11 disaster, we're reaching for it."*

*"No, I cannot watch it (the twin towers attack). After 5 days I'd had enough of watching catastrophe."*

*"It all has a sense of unreality to me: India versus Pakistan, why do they want to bomb each other?"*

*"All the best wars are with the people who are closest to you."*

*"Yes, like your brother or your neighbour, India and Pakistan are so similar."*

*"We're the mummies, stuffed with no feelings."*

*"We could be reborn."*

*"There's a sleepiness here, we're not connected. There's no spontaneity. These dreams are mosaical."*

*"It's really an untruth that we cannot live with. It takes me back to the cold war of the 70's. The lie is that the world is simple."*

*"Well the world is very complex. Anyone could be a terrorist— but at the same time things are being ironed out, positions are being taken."*

*"When God turns away from us, the world falls apart."*

"*There's a sense of hopelessness, the meter's running down.*"

"*What is the matrix responding to in this depressed, ineffable, unspontaneous state?*"

"*The problem is we don't know what is real—so we cannot play with ideas. Last year we were playful but we did not realize what out dreams were about. There's no delight about what's in our unconscious now.*"

"*Being in the wrong place, things are not where they should be. There is no system to trust.*"

This nostalgic memory of innocence seems like the realization after The Fall. Reality comes in with disillusionment. And yet, amidst the wreckage of disaster—this inability to use dreams for thinking—signs appeared of what was eventually to emerge. At first it was literally signs inscribed on stone. Then in the next matrix came the following dreams, all reported by women:

## Dreams of fire and the mob

1. *I was in Delhi at a wedding party. They did the conga, it was like a concert...then it got nasty and there were mobs coming. I saw a church with flames inside. The mob had not arrived but people set fire to the building anyway. A girl came and said "I've booked you on Virgin Airways to London." Then I got the standard anxiety dream. Would I get to the airport in time etc., A taxi arrived with an Islington councillor rescuing people from the mob, then off he went.*

2. *I had the same dream. Going to a meeting in another town, it was so slow, there were huge jams and I had to change at suburban Reigate. At first I didn't worry but later as I waited in a queue in a house opposite there was a fire.*

3. *I also had a mob dream. I was asked to run a group and it was in a large auditorium on a slope. Not sure why I was there. People came into a circle, the whole place filled with masses of people. So I said, you can see the body of a group. As it piled up with people a slurry of clay came over the top, people walked on top of others. It was pleasurable, people were in ecstasy. The crowd broke up and military men appeared, they'd asked me to do the group. So I flung a man down a slope and then apologized.*

*Sweet honey in the rock dream*

4. *I was selected to be in the singing group, "Sweet Honey in the Rock". I'm flabbergasted, why me? I'm white, I don't know the songs. I was walking behind them in a gorgeous setting at the top of a mountain. I hope I don't have to do a solo.* (Sweet Honey in the Rock are a female a capella singing group popular in the 1980s)
5. *I'm at an international conference and I'm chosen to sing a song with Maya Angelou*

Members remarked on the synchronicity of these dreams:

> "It's fear of the mob, joy of the group, ideas both benign and sinister.
> The ground trampling reminded me of Dante's Inferno.
> Or the mud at Glastonbury.
> It's like the auditorium of a Greek drama, or social dreaming—with merging, no boundaries and then feeling better, as in social dreaming.
> Slurry and clay—it's like being recreated
> It's like mob and ante mob—heaven and hell, ways of being together in a group.
> Like a good idea of Glastonbury.
> Can anything good come out of it?
> The myth is, "If you hit a rock, honey will come out."

Amidst the fear of flames and the mob, a woman's voice was being chosen and there was a reference to something sweet emerging from stone (sweet honey in the rock).

(The initial reference to sweet honey in the rocks comes from early Aegean cultures where the bee was believed to be a sacred insect that bridged the natural world to the underworld. The bees made their nests in rock and were eventually featured as tomb decorations of bee-winged goddesses: literally, there was sweet honey in the rock As we have seen in the Chapter on Social Dreaming and the Self, the maternal is source of the sense of 'being' for the growing infant. Thus the sacred insect here is the honey bee, signifying 'bee-ing').

## The whale dream

*Next came the following two dreams*

1. *I was on Tower Bridge and a guy was fishing. His line goes taught, the rod bends—Oh! It's a big fish, it's like a boat scudding along the river. The surface of the Thames starts to swell and a big black head emerges. It leaps out and crashes down and it's an enormous whale. Next a behemoth gets out and clambers onto the bank. Panic! It's morphing into a duck-billed platypus. People scatter. I burst into a club. People are dancing, the rappers have green spiky hair. A voice said, "Oh! After the whale people cannot do that kind of thing". The whale had disconnected things.*

## The tower of books dream

2. *In the next dream, I'm landing a shark and there's a tower of purple granite, which erupts out of the ground. Hubris. This stone tower is actually made out of books.*

The whale dream evoked powerful associations of a huge sea change in the matrix, a shift which unbalanced the equilibrium. The dream announces disconnection and hubris. Dreamers responded imaginatively but with alarm. The process of catching a fish was seen to parallel the process of social dreaming, catching and then following the myriad images which emerge from the unconscious deep. As one dreamer put it, "The whale is like a social dream." Another, thinking of Jonah and the Whale, connected this to the Gershwin song, "It Ain't Necessarily So" implying that what is already written is not necessarily true.

> *Now Jonah he lived in a whale,*
> *Yes Jonah he lived in a whale,*
> *The things that you're liable,*
> *To read in the bible,*
> *It ain't necessarily so.*

Perhaps the inference here was one of scepticism to the whale dream. 'It ain't necessarily so.' This dream of disconnection and hubris unbalanced the matrix—and yet hidden in the fishing dreams had been another reference to *words and stone* (a tower of books). There were rich and varied responses to whales and behemoths, from Moby Dick to the Bible, from Golam to Myra Hindley, from Douglas Bader to the idea of a Second Coming. The dream had been of a man fishing (although of course a whale is not a fish). This evoked the Arthurian legend of the Fisher King, a leader with a wounded thigh who is kept alive by the existence of the grail—the stone bowl or dish which makes him whole. (Percival the knight asks this maimed king "What ails thee, Fisher King?" and it is this question which heals his wound. Just as in the rite of passage for Jonah who emerged as a changed man from the belly of the whale, the Fisher King is the story of healing and growth that comes through the power of relatedness, typically associated with the feminine qualities of empathy and compassion. His realm had become a wasteland where he was unable to connect with the life-saving contents in the waters of the unconscious).

The whale is an ubiquitous archetypal image signifying stability and a sound base. As a container it recalls the grail, the ark, the womb—the place of safety, of healing. It is striking that such ancient myths reoccur in the social dreaming matrix as known archetypes, stories of universal application. They are repeated in, for example, T.S. Eliot's The Wasteland and in Jungian psychology where the search for the grail becomes the key to personal identity and of course with Christ's cup at the Last Supper.

However, in this matrix the dreamer of the whale dream strongly rejected any hermeneutic or referential model, saying, "The whales I catch are social dreams, like a form of Western yoga. Yes, we can say the dream means this or that but it (my dream) is about the process which puts you into a dream state. It is dreaming. I reject any form of interpretation, I go to sleep." Here was passionate resistance to the thoughts his dream evoked in others. As if it was a private not a social dream. His point that the dream should not be interpreted underlines a paradox. Of course dreams can, will and sometimes *should* be interpreted—Charlotte Beradt demonstrates this in *The Third Reich of Dreams*—and yet this dreamer talks of a process that puts you into a dream state that needs to remain untouched. This implies a form which is holy, sacred, as of course dreams have been in a wide variety of cultures. There is a mystical-religious aspect. As with art, music, mythology, poetry, these are forms traditionally connected in some way to the sacred. Perhaps dreams have the same quality. We are in them, they have us, we speak them out, they represent some other reality, beyond the self and yet connected to it immutably. It is tempting to view the 'no interpretation' decree as a ban on thinking, rather like a fatwa issued by the Ayatollahs forbidding trespass into the sacred. And yet we need to be careful not to fall into what Edward Said calls the 'Orientalist' trap, as if ours is the righteous ground. East and West have different worldviews, different ways of thinking. Things cannot be interpreted so easily in the light of vastly different cultural understandings. The whale dream shows us a conundrum—to be faced by the wonder and majesty of a hybrid mammal form which shows us our limitations and also enables us to be in touch with 'not-knowing'; It points up the fallacy in believing we can interpret things so easily.

Yet this dream conveys another truth. What happens in a community if certain forms of discourse are forbidden? Prohibition—the *rejection* of the idea that dreams have meaning—places a taboo on thought, on insight. According to this doctrine, a dream must not be played with, elaborated, opened up to infinite stories. As in totalitarian societies, there can be no other version. Here, in this matrix, there is a clear parallel with events after 9/11. With the destruction of the Twin Towers, thinking became impossible, flattened out. America was apparently not able to stop and think, 'Why do they hate us? What does this mean?' If you cannot comprehend what's happened to you and why, the outcome next time maybe something beyond your darkest nightmares. "No more water, the fire next time". When New York sustained that terrible attack, it found out what some people in third world countries had been experiencing for years. America now discovered *the real*, which was hitherto always out there, somewhere else, or as the "problem" to be solved by Star Wars, John Wayne or Superman. The Twin Towers attack was the future happening in the present, the disaster movie come true in the here-and-now. If, as Freud stated, a dream is the fulfilment of a repressed wish, could it be that after decades of sci-fi fantasies, war films about ruthless, cruel barbarians who are always outside and threatening, America got what it unconsciously longed-for—contact with the real? Slavov Zizek suggests that the threat of American vulnerability was always libidinally invested. "The unthinkable which happened was thus the object of fantasy, America got what it fantasized about and this was the greatest surprise" (Zizek, 2001, p. 2). Thus the impact of the bombings is accounted for by the background of a borderline that separates the digitalized First World from the Third World "desert of the real". Living in an insulated, artificial universe has created the notion that some ominous agent is threatening destruction from outside. As Lawrence puts it, the more we deny tragedy, the more we bring it into being, because somebody, somewhere is having the psychotic kind of thinking that generates tragedy (Lawrence, 2000, pp. 208–231).

The sudden explosion of the whale dream undermined thinking. Something emerged in the matrix which reflected what took place in the collective psyche, as represented by Bin Laden and George Bush. Bin Laden released a video which reported seven dreams of his own followers, prior to 9/11, which envisaged the Twin Towers attacks. Bin Laden told them not to tell anyone (Lawrence, 2005, pp. 81–2). During the same period, several hundred similar dreams of American citizens are reported—of plane crashes, buildings exploding, twin towers etc.: the same dreams but with different emotions; Americans experiencing fear and vulnerability, Islamists rejoicing at these 'good omens' (Bulkeley, 2002). After the attack the Bush administration responded immediately and without reflection, with an ill-conceived war on a distant country, eventually constructing the horrors of Guantanamo Bay—a prison worthy of any totalitarian state trying to control free-thinking. You can stop people talking about dreams but you can't stop them dreaming. Just as in the USA and Saudi Arabia—and despite the split developing in the matrix at this time—the dreams insisted on illuminating what was happening, both in the matrix and in the world at large.

In the famous analysis of his own dream of Irma, Freud showed how the most trivial feature may contain the brightest clue. (Freud, 1900). Hidden in the two whale/fishing dreams had been another and quite different reference to *words and stone*—'a tower of books' This did not go unnoticed. One person's association to this image was of the Holocaust memorial in Austria, which featured Ann Whiteread's concrete sculpture of the "Nameless Library," an inverted concrete room of books. Another member thought of the Library of Alexandria which was destroyed by Muslims in 800AD. They did not like the idea that books contained pictures of other religions. In retrospect, these linkages have a profound resonance in the present context and point to the consequences of disregarding danger signs when they appear in our dreams. Whiteread's sculpture was defaced by right wing vandals from the neo-Nazi FPO party who actively deny the holocaust. The "Nameless Library" is a potent motif. The destruction of books is a concrete symbol for the prohibition of thinking. The Nazis burned books as a prelude to genocide. Thirteen hundred years later the totalitarian fascist ideal still threatens world peace. Both the Austrian Nazis and the mediaevalists were stating, "You are forbidden to talk about our dream, further thinking is forbidden on pain of death." At the end of this matrix someone remarked that a stone had been found in Yugoslavia which was inscribed with an unknown language.

Ensuing matrixes began to reveal the hidden dread of the earlier sessions, the unthinkable monsters concealed under the flimflam and deception of disconnected images. One man described a dream in eight parts, the fragments of which read like a text for the apocalypse. From this dream people constructed a scenario of unconscious dread:

• we are approaching the terminus
• we feel powerless in facing what might happen
• Barbie dolls are connected with Klaus Barbie the French mass-murderer of Jews
• you cannot frighten people who are prepared to die as suicide bombers
• the horror of controlling people's minds by corporate companies who create desires in order to sell new products
• 'Alzheimer's disease' as a general state of mind in the face of world-conflict, the mind deadness required by any form of totalitarian state.
• A quote from Philip Roth's novel, The Dying Animal, that, "In every calm and reasonable person there is hidden a second person scared witless about death."

The dangers of mindlessness—of dismissing our dreams and ignoring the wisdom of others—were emphasized in other dreams:

I was attacked by a paranoid schizophrenic who tried to stick a biro into a spot on my head...when the police arrive I'm about to tell them my *experience and then realize "Oh! It was only a dream"* (The dreamer rejects his own dream while dreaming!).

*I'm in a New York hospital on a bed waiting for a diagnosis and expecting the worst. Fearing how much I've smoked. Do I come clean and tell the doctors or is it too late? I meet some young black criminologists but their Navaho Indian theories seem naïve and I can't be bothered to argue with them. It's strange as normally I really would have taken them seriously.*

## The suicidal dog dream

The images in the next matrix signalled death, the finishing point, claustrophobia, something being cut off.

*I was in Jerusalem, the trees were heavily pollarded, cut-off short— parallel to it was a street, rubbishy and neglected. I was walking with the widow of a German translator. Then along came a car and a little dog got in the way and was run over. A red stripe of powdery material was left, like something that was over. The dog got itself killed.*

After this matrix, the author of this dream left and never came back. Encoded in his dream was a sense that something had been cut down, the dreaming was over. Something could no longer be translated. Whether the dog stood for a suicide bomber or for the matrix, something was over. The split, the challenge to free association and meaning of dreams was invidious. Because there had been silence in the face of this prohibition, something fundamental to the process was being ignored, dismissed. The process began to close down. To dream you need to think symbolically. There had been a breakdown in symbolization in the matrix. Only the dreams refused to obey.

In the next session, there were now four dreams about babies which were abused, starving, had a hole in the heart, legs cut off. It was suggested that these babies were the social dreaming process which was being abused. The question arose, can we criticize and then forgive someone in the matrix instead of leaving. In retrospect it seems likely that this referred to the 'killed dog' dream of the previous meeting but it was not picked up. The scenario described in the dream could not be spoken, instead it was acted out: literally by 'walking out'. It was a tense point. As one person put it, "Something is undreamed which we experience. Something seer-like from which we dissociate."

In a dream about a wedding, a brother was pushed down into the tarmac until he disappeared. It seemed the matrix had been flattened like a battered baby. There was a sense there was no way back, we were stuck. There was a claustrophobic dream about a tunnel. The insistence on dream telling without associations remained unchallenged as if invisible. This certainty had been destructive of the potential space, where it had become impossible to stay with the idea of not-knowing and just waiting to see where the free associations led us. A dilemma had been created of ritual versus epistemology. But social dreaming is neither: it is more than just the habit of dream telling. At the same time, as a form of knowledge it depends on not knowing. In the claustrophobia of the matrix described here the task became stymied. The matrix is more a subliminal environment than a place of certainty. Social dreaming is an uncharted journey to find an identity which is not based on ego. This involves taken for granted rules which, when broken, cause a breach in the process. The dreams demonstrated this but the thinking did not get there. Conviction is not the same as certainty. The matrix had attempted to contain its own conflict and failed but the dreams remained as markers for future use.

What is social dreaming for, if anything? The implication of this chapter is that social dreaming can be useful, can have a purpose, create insight, reveal hidden conflict and aid communication. The paradox is that this is only possible if we give up the search for truth or end product. It functions only by having no function. What is required is to trust the process—speaking the dream, following the associations, waiting and listening—and abandon any attempt to 'get somewhere.'

At this point (July 2002) we recessed for the summer break eventually to resume the following October. The ensuing year of social dreaming is the subject of the next chapter.

# CHAPTER FOUR

# Sweet honey in the rock

"When there are two people, one of whom can say what life is, the other (almost) what the soul is, it is only right that they should see each other and talk together often."

—Freud quoted in Bettleheim, 1989, p. 46

When we reconvened in October 2002, it was with a smaller matrix of dreamers. At the same time we were joined by four new members. Despite this turnover in participants many of the earlier dream themes continued. It was clear that the difficulties described in the last chapter had been a constructive part of an inevitable process after a traumatic scenario. Although much of the anxiety and uncertainty remained and splits and tensions arose, this time there was a more thoughtful and direct response to the tendency to neglect, avoid, suppress and prohibit.

## Fear of not being afraid

In earlier matrixes there had been an avoidance and displacement of fear. Perhaps we were in a state where reality felt so awful that it had to be denied. It was suggested that sometimes it is appropriate to be frightened. People were feeling very near the edge. The psychoanalyst Donald Winnicott had shown in his work on vertigo that this is actually a fear of *not being afraid*. If you are not frightened you may go too near the edge and fall off. Milan Kundera similarly sees vertigo as the *desire* to fall, to fail, to go down, to be weak and warns us to beware of this tendency in western society. At this time there was understandable anxiety amongst participants and probably in society at large. There was fear of further terrorist attacks on British soil, the Bali disaster had just occurred with the deaths of over two hundred people, and Britain had, with the USA, embarked on war in Afghanistan and was contemplating the invasion of Iraq. Underlying this atmosphere of being 'scared witless' was the 'Alzheimer's' state of mind—imagination dead, unthinking, reality being wiped out, forgotten. The real danger was of being in a world in which people were not actually frightened enough. A German woman reported a dream:

> "I was staying in Bristol with friends and to get to the toilet you went into the dark. I switched on the light and the bulb blew. Then I dreamed that I organized a new bulb and had to get up and put it in before the lady of the house came down."

Later in the matrix she said that, since telling the dream, she had noticed her anxiety had noticeably lessened. "I feel relieved after describing the bulb. If more people could do it they would feel better. Guilt can be shared—absolutely. The dream said, 'I blew it'. I carry the guilt of the Second World War. I am German. Actually my bulb dream took place when I was in the house of some Jews. Clearly this is very significant. J. is right; we *do* need to be frightened about these things."

Another member said, "What is a dream of the world, in a culture? What should it be? I went to buy some meat and this Muslim man wanted to talk about vegetarianism. He started to proselytize and told me, 'Islam is the only thing which will give you hope. (I'm Jewish). He tried to pull me round. I said 'Do we have to fight, can't we be side by side?' He had a whole other construct. People fear that if you don't join in, this is the end of the world. As if they're saying, 'You must dream my dream.'"

In the post 9/11 context of mistrust and fear this story is a touching vignette of the fragility of identity and the disparate need to hang on to it. In the face of difference—whether Islamist fundamentalism or America's homogeneity in globalization—dreams are a source of resilience to survive. *But only if we take them seriously.* As Charlotte Beradt shows in her study of pre-war Germany, people were actually dreaming of how subservient and compliant they would soon become to a brutal fascist regime. They 'knew' what was going to happen but did not speak about it. (Beradt op cit)

## Creativity out of destruction

Synchronicity in the dream content continued. In the next matrix, people dreamed of more books—a blue book of wisdom, one of fairy tales, then a dictionary:

> *King James the First had a bill of no pounds, no shillings and no pence against him. A group of people in Oxford were deciding on statutes for the revision of a dictionary, stating:*
>
> *"It shall be to such a person, on such terms, for such remuneration as the governors in council shall determine." It was a parameter of contract where governors would get their power from a group of people. It involved the language and words of a New End.*

A blank bill was perceived to be 'wiping the slate clean.' Associations suggested a desire for a new social contract, a language to define culture, a language connected to emotional experience. If a dictionary was a dream it would be about how to formulate new thoughts, looking up one word to find another on a journey of infinite conjecture. As one person put it: 'This is a plea for a revised edition, as if we feel things cannot be defined any more. And revise also means to remember.' This dream also enigmatically promised us a New End. There was now a mélange of meanings, different perceptions of content and process. While new thoughts were crystallizing, there was disagreement amongst dreamers in the thinking section as to what a constellation of conflicting dreams signified, or whether they had to signify anything at all: perhaps the *process* was the crucial element. To some it seemed there was too much information, others disagreed, in that we were each 'looking through a different window' and just needed to 'sift through it all'. There was also a sense of intense emotional communication, lack of inhibition amidst free-flowing dialogue. It seemed that the anticipation of discovery pushed the matrix into full-throttle. Dreamers noticed this spontaneity with pleasure:

> "The past three matrixes have had a strong emotional effect. It's remarkable. We are revising the dictionary and seeing emotion as part of that language. The book is empty. It's not the dreams we take out of here but the experience of thinking together."

An idea was taking shape of another kind of submerged emotional language. This was captured, for example, in a dream about old musical instruments preserved under water.

It was not the content or the meaning of the dreams at this stage but the emotional experience of engaging in a rich pattern of complex thoughts and feelings. The following dreams give a sense of this variety.

> *I was taking a group of Americans on a tour of the village in Africa where I used to live. I go to get a beer; they've only got long sticky nosebags. I can take a right or a left path. I take them back to my childhood and want to show them the original unspoilt landscape but instead I find a theme park of world religions, crazy golf etc. It's all homogenized. The received languages were all burned out; they were going back to something more primitive.*
>
> *I had a dream of a carpet. I'm cleaning a room with a friend, putting water on wood; the carpet is a mixture of Asian and Bedouin. At the edge it's got tiny moth eggs. Then it becomes a swimming pool, with a Jewish man on the other side. I've got to dive in because on the bottom is a bacon sandwich.*
>
> *I'm on a football pitch ready to play behind the substitute. The captain shakes my hand and seems interesting. He starts singing "Onward Christian Soldiers". Then girls arrive and he knocks against a sharp edge and I realize he is a double-sided man—like Christianity.*

Homogenization and the burning out of languages signify differences, which cannot be tolerated, and this links to the notion of a double-sided Christianity, which cannot face its other 'shadow' side. Jung suggested that if you turn God around, the Devil is on his other side—a form of dissociation, an unintegrated God.

## The tiger, fox and lipstick dream

*I covered my lips with lipstick. I was on a plane, increasingly dehy-drated, there was not enough water, and people were getting desper-ate. The back of the plane was open, revealing neat, green fields. Some people jumped out in the USA. There was not enough to eat here. We went to a restaurant, no food. Then I found half of a dead tiger—then a horrible black fox wanted to steal our food including the tiger. I killed the fox with a shoe. We ate the tiger and then the fox, black and hor-rible. I reapplied the lipstick and that was that.*

## The dreamer's association was

"I think this was a dream about the inhumanity of humans. The lipstick makes me think how thin a veneer civilization offers us. I think of Rwanda, where I've just been. There is no sign of the genocide after eight years. Material well-being, which is supplied by the Americans, covers up what happened. We seem to be on the edge of a return to mediaeval violence and war."

This describes loss of life, loss of meaning and loss of context. There is a materialist misinterpretation of Rwanda's needs by the Americans where Rwanda as a place with a culture and a history gets lost.[1]

## *It's up to us women*

In the next matrix there was a dearth of dreams. War was imminent in Iraq and London was on high alert for a terrorist attack. As one participant said:

"We're all saying we are not panicky or anxious. I wonder why? There are troops at Heathrow airport. I cannot remember my dreams of the last three weeks. Maybe it's not possible to dream at present."

A female member, who I will call Jean, remarked that at times like this there seemed to be a lack of female authority in the world. In her words: "We allow it to happen, we allow men to behave like this." This thought-provoking statement came after her reported dream that she was pregnant and felt she should give birth but was told she could wait a month. It was felt this dream held a paradox—

"We're relieved at the lack of pain in birth and yet the joy of creativity we want now." *It* reminds me of a paper I read, called "Destruction as a cause of coming into being".

This led to a discussion of Winnicott's notion of the uses of hatred and of the importance of ruthlessness in the creative process (Winnicott, 1947). None of the other women in the matrix had spoken and so Jean returned to her earlier statement. "What do you think of my idea earlier that women allow all this to happen? Perhaps it is sometimes the case that you have to argue violently in the cause of peace." The idea was not directly taken up.

Perhaps, someone suggested, such an absence of dreams only happens when the nightmare is real and taking place out there; then dreams revert to being private and the link between the public and the private is severed. What connects people is so broken that the language of dreaming cannot be shared. Thus there is a loss of the symbolic. Everything becomes concretized.

At this point in the dialogue Jean stuck to her dream—the birth of an idea:

> "This is a new concept of authority which is neither oedipal nor the old feminism. It's up to us women that is my dream: there has been a loss of the father and of male authority in the world. It's not just that women must start doing something—but that we need to realize the dream in all its forms. Solutions come through dreams. People seem to not dare to associate to what I am saying but something new is being forged."

Jean had to be courageous to insist that her dream be worked on. People try and get away from some dreams and back into complexities of ego structure or the idea of group process. The dialogue can become personal and defensive to avoid unpalatable notions. There was a now a tense contretemps in the matrix with arguments of political correctness and erudite interpretations of group dynamics. The free flow of ideas dissipated. Indeed one female member dropped out after this difficult session. It is not always easy to trust the process and just wait for the next dream. However, the following dream was told near the end of this meeting:

> *I was in a big temple, there were hieroglyphs; not letters but sacred writing. I was transfixed, trying to understand. I seemed to get one of*

*these hieroglyphs and then I read it in a dream. It connects to music.*
*There was also sound relating to these.*

Again, we find writings, signs and sounds. Regardless of individual feelings, group dynamics, hurt egos, or defensive structures, the matrix just goes on. The process is not about what A is doing to B but about what one person's dream creates in another's unconscious, thus producing further dreams and ideas. The focus is the dream and not the dreamer. One dream leads to another. There is a space in which we can create material for the dream work to operate. Everything, which happens in a session, combines to provide stimuli for a dream, a single unity. The dream becomes what Winnicott called a transitional object, linking us with emerging experience. This is always connected to play. When children play they are not thinking about who they are supposed to be. The pleasurable lightness of being of the social dreaming experience is that we forget our *selves*. When we give up the struggle to present a coherent, consistent, non-contradictory identity we lose ourselves in the process: we start just to be. The process is to speak the dreams and freely associate to them, saying whatever comes to mind, without too much censorship. The scrutiny and surveillance of our own split off alter ego, watching and criticizing us, surprisingly dissolves if we dare to trust the dream. As with listening to, or playing, music, an unmediated part of our character is allowed to hold forth and sing. When there is a confrontation between the clever and the playful, the matrix versus the group, or dream versus ego, then the potential space is disrupted. In this session it had been difficult to play with the question, "What do you think of my idea—it's up to us women?" However, the matrix continued regardless. Something profound was emerging. Perhaps it had taken a certain amount of aggressive disagreement to engender a creative idea. The next dream continued an earlier theme.

## Psyche and Eros

### Symbol on the mountain dream

*I looked at a map of a mountainside with a cable car, which came down to the base station. Higher up on the middle stages there were two others feeding into the main one coming down. The name of the station was Long*

*Hours—it was about a decision as to which way to go. I associate this dream to L's reference to cave paintings—our ancestors started to realize they could imagine and symbolize. The shamans were dreaming their dreams.*

*In my dream the symbol on the map was in the shape of a psi, a letter of some kind.*

She drew it (the symbol of the Greek letter psi)
Associations now came swiftly:

> *- It's a bird's foot.*
> *Or a vagina—a symbol of creativity, fertility.*
> > *I love hills and mountains—strength and majesty—*
> > *I will lift up mine eyes to the hills, from thence cometh my strength*
> > *They're signs of the eruption of the world, upheaval.*
> > *Yes, "Destruction as a cause for coming into being"*
> > *Matterhorn—the horns matter*
> > *In Switzerland they did not take part in wars. How did they do it?*
> > *They didn't know the rules of war in the Fifteenth Century and refused to play the game with England.*
> > *So everyone knows what's going to happen.*
> > *The pervert always knows what's going to happen, it's about being in control.*
> > *What did the sadist say to the masochist who begged him for punishment?—He said, "No."*
> > *This is about alliances—you can change camps.*
> > *Certain things can come in from the past and it's alright, other things should not. A good man becomes bad, or vice versa.*
> > *The Lysistrata is a play about women who try and stop the men going to war. They do this by going on strike sexually, by withdrawing their favours.*
> > *The horn will be deprived of its pleasure, that is the matter.*
> > *The perversion is of the USA wanting a war which they know they will win. If you destroy, then you have to rebuild.*
> > *This matrix flies like a bird, what makes it so? Was it the 27th letter in the alphabet, the psi?*

*Maybe we are in the process of discovering a new language. What we have so far is 'a', the first letter. The alphabet had to be constructed in the first*

*place, just as with the first person to point and say, 'That is a mountain'.*
*The environment is brought into reality by the word. It is a symbiotic*
*relationship, one cannot exist without the other, it's reciprocal.*

*The word is 'psi' and this also means soul. Clearly there is an association*
*between the Soul and the matrix. Psi is the origin of the word psyche.*

(The word 'psyche' was mistranslated in Freud's work to mean
'mind' but actually, as Bruno Bettleheim shows, it means 'soul.')
(Bettleheim, 1989)

## Jean continued

*This makes me think of the myth of Eros and Psyche. She is married to*
*the god, Eros. Psyche is not supposed to know who he is but she disobeys*
*and sees him in an oil lamp and he wakes up burnt and flies off. Psyche is*
*then bereft and ends up at the home of Aphrodite Venus (Eros's mother)*
*who gives Psyche impossible tasks to fulfil. Somehow, she does not know*
*how, she finds help. She learns to think laterally not logically. She always*
*fails and this is the solution. It is about the significance of not knowing the*
*answer. Aphrodite Venus was born from the dark night of chaos. She stands*
*for the old feminine which is inimical to the masculine, whereas Psyche*
*represents a new way of relating—of relatedness between the masculine*
*and the feminine. This is very hopeful. No egos mean it is free. When we*
*forget who we are, the matrix comes into the foreground. When we remem-*
*ber, it recedes and the group re-emerges with all its fears, competition and*
*inhibitions.*

There are three critical ideas here

(1) Creativity generated by destruction
With *The Tiger, Fox and Lipstick Dream*, we witness how crucial
it is to be able to express aggressive and destructive feelings in
some containable way. The reference to the murder of two million people in Rwanda is a chilling reminder of what lies beneath
the surface of civilization. It is easy to forget that we are animals.
Perhaps the tiger and fox are there to remind us what humans
are capable of in desperation and anger. The psychopathic killer
reference (endnote) underlines the danger when hatred and rage
cannot be safely expressed in childhood. Donald Winnicott wrote
extensively on the central role of destructiveness in the child's

emotional development. His paper on *The Use of an Object* stresses how important it is for an infant:

- To be able to express aggression
- To witness that the object (parent) survives its anger.
- To experience separateness through the realization that the surviving object has a life of its own and that omnipotence is therefore not possible. (Winnicott 1971)

In *Hate in the Countertransference* he underlined the value of acknowledging the hatred that we sometimes all feel, including towards those about whom we care. (Winnicott, 1947)

Conversely he also notes the role of ruthlessness and destruction in the creative process. Sometimes it may be essential to be single minded. Resistance can be a sign of health. Being nice or polite can be ineffective or inappropriate. Sometimes individuals walk away from situations rather than say what's really on their minds. The idea of the matrix is to speak clearly whatever is the next thought. There was an aliveness in the exchange of ideas about feminism within this matrix. Jean was not compliant and spoke out when she felt not taken seriously. It was a destructive process, there was anger, hurt and disagreement—but this was necessary to give birth to an idea.

(2) Women going on strike
Lysistrata is a play about female power and authority, written by Aristophanes. Although not greatly influential in Ancient Greece, it has more recently been effective as an idea in a variety of settings. In 1997 during the drug wars in Columbia, women employed a 'sex strike' to enable an end to violence in which men could lay down their arms and talk. They achieved a brief but significant cease-fire. Then in 2001, in the Turkish village of Sirt, women similarly went on strike in response to the inaction of their lazy men folk. They were successful and managed, for the first time, to get a new pipeline of clean water laid on. This was achieved by the withdrawal of sexual relations.' Probably the most convincing example was in Iceland in 1979, where in the "women's day off," 90% of women went on strike. Since nearly all

women worked in the home this affected almost every household and led to the world's first equality legislation. Then four years later the head of this women's movement was elected head of parliament.

(3) A new way of relating

The imago of Psyche stands for differentiation of the conscious from the unconscious. She represents a significant step in history, where woman becomes responsible for her own decision-making. She had to undergo a variety of tasks. Unlike the mythical male's act of heroism (against the whale, the dragon, monster etc), her deed of autonomy is an act of love. Psyche represents a fruitful embodiment of the masculine and the feminine, similar to Jung's idea of individuation. Here, the female meets aggression with wisdom not force, being prepared to wait in order to avoid violent confrontation. Jung saw the essence of the feminine in personal relatedness. Winnicott talked of the 'good enough mother' who could patiently allow the baby to create the world as if it was the child's invention; who could enable the child to be alone in her presence without impingement or intrusion. Bion describes the 'reverie' of the mother in taking in and containing the child's anxiety until it can appropriately be thought about and given back to the child in a measured, bearable way.

Each of these aspects of the feminine is touched upon in this matrix. They are far removed from contemporary conventional 'masculine' approaches. Not logical, rational, scientific, prescriptive, or aggressive, they represent a totally different concept of power and interaction. They emphasise relatedness, protectiveness, patience and tolerance; negative capability, the possibility of not knowing. By 'reverie' is meant the possibility that difficult emotions—such as dread, anxiety, hatred—can be safely contained, and when possible, thought about carefully and calmly. Psyche, this other notion of the feminine, makes viable a space in which the dream can occur and can be processed, symbolically close to the mother's body and to the sound of her voice. Many of the dreams and associations hinted at this life-giving space, this 'sweet honey in the rock.' It is, we believe, a model for human relationships, which is greatly lacking in contemporary society. But children need *both* parents. Relationship is the very basis of sanity. Ironically, the essential ingredient so often absent is the very presence of the masculine, strong, protective and logical father: a figure who defines and maintains the space so that relatedness and containment can exist. As the free association put it, 'Horns matter', the phallus, the male capacity for reflection, knowledge and order, is significantly absent from contemporary society—the creative notion of male power. The idea of the father in our society has declined. In many ways it is this loss, literally and symbolically, which these dreams highlighted.

## A new end

Dreams are great levellers. There is no hierarchy of motifs. The most trivial objects take on significance, profound issues jostle with the mundane, memories are mixed-in with the here and now. In this chapter I hope to have shown how in this ongoing matrix, after a long and difficult labour, the dreams gave birth to serious ideas: about the need for new ways of thinking, the profound impor- tance of reverie and empathy—as opposed to temporal 'masculine' logic—and for a radically different form of authority in the face of potential catastrophe. Through protest, debate and the dialogue of memory, consciousness is established and relationship strength- ened. And yet, as we approached the final meetings of this three year experience, other themes returned, in particular the encroach- ing end point, the loss of relationship and connection, thoughts of death, contemplation of the infinite void. All dreams are inevitably related; traces of one live on in another. As we dreamt of death, child- hood returned. Water and the sea were ever present and the search for good, safe, alive containers surfaced in the dreams—ways of thinking, ways of surviving, of work and pleasure. In one of these late dreams was a memory of a good boat—a container—near some marvellous rocks:

### Golden Pond Dream (2003)

*As in 'On Golden Pond', I was in a boat near some rocks. It was a boat which belonged to a Northern Irish friend I've known for forty years. His father made sausages. As I stood at the prow I marvelled at the rocks. Somehow we never hit them, we just squeezed through. Whoever was steering the boat did it with a sixth sense.*

As I write this paragraph, it is uncanny to remember that this dream echoes a similar dream at the start of the very first matrix three years earlier:

## The Ferry Dream (2000)

*I was on a large ferry. It was not out of the harbour before it turned, a huge turning of the boat. We just made it, though it touched the quay as it went. There were police, who shouted, "Did you touch the side?" It was either a brilliant manoeuvre or very dangerous. If you looked at the quay you could see a bit of the paintwork had come off. I'd thought I would not be allowed on. I'd left my luggage behind on the quay.*

The Golden Pond dream evoked the faculty of intuition; the subtlety of judgement required, when the prow points in one direction but you steer from the stern. We tackle something in one place and it has effect elsewhere, thus negotiating a series of opposites. Wonder was expressed at the instinctive navigational power of migrating birds; there were memories of leaving by ship and wanting to turn back; thoughts of The Perfect Storm. The essential reference here is to the *insight* of social dreaming. The dream directs us to trust a 'sixth sense', an intuitive, non-rational, 'seeing' part of the mind, which guides us throughout the process. Trusting the dream, the matrix had steered its way into different waters. The denouement, after three years of social dreaming, came with this notion of a new but unformed vocabulary, a different map of the psyche, the potential depth of a 'feminine' wisdom, to steer with a different touch. Quintessentially, this was about *not knowing*, about not trying to find some absolute truth but instead trusting a different way of seeking and of relating to each other from a non-egotistical, non-ideological position. Here was the honey in the rock.

In the Ferry Dream, the key—'quay'—was to trust the unconscious, to dare to embark on an unknown journey, which allowed the dreams to take you where they would. All baggage could be left behind. And this just by speaking freely in response to the dreams without the critical eye of the 'thought police'—the ego, the group, the clever, the politically correct. This is not about proving that we are right and have the only truth. In the Twentieth century millions of people were killed by others who knew what was best for them. As Adam Phillips says:

> *We are living now in the aftermath of the horrifying consequences of politically defined Good Lives; of the most militant and coercive blueprints of what people should be and want to do with their lives. And it is not incidental that the languages of so-called mental health—of who is sane and who is mad—were so easily co-optable by fascists and communists alike.* (Phillips, 2005, p. 119).

The 'key' exists in the development of a different vocabulary—perhaps beginning with the letter Psi (soul)—in which we are seen to share the same kinds of experiences as others. In the novels *Animal Farm and 1984* George Orwell sensitizes us to a view that the rhetoric of "human equality" has been used by intellectuals of different persuasions to defend the commonplace cruelties of communism and capitalism alike. Orwell gives us an alternative perspective. Instead of answering the question "What is to be done?" he suggests how *not* to answer it, because our previous political vocabulary is no longer relevant. What we need, now as then, are new scenarios, different metaphors, new dreams—not to stand for an existing idea but as new creations in their own right. In social dreaming it does not matter whether the truth is subjective or whether it relates to external reality. All that matters is that you can say it without getting hurt. This is the essence of free association.

> *What matters is your ability to talk to others about what seems to you to be true, not what is in fact true. If we take care of freedom, truth can take care of itself. If we are ironic enough about our own final vocabularies, and curious enough about everyone else's, we do not have to worry about whether we are in direct contact with moral reality, or whether we are blinded by ideology, or whether we are being weakly relativistic. (Rorty, 1989, pp. 176–177)*

There are some societies in which the sharing of dreams is illegal and risks imprisonment. The freedom to dream and think together creates the circumstances where "me" merges into "we", and then "we" extends to "them". It is the freedom and contingency of the matrix, which can generate a sense of solidarity. This idea is not inevitable but it is worth pursuing. It is not about some basic inner or external truth but about the irrelevance of religious or racial differences in the face of pain and humiliation. It is the ability to think of people different to us as being just like us.

\* \* \* \*

## Note

1. The psychotherapist who had this dream had recently worked in a psychiatric hospital with an undetected serial killer who went on to commit several gruesome murders with severed body parts. The therapist knew nothing of this person's history but dreamed of these murders in some detail before they were detected and *before* the identity of the killer was known. She had dreamed something, which she *knew* but had been unable to consciously *think*. It is a dramatic example of the intricate details we actually take in of our surroundings but which are hidden from consciousness until made manifest in a dream. She had *known* he was a murderer without being able to consciously *think* it. There was a visceral intensity in the closeness of this dream to a real murder out there in the world but only two miles from where we sat. This was a personal dream but not a dream of the dreamer's inner world, rather of the horrific internal world of another human being. This is what in the psychoanalytic jargon is referred to as *projective identification*, specifically experienced in the presence of psychotic people.)

# CHAPTER FIVE

# The end of the dance: Dreams at a literary festival

*Addendum by Jane Storr*

> "Global momentum is driving unmindfully towards a landscape of consumer-robots and social instability with the chance of self-determination probably diminishing for most people in most countries."
>
> —DeLillo, 2001, ibid

For two years running, we ran a three-day social dreaming matrix during the annual literary festival in the Welsh/English border town of Hay-on-Wye. The first programme in 2003 has been written about elsewhere (Zarbafi, Clare and Lawrence, 2006). We were eager to repeat what had been a stimulating and enriching experience with more participants who were new to social dreaming.

The first year's matrix had addressed the question of "What is Creativity?" and produced a fascinating tapestry of dreams and associations. It delineated the need for uncertainty and risk in order to take a creative leap; the importance of letting go in order to discover a measure of freedom in a world of conformity. Dreamers emphasised the value of the shared experience itself, which creates an "opening up" of the unthought and leads to a flowering of the mind that is the essence of the creative.

At the start of the festival, in May 2004, fifteen people arrived at 9.00 a.m. as we embarked on a new voyage of dreams and associations. Most dreamers were festival goers. Ages ranged from 19 to 75 and participants included writers, teachers, farmers, students, housewives, counsellors, booksellers and various business activities. As ever the introduction to the matrix was simple. Each day we would meet for 90 minutes, the task was to report any dreams which were remembered, no prior experience was required, just the ability to tell your dreams and to respond to the dreams of others, speaking freely with whatever came to mind.

## Day one

### Dream 1

> I am at an event and J arrives as a schoolboy, a child with no beard and a pudding basin haircut. He said, "I want a dream." I dreamt of a Jew. What is a Jew?—maybe a local watchmaker or other? Then there was a film of dreams with a ballet dancer and a chair. She came in on points, put the chairs on top of one another and then hung herself. This was all in the film and we were then supposed to talk about it.

### Dream 2

> I was in a big, big space, unfamiliar and dripping with water. There was a sense of dread. It was an alien place though there was also a sense that it was located and there was a sense of hope.

The dream matrixes this year suggested a changing climate in the world, ambivalent, menacing, suffused with paranoia and yet mindlessly oblivious. These first two dreams set a tone of hope and dread. There is a Jew, the 'other', perhaps another alien part of the self, separate and always watching us. We can 'see' what is going on in the world but we are unable to consciously think it. Then there is a catastrophe. A woman commits suicide after dancing on her toes: all this takes place within the dislocated, split off realm of film; a space of otherness, of unreality, projected onto a screen. In this first dream there is a sense of the transience of life: as one dreamer put it, 'dreaming is like a shorter life', as if a glimpse of our life flashes by during sleep. Another participant said, 'We live, work and then we die, just as the girl in this dream danced on the table and then hanged herself.' Sometimes death can be an abrupt and final ending after a many layered and but 'unfinished' life.

Another dream told of buying Finnish vodka at passport control where 'we felt greedy but we were saved'. A world on the brink of self-destruction has been an image in social dreams since our work began in the 1990s and this theme of a self-destructive ending, a finish, was continued in this matrix. The difference now was that this dream included salvation, a taken-for-granted notion that somehow Europeans would escape this violent finale. A dream may contain the fulfilment of a wish but this dream also implies survivor guilt— we were greedy but we imagined we would be saved. Dream 2 describes a big, alien space and makes a connection between dripping water and a sense of dread—though there is also a trickle of hope in sight.

## Dreams of premonition

Three subsequent dreams repeated this image of water, simultaneously treacherous and promising. We are in dangerous waters but there is yet some possible solution. If we treat life merely as film we may disregard the dreadful nature of the threat, like something on the other side, not real, behind the screen. Both dreams suggested a fear of things getting out of control, of potential catastrophe if our dreams get built up and then we fall. However, right from the start there is the definitive statement, "I want a dream" echoing Shakespeare's reflection in Hamlet ('to sleep perchance to dream') and Martin Luther King's heroic vision—'I have a dream'—underlining the danger of a dreamless world. The dance, which gets destroyed, suggests obliteration of the imaginary, the unconscious, the lyrical, the dance of life. Gordon Lawrence has suggested that the first dream spoken in a matrix can be a hologram of the whole body of dreams to come. This dream of the dance is foreboding. It is a signpost of what is to follow. The connection to the female body which is lost in the first dream—she commits suicide—is a telling statement at the start of the matrix. The dance is curtailed—the dance, the myth, the fairy-tale, the novel, the poem, the play, the song—each speaks of our early connection to the mother's body, our capacity to dream in the safety of the maternal embrace, the possibility of letting our mind go playfully where it will.

> *"...to make the dream is to think like an infant again: in intense hallucinatory imagery that conjures a reality. To recline next to a quiet yet present other, evokes the half-dreamy state of a free associative being—infant and mother engaged in differing states of solitude and relatedness."* (Bollas, 1999, p. 31)

When we lose this closeness with the feminine we lose the ability to dream, we lose contact with the unconscious and with our capacity to stop and think. Imagination is slipping away in a consumerist world of social instability, privatisation and loneliness: a world preoccupied with surface and appearance, with shopping and celebrity. As our internal world shrinks with the lack of anything deep to be expressed, we flick the channel for the next quick fix. There is no time to reflect on what is happening to us. With this ominous waning of affect at the start of the Twentieth First Century we are indeed in dangerous waters. Something vital and alive is melting, dripping away from us, just as in the same way we allow global warming, the erosion of natural resources, the pollution of the air and sea to destroy the natural world on which we depend and which depends on us. And yet, despite this erosion of the imaginative, clear water appeared in many of these dreams. Water, as in the river or the sea, evokes the flowing passage of life, the ebb and flow of the seasons, night and day, the waves and recessions of our comings and goings. The world of water is the ocean, the location in classical mythology of dread and desire. The sea signifies the ocean depths of unconscious life, the internal body of the place we came from, the infinity of the imagination. Thus the dream could be a place of hope and depth. The following dream of water illustrates the vitality of the dream space as a place to process the joys and losses in the ordinary river of life.

## Dream 5

> *I'm in a river near the Border Hills. Me and my sister have a mile to swim and slide. My sister died of breast cancer and there was a joy in being together going down the river. It was a nice dream.*

## Military dreams

Further on in the matrix, however, there is more foreboding.

### Dream 7

> *There is a market place with hot headed men having a fight. Some American women are saying, "They are Japanese", no, they are Chinese". There are knives and swords. Chinese men are being killed. I smelt the blood. The knife coming up through the body. They are killed by military men. They are cutting up Chinese men into pieces and putting them on a table to sell them so there will be no witnesses.*

As one member commented, 'If you can't tell the difference between the Japanese and the Chinese you miss an entire world'. In this dream, something serious can be smelled, a bloody aroma is detected in the imagery and yet, as another dreamer said, if the dreams are cut up into pieces and got rid of then the meanings may be lost, discarded in the attempt to make something digestible. If you cannot tolerate hate, then something awful happens. If there are no witnesses to the violence because of fear or shame, then the trauma will not be remembered, nothing will be passed on to future generations, history and fairy stories become defunct.

### Dream 8

> *For 25 years I've been dreaming I'm being attacked by people in uniform. There are barriers and I am moving home. It is very violent at the point of violence.*

'The dream stopped ten years ago when I realized that the authoritarianism in the dream was me. I'm sure this is about my own fear of authority and my belligerence. My father was a gentle figure but in uniform he was diabolical.'

## Dreams of grandmothers

### Dream 9

> *Two elderly women were buried under a sheet of glass with their faces pressed up. They are undead. They tried to communicate that ways are*

*needed in order to understand. It was very disturbing. They needed to get ideas across and were, at the same time, very trapped.*

## Dream 10

*I was in a dream with my mother. There was something about trans-generational repression and what one passes on to children. It made sense of mothers and grandmothers. There was a dragon with fire and women needing to beat out the fire. It was something to do with femininity and masculinity.*

## Dream 11

*I dreamt I was a grandmother at a jumble sale with pottery and a crinoline skirt. Blackbirds were put back into a pie to let the steam out of the pie. Bring it on down to the beach and we will play with it. Lots of steam[1].*

The synchronicity of these grandmother dreams is remarkable. After the failure of male authority (men in uniforms), we find the grandmothers trapped across time, the carriers of memory and wisdom; older women who are powerless and unheeded in a society where youth and masculinity as are seen as the primary agencies of knowledge. The maternal role functions to take the steam out of things, to still aggression when it threatens to get out of control. Female authority—non aggressive, reflective, containing and conciliatory—is paramount in situations where religious belief, or racial difference, or colonial conflict puts life at risk. (This failure of authority applies to oppressed minority groups as well as capitalist oppressors. A group whose whole *raison d'etre* is violence at all costs ultimately produces more suffering. The 'Real' IRA bomb in Omagh, after the negotiation of the peace process, is a case in point).

I use the phrase *maternal function* here to make it clear that this is not a reference just to the need for more women in the decision making process—vital though this no doubt is—but to point to the need for a *different kind of thinking* after a century of destruction in which the male order of authority has failed so catastrophically. It is not about what sex we are but the need for two kinds of thinking, the imaginary and the symbolic, the father *and* the mother—thinking that could be done by men as well as women.

The associations which followed these dreams highlighted a fear of what is missing in a world on the edge of apocalyptic conflict— wars in Iraq, Darfur, Afghanistan and the AIDS crisis in Africa were all ongoing at this time. There was a repeated fear of things getting out of control, of the dangers in hating people who are different from us, the cost of forgetting history. As one man put it:

*The enemy are who you hate, they have no identity. If they are on the other side of the track they are the enemy. I was brought up in Wales in my boyhood in what was Plaid Cwmru territory. There was a lot of anger and hatred against the British. Why? 800 years ago someone marched in here. In 800 years time will the Iraqis be feeling the same? What makes men and women impose their will?*

## Dreams of powerlessness

### Dream 12

*I've only ever smelt anything in a dream. I was enraged but I kept wondering—why can't I smell it? Why can't I smell it? I feel shame about a war where I am powerless to stop it.*

A subsequent association was the phrase 'Fee-fi-fo-fum, I smell the blood of an Englishman' from the story of Jack and the Beanstalk.

### Dream 13

*There is an attack on London at Tate London and Battersea Power Station. A menace and it came along the river.*

This dream evoked a wealth of associations about powerlessness in the face of danger. It was felt a terrorist attack on London was imminent (in fact it took another year to become reality), there were references to the Great Plague brought by rats from abroad, a fear of virus or a virus of fear, the Pied Piper of Hamlin who led the children away when he did not get paid. (One lame child was left who was saved and became recognized, which evoked a touching memory of a child who felt misunderstood by her father). Many associations of were of helplessness, paralysis, a feeling of not having a voice in the real world and the idea that a way of life was being eradicated. Someone suggested that the very reason for being in this social dreaming matrix was to try and escape from this state of paralysis. Ironically the following days revealed just how strong the urge was to *stay* in this state of paralysis. Several dreamers did not turn up for the next session. It was as if anything was easier than coming face to face with meaning of these opening dreams. On this first day the freely spoken associations to the dreams of menace, dread and violence had been manifold. There was a busy discussion which took in war in Iraq, Bush and Blair, Ghandi and Martin Luther King, the mental health problems of soldiers, the capture and humiliation of Saddam Hussein, Bill Clinton, abuse of power, pornographic images, transvestites, sexual degradation and the powerlessness of men. Despite people's resistance, the dreams were insisting on revealing our fears of what would happen. A dreamer suggested that when we are asleep perhaps dreaming is a shorter version of life—as in the pessimism of the cliché, "You're born, you work, and then you die"—but there was a sense in which people were saying in the dream work, how is it all going to end? How is Britain going to die? Civilisations come and go. With global warming, nuclear confrontation, resources dwindling, extremes of affluence and poverty, the growth of China, there was an idea that we had reached the apogee in 1900 and since then events have been all down hill.

It is likely that, in 2004, people all over Britain were having this 'London attack' dream about an invisible enemy, an unpredictable catastrophe, a virus of fear, of impending doom, of 'Fe- fi- fo- fum, I smell the blood of an Englishman'. As we now know the London bomb attack, killing 52 and injuring over 700 'Englishmen' and many other people, followed in July 2005.

* * * *

Alistair Bain has written of the problems of trying to describe exactly what happens in a matrix (Lawrence, 2003). Social dreaming threatens the fabric of our "common sense" awareness of space and time. It can be difficult to remember events from the matrix because of a different space-time reality from ordinary life. He suggests that we are looking at a different reality because social dreaming is about a new identity for us which is not based on "I". He thus uses poems, gleaned from the dreams, to convey this different quality. The social dreaming matrix in Hay on Wye 2004 was a place where doubts and fears evinced poetic language. If we put together verbatim phrases taken from this first day's matrix, a sense of this rarefied expressiveness is conveyed in the following 'dream poem':

**Dreaming is like a shorter life**

*Even now there are places where a thought may grow.*
*It took a year to come here today and*
*Needed courage—a terror of fear.*
*The instinct is to want to look away but we cannot wake up*
    *from the dream or ourselves.*
*The enemy are who you hate,*
*They have no identity.*
*As opposed to fire,*
*Steam is gentle,*
*Take the steam out of our pie.*
*Fe fi fo fum, I smell the blood of an Englishman.*
*Fear of virus, virus of fear.*
*I want a dream,*
*Dreaming is like a shorter life,*
*Life and then we die.*
*Reality is more like a dream world*
*I am baffled by people who see things clearly*
*Things are so complex and*
*The dream world is more like reality*
*Dreams get shot*
*What lives on is the dance.*
*The Ministry of Food and Cockles,*
*Stop things from escalating shame,*
*Bill was a fat boy obsessed with health*
*The dark-skinned ones keep the rest of the world alive.*

\* \* \* \*

## Day two—The disconnected matrix

To use an idea developed by the psychoanalyst Wilfred Bion, we could ask what is the emotional truth of a Social Dreaming matrix, what is the essential affect contained in a dream? Behind the content of individual dreams, what is the underlying theme? The second day's dreams, which follow, are sophisticated and evasive but it is possible to glean a strand of meaning, like a long necklace of beads, running from dream to dream.

## Dream 1

*I had a memory about a colleague who committed suicide last month. He left a note. A car was found but no body. This was shocking. There was some doubt about the body, as to whether he'd actually died or not. What is real or being real? Then I dreamed: I was trying to get some work but could only get it if I dyed my hair so it was not grey. I was hugely offended but then agreed to it.*

Here we see more self-destruction, a suicide, a missing body with a sense of disconnection. The dream asks, 'What is real?'—there is a lack of authenticity; an attitude of compliance—he felt offended but then agreed. 'Dyed my hair' was misconstrued as 'died my her', the killing off of the feminine. These themes—of disconnection, destruction and bad faith—were echoed in the oncoming matrix.

## Dream 2

*I was trying to change the church constitution, or congregation. I had torn off strips of paper and needed the permission of the congregation to validate it. But the strips of paper got mixed up. There was no body—we were in the presence of a huge sense of authority but I was fucking up.*

Associations were of failure of authority, being torn off a strip—ineptitude, helplessness, the fear of chaos.

## Dream 3

*I was cycling into the city and there were some barriers or fencing round a hole. A huge chasm of road works in the city centre. There was something else in it which I will not mention.*

Here we encounter a hole, nothingness, barriers—defensiveness: the unmentionable, a thing which cannot be named. A fear of exposure in this dreamer's reluctance to say more, implies fear of psychic exposure which paralleled the mood amongst dreamers at this stage of the work.

## Dream 4

> I was a crab lying on my back. I was revisiting my team at the psychiatric hospital. I felt different and apart from these people. I lay on my back, a crab with a bell jar which I carried with a little candle of nightlife and a rat inside. I lifted the glass bell up and let the rat out. There was a woman wearing a garland, a necklace. Some vibrant red beans were missing. I'd gone down to my alternative placement in Southampton. The headmaster had a heart attack and the school was called Anders School.

Associations were of helplessness, depression, suicide. The reference to Sylvia Plath's novel, *The Bell Jar*, about her depression before her eventual suicide was noted. The mood was sombre with another image of sudden death, the loss of a vibrant object. There was an idea that something (a rat) needed to be let out. Metamorphosis by Kafka, the story of a man who woke up and discovered he had turned into a cockroach, was mentioned.

## Dream 5

> I was a young girl. My father was in the dream. He had lost a beautiful pin—a triangle ebony pin with a diamond in it. I was angry about it:

This time we see the loss of something of aesthetic value—a mind that can think and imagine?—an association was to a bracelet with a triangle denoting a secret society, the importance of the eternal (oedipal) triangle with its possibly sinister connotations. Next came a dream of a terrorist bomb on a children's bus. Further dreams told of chaos and mindless violence, one producing the following association of coercion versus listening:

"I came here from a conference in Chicago and there was a man on the plane who took up a lot of space. He could not listen. Every time we meet a person we think instantly he's either going to listen to me or kill me. But today I thought when a woman meets a man it's, "Are you going to put me down or make love to me?"

In his book about sanity, Adam Phillips writes acutely about listening and coercion. "There are better ways of paying tribute to people than getting revenge on them. Revenge is no good to the sane because it is an attempt to coerce agreement in the form of submission and/or despair. Only people who don't expect to be listened to need people to agree with them. The sane prefer listening to speaking: indeed, they regard most speaking as a defence against listening; though they realize of course what would happen in the unlikely situation of everyone wanting only to listen" (Phillips, 2005, p. 229).

There is not enough listening in the world. Here the Chicago conference memory emphasises our great and urgent need to be found, discovered, listened to, heard—our great insecurity and insistence on compliance whenever we feel insignificant. It speaks of our need to be listened to, but also to listen. It is a noticeable feature of the present century that people seem to find it increasingly unbearable to listen to one another without either interruption or reference to their own experience. In the words of one psychoanalyst who listened a great deal and said very little, 'It is a joy to be hidden and a disaster not to be found' (Winnicott, 1971, p. 186).

*Dream 9*

> *In a theatre—lots of dark, velvet red seats and curtains. I go into a room and there is a hooded figure in bed. The figure is important. I can see a slit eye and a closed one and a slightly deformed mouth through the shadow of the hood. There are many cloaked elders around—masters going to see this figure—an evil figure who is about to be reborn or reformed into another body. I leave but as I look back I notice that the body this figure is turning into is a blond young woman—a very American evil, I think, a watered down attractive evil. Not the real thing. I go to the concert and am standing with two gay men. I notice I am in my pants and tee shirt. We are waiting for the new star to emerge. Is this who they call 'golden bollocks'? I say to a gay guy standing next to me. Yes, he says. We chat but there is a feeling he will be disappointing. The guy tries to put his hands into the back of my pants. I take it away firmly and he desists knowing I am serious. Many actors start arriving with poles all dressed up in shiny outfits. They are late. The whole thing is late.*

Again there is the sense is of something not real, fear of metamorphosis, disappointment, intrusion, the need to be serious, a sense that it's too late.

We could take this sophisticated dream as a warning of a sinister threat from a hooded figure such as Osama Bin Laden, or for a bland temptress of the American dream, where both images stand for the embodiment of evil with dire consequences for world peace. Also there is again a notion of transformation. However, peoples' associations at this stage of the process were much more complex— supping with the devil, spoons on long poles, fear of madness, hammers, sex, the bell jar, psychotic depression, *fear of a bomb exploding in the matrix*. Thus on further reflection the dream actually seemed to be about the matrix. Perhaps something horrific might emerge. Someone wondered what lay beneath the golden bollocks. Was it masculine strength or rubbish and failure? 'Bollocks or bollox?' as one person put it, differentiating between the literal and the metaphorical. It seemed that members realized that the dream referred to the difficulty of relating to the horrific material of day one. Something was being formed into another body. A sexual act of sameness was attempted out of which no baby could be born, no new and alive idea could emerge. The sophistry of the dream is in its paradoxical hiding and revealing of denial. The dream speaks of something cloaked at the same time as it cloaks the truth. It does, however, clearly state that this is 'not the real thing'. In a sense, these dreams which obscure *are* 'a load of bollox,' inauthentic and duplicitous, preventing us from returning to the dark material. The next dream told of walking through thick mud and slurry. Amongst the dreamers, as the stream of conversation flowed, the idea arose that we were jousting with the unconscious rather than playing with it. The phrase *'nostalgie de la boue'* (literally, nostalgia for mud, yearning for the low life) emerged. This was used by Tom Wolfe to describe New York intellectuals' flirtation in the 60's with the Black Panthers Movement (Wolfe, 1972).

Wolfe saw their stance as a sentimental and pretentious longing for dirt and danger on the part of privileged wealthy Americans. Here is another reference to inauthenticity and false consciousness when we know something important is being left unspoken. Indeed it was suggested in the matrix that fact and fiction were like navigators guiding us in and out of different dimensions. The fictions in the first day's matrix had been The Pied Piper, Jack and the Beanstalk, chopping up dreams and getting away from uncomfortable truths. The thing that frightens us also helps us, like the grand mother in Little Red Riding hood. Facing up to horror can often lead to strength and resolution. It may be important, the dreams seemed to be telling us, to let the rat out of the jar. If we ignore the unpalatable we risk catastrophe. The associations now flowed thick and fast and then came the following dream.

### Dream 12

> I am standing on a cliff with my wife. Just below is a ledge and Adam our Two year-old is standing there. We are concerned as it is dangerous. Another little child to his right runs off and drops 60 or 70 feet. We are shouting at him to stand still but he doesn't hear us. For some reason we do not go down and do something other than speaking or shouting. Finally he goes over the ledge. It is a terrible feeling and I start running down. Oh God this is terrible. I wake up and am relieved it was a dream.

### Dream 13

> There was a group of people in a crowded square. A man fell over into a long drop. People shouted. "Watch out".[1]

Associations were of the birth of man, (Adam), the fall of man, and the question where was Eve? Was she paralysed with fear? There is a clear dread of going into the void. The obvious 'surface' meaning here is of every parent's very real fear of losing a child, or of the danger of falling if we don't watch out for ourselves. We could also see these dreams as fear of our own death, or of imminent attack from terrorism, American acts of aggression and so on. However, it is also possible that the void is the Unconscious, the infinite chasm of the dream world which can connect us to unthought reality—but only if we have the courage to take that leap into the great unknown. There is a manifest anxiety about the consequences of letting go of the self in the dream-telling and associating. Again there is fear of exposure, of what happens if we dare to speak the thoughts and feelings within. Could it be that the dream contains the hidden wish to let ourselves fall, to let go, to speak our vulnerability and our desire?

## Dream 14

*There is a large room and we are trying to get tickets. There is one older lady there handing them out. There are hundreds of people cramming into the room. There is a big expectation but there are only five tickets left all day. People are really angry and there is a massive sense of loss—opportunity. She was the key and had the discretionary power.*

The associations which followed were of Eve as enlightened, the source of all knowledge. Moreover the feminine also stood for the void, the abyss, Freud's 'dark continent.' "Don't we need her wisdom and knowledge to deal with the vagaries of life and death?" There was intense unease about the shallowness of the contemporary world. As one person put it:

'Yesterday I was thinking about death and grief, I thought of the little boy in' The Go-Between' trying to negotiate the adult world. But life nowadays feels like a meeting with a slick documentary maker, all gloss and surface and no content. Whereas this experience feels real. Social Dreaming is an opportunity to connect. Where has experience gone? I feel happy in my internal world and yet the world is persecuting me.'

The matrix at this stage had become more alive and fast moving with dreams and associations displaying a more determined search for meaning and connection.

## Dream 15

*There is a hole in the road and I go and tell the person who is managing the hole. I was trying to persecute the guy because I was cross. I sounded off, he smiled. He treated me with marvellous patronising disdain and then disappeared. We got on the floor together, I turned and said, 'He's disappeared, hasn't he?' I've come, he's gone and now I'm going to go. I felt much better and went on my way.*

The ideas which came after this dream evinced hope. Finding gold in alchemy was the highest form of coming together. There was a manager who could survive another's anger. The hole had become more wholesome, as a work in progress, a to-ing and fro-ing, a never-ending quest in which dreams were valued and given some authority. Ordinariness could be valued. Transience—the comings and goings in life—could be accepted. As one woman said: "My life is a work in progress; which is a creative act. My grief is that I cannot express more in settings like this because the world seems unlikely to receive it; I suppose it's just the times we live in."

### Dream 16

> Be careful at Hay-on-Wye because they steal things. An image of Margaret Thatcher with a hand going into a bag. A sign saying, 'Beware, street crime'. A bag of dreams was being stolen.

Again the flow of associations was intense:

"We are without religion in Western Society. We have had our dreams stolen and we need them."

"Someone has stolen my hot flushes and I miss them in Wales. They come in waves like the waves of the ocean."

'On the seashore of endless worlds, children meet.'

"Margaret Thatcher stole milk. Mother's milk."

"In the film 'Women in Love' they make love on the mat. Alan Bates wrestling on the mat; he was in the Go-Between."

"A menopausal way of love. Menopause. Men, Oh! Pause and look at me."

This stealing dream was seen in stark contrast to the day's first dream of compliance and dying your hair to get a job.

### Dream 17

> I am on the top deck of a bus I give the conductor money but it slips away from him. I have to take a risk. The conductor falls off the bus and the bus stops. I go back to get him. I have a little girl on my shoulders and feel frustrated as I want to get to my wife and children. I am wasting time. A boat is leaving and the family are sailing onto a beautiful island on the horizon. I look into the clear water and then get into it. There is a boy's dingy with an outboard motor. They offer to take me but I wonder—can I trust them? The boy has beautiful shells attached to his spine.

Again, something of value slips away and yet another man falls to the ground although this time he is retrieved. But here someone takes a risk, there is the image of a protective father, we glimpse something promising in the distance but there is still ambivalence. Can other people be trusted? And once more we are left with a vision of luminous objects, the shells, symbols of health and protection.

Despite its ambivalence this final dream served as a denouement, a hopeful drawing together of the strands of the matrix. Something is lost and then saved, something hazardous is being undertaken which involves daring, a man is trying to get to a woman, ultimately there is uncertainty but the water is clear with a beautiful view ahead. This uplifting mood of the matrix was reflected in the eagerness and alacrity of people's associations. There was a growing rapport—"there is a link, a coming together"—the thought of a connection between worlds, of Bruce Chatwin's book *Song Lines* about the Aboriginals' complex use of dreaming as a form of knowledge, where dreams were central to life: the need to trust the dream, Venice, children in Canada, Niagra Falls, "You can be connected by water." "We have forgotten how to make children central to our life, childcare is now a perennial problem as if children are an inconvenience, this is not what life is really about. We need fairy tales and playfulness."

\* \* \* \*

## Day three

The final day began with a complex and dramatic dream.

### 1. Dream of deformity and exclusion

> A woman in her late forties comes to my home with a boy of 18. They are having a sexual relationship and I am aghast so much so that I find my self gulping for air. They have brought with them the product of their union, which is a round, furry teddy bear with a baby's head but a creature's penis. I feel I have to put it right but I am not a doctor. On the sideboard there are two phials filled with alcohol. There is a red box in the middle with a clitoris and there is alcohol running into it. I feel it is too late. I light a match and it catches fire. I go and move my car in the street. As I am parking it a four-wheel drive slid like an alligator into my space, and two huge black men and an elegantly dressed lady appeared. The woman in the house pulls me back and screams, 'That

*woman has come back, don't let her in.' I shut the door and there is a*
*little fight at the door.*

The disturbing narrative of this dream could be seen as an answer
to the conundrum of the previous days' dilemma; i.e., of the trauma
which is both acknowledged and denied simultaneously. A disparate
sexual intercourse creates a crazy malformed offspring: something
is born which has gone wrong and needs rectifying, though perhaps
it is too late to undo the damage. There is fear of a conflagration—
sexual or racial—and these ideas of dread have to be put outside.
A woman and two black men must be excluded.

The imagery here is of incest, irresponsible adults, the suf-
focating claustrophobic atmosphere of trauma, a cuddly toy of
comfort transformed into a perverse amalgam of baby and animal's penis. There is a suggestion of parental neglect and abuse.
Things are disconnected. The clitoris and penis are 'part objects'
detached from the whole body. Something cannot be rectified, it
is too late for reparation. This is a picture of a world in bits which
does not make sense and which could catch fire at any moment.
As in so many families, there is no grown up male presence in the
house. At the same time the female imago remains cut off, as in
'do not let that woman in'. Women and black men are kept out of
the picture.

Another more benign dream has a radically different tenor of
movement and pleasure.

### 3. Dream of playing in the river

*I'm near a wide, teeming river. There is an Oxford college at the*
*side plus a bridge and people sitting on the bank. They are jumping*
*into the river with mattresses and lilos and then coming out. People*
*said 'You'll get your pillow wet. I keep it with me. Nobody knows*
*how much I need this pillow to sleep.' The river is a playing place.*
*The currents were taking people off into channels of clear water and*
*beautiful dark reeds. Some people are going down and others are*
*playing.*

Here again here we find a comfort blanket, but this time it is as a
familiar pillow, a reassuring aid to sleep. Perhaps this reflexive dream

is a comment on the playful, flowing nature of social dreaming itself. The teeming river is the unconscious, living river of dreaming into which people jump playfully together. The comforting pillow, or *transitional object*, (See Chapter 1) is vital. It enables us to stay asleep in order to stay in touch with the unconscious dreaming self.

Next came another playful watery dream.

## 4. Dream of laughter and water

> People are coming down the mountain with lots of water. Everybody is doing something different—somersaults, dancing etc. It is very colourful and I am laughing so much I have to wake up.

At this point many associations arose to these opening dreams of day three. It was suggested that some societies have foundation myths connected to water. A specific example came from the mythology of the Australian Aboriginals. They believed that at the beginning of the world a giant frog swallowed all of the earth's water. It was released only when the other animals of the world, dying with thirst, made the frog burst out laughing. Clearly, the dream suggests, a sense of humour is basic to our survival. These playful dreams could be called 'good dreams' in that they guide us towards the real, towards relationship, towards what life is about, towards *being alive*. They are the opposite of a nightmare. Celebrating diversity, they are a clear counterpoint to the dreams of 'no difference.'

However, the disturbing imagery of the first dream of the morning remained vividly present in the matrix. The dreamer who had been reluctant to give more detail of the anger at the hole dream, now said that he had omitted to say that the person he'd felt cross with (in real life) was black man. This participant was greatly experienced in the work of race relations. It was a deep paradox, he felt, that the black person knew, when confronted, that there is a question mark in society about confronting black people. On the same subject, someone else said, "But colour is only one thing and you might have thousands of similarities." Next came a memory of immigration officers in Tottenham who had been guilty of the murder of a black woman named Cherry Gross. They shackled her and then she died.

Associations to the name Cherry threw up references to Jeanette Winterson's novel 'Sexing the Cherry—a fairy tale of a boy and a large dog woman—and this led on to a joke which a participant had heard the night before. The joke: *What do the clitoris, birthdays and toilets each have in common? Answer: men miss them all the time.* Uneasy laughter in the matrix followed. Essentially this is a joke about the ineffectiveness of men, their ignorance of women's needs and their child-like lack of control. We laugh at jokes when we recognize the unpalatable. If all jokes are in some way true, does this jibe towards men harbour a contemporary truth?—Is it pointing to a sense of their inability to really connect, to have a pleasurable intercourse which satisfies both partners, and to maintain adult control over bodily functions? This joke underlines—for both men and women—the destructive capacity we all have to marginalize our own dreams and creativity, through ignorance, forgetting and lack of curiosity. As Ted Cohen remarks, such a joke also provides a way of striking back for oppressed groups and may restore enough power and control for people to speak the unspeakable (Cohen, 1999).

There was an idea, amongst dreamers, that blackness was associated with evil; where the stranger, outsider or 'other' is often connected to fear. Thus something unbearable in the self must be evacuated and then symbolised by this 'other'. We heard the acknowledgement of racism amongst white people in the room. People emphasised the value of difference, of 'otherness', of opposites, of black/white paradigms. Skin colour was just one example of this. There are more similarities *within* races than between them (World Health Organization Symposium, 1966). Significantly, in the matrix, this otherness lead onto to sexual difference, to the categories of male and female which repeatedly failed to come together in the dreams. To some extent racial and sexual difference were interchangeable in the discourse.

However, the first association to this dream—also about difference—had a more benign tone. One dreamer reported:

> *I awoke 4.00 am this morning to the beautiful sound of a nightingale outside the room. This is 'the bird with a hundred tongues'. I wondered how many ways are there to sing. I found myself counting the patterns.'*

(This association actually came immediately after the dream of laughter and water.) It repeats a clear recognition of the value of *difference*, the beauty of a hundred different tongues. Whereas the first dream created a clitoris and a penis—two similar objects emanating from the same biological origin—here was an idea stressing the importance and beauty of difference, the danger of a world without opposites. Two men and an elegant woman were kept outside ('don't let her in') while a woman and an adolescent remained inside with their disturbing offspring, a clitoral box and dripping alcohol with matches. One member of the matrix remarked that the repeated themes of the day were of 'holes separate from penises, the container separate from the water, of disconnection and then playful release.'

## 5. Dream of sexual discontinuity

> I am at a place where the water is not free flowing. A woman stands in the water with her husband and they are about to make love or have sex. He urinates in the water and that pushes her away, puts her off. I said, "Why allow that contamination?"
>
> Next she's in the bathroom. There are hundreds of sunglasses, 1950's style. This was not the sun in the sky but the son, the son-glasses. This is the male who is not able to see properly.

Here again we witness the difficulty of being creative, free flowing, spontaneous. Once more a sexual intercourse is not possible, somehow the man just cannot see what's in front of his eyes. The associations which followed elaborated and played with this theme:

"If we don't marginalize these dreams we stay in this flowing water—we are part of this rich world."

"It matters how you treat a black person."

"We are confronted by that aspect in dreams where we lay ourselves open to all sorts of opposites. Creativity comes through opposites. Babies are born through the connection between opposites—a man and a woman."

"There is such ambiguity in the quality of male and female in the clitoris dream."

The next dream continued this theme.

## 6. Dream of interrupted sex

> I was in a room—a study room with a man who is the boy friend of a best friend. We are about to have sex and there is some aggressive foreplay.

*The girlfriend walks in. I was on my back, angry, horrified and afraid. The man is very nonchalant about the whole thing. The sex then progressed and she came back into the room. We are in the middle of the act. She yells at me. 'What are you doing?! She says. I say to her 'You already knew. We agreed to share this man.' She says, 'You are not supposed to act on the agreement'. The man just stands there waiting for a resolution.*

*At the end she just yelled, 'Why did you enter the agreement? You are just destined to have my leftovers.' The sex is never completed.*

The synchronicity between dreams is impressive. An act of union is not possible, something is left undone, the women do not stand together, the male is passive and complicit, an agreement is broken, intercourse is incomplete. It was striking how dreams of sexual discord now evoked associations with political and racial meanings:

Again the associations in the matrix were immediate and urgent:

"The rich First World just gives leftovers to the undeveloped world."

"We are in serious trouble and it is too frightening to think of the consequences."

"We have missed the boat and cannot get to the island."

"I felt profoundly sad. There was a sense in which she was right. There was no fighting back, just acceptance."

"We feel guilty about what is going on in the world and yet hopeless."

"If dreams are not the remnants, you are more than the discards."

"To just accept the world is topsy-turvy. Martin Luther King recognized this ongoing tragedy and he moved people."

"In Buddhism the Lotus flower grows out of mud, thrives in it, yet is beautiful. This is cause and effect. The mud is necessary, they are interdependent."

Thus an idea emerged about the inevitable interdependence between the rich white world and the poor non-white countries, between men and women, between waking and sleeping, between conscious life and the dreamtime. We need one another. If you discard one thing, you damage another.

### Dream 7- staying above the hole

*There are all these people in a warehouse when the floor starts moving down. They all move to the sides moving delicately around the wall and staying above the hole. Nobody fell down. It was tightrope like.*

Perhaps in this matrix, the dream is saying, nobody dares to look into the black hole which threatens us. A vivid association to this dream was the memory of a fresco in Pompeii of a black man in mid air, diving into water. A further torrent of dreams about brothers and water now ensued, echoing the water dreams above.

## Dream 8

*My beloved brother dived into a swimming pool but there was no water in the bottom and he exploded.*

## Dream 9

*My brother is standing there in Denims.*

Denim material originates from Nimes in France—'de Nimes'—which is the site of a famous Roman water system on a triple aqueduct.

## Dream 10

*My brother fell into a swimming pool and I hesitated and did not dive in to save him. M's brother dived in and saved him.*

## Dream 11

*I had forgotten my son was going on a residential trip. I had not realized and started running. I feared he would drown on this trip. I feel like an absent father.*

These led to wealth of associations about powerlessness and responsibility in a world which seems to have lost contact with the essence of humanness, the tenderness of motherly care and the knowledge and memory of fatherly authority. People reflected on the hope and optimism of good parenting. There was a heartfelt critique of a shallow and fragmented world, unhappy and overly preoccupied with the superficial:

*If you take the skin colour off, nationality off, take away where a person is from, take their gender away and look at the soul, then is it possible to meet?*

*Layers are also boundaries, full of senses and feelings. They are a very active part of who we are.*

*My hand-wringing mum left and I was raised by my dad. It had a big impact on me. This made me the person I am.*

*I work in the world of education which is not a happy or a hopeful place. It's clear that, in a way, pre-school children are socially dreaming together. And yet if I tried to introduce social dreaming into an educational setting, I'd be taken away. This madness makes me feel without hope.*

*Thinking of parental neglect, at the age of seven I found myself drowning in the Caspian Sea. Then a man saw me, pulled me out and put me on the sand. It was just chance that he happened to see me drowning.*

*That's contingency, you just never know what's going to happen but the question is, when something turns up, what do you make of it? What can you do with contingency—just resign yourself to fate or take some sort of positive action?*

The final reference at this point was to 'Bury My Heart at Wounded Knee', the book about the final massacre of the North American Indians. It was suggested that a sense of omnipotence had made the Indians believe they were invincible to bullets. But perhaps there was a genuine human trust in their stance. The Indians' ideology was of respect to animals, the value of mother Earth, the idea that what you put in you get back, whatever you take you give thanks for. It was in this spirit that they welcomed the first settlers by sharing food. Was it this idea of authenticity and equality in human relations that the matrix was trying to relocate in a world of greed, acquisitiveness and inequality?

* * * *

## Holes

### Dream 12

> *I was with friends and there were lots of holes in this field. It seemed a more difficult place than before.*

This was the final dream of the three day-matrix. Associations to it were bleak:

- The nostalgia of a lost landscape—'The Green Where I Used to Play'
- A fundamentalist movement that spread like a virus
- Totalitarianism
- Mass psychosis
- A fundamentalist preacher separating couples to stop them having sex
- A preacher threatening doom

At the start of the 21st Century we are in a different landscape. These chilling apocalyptic images are a revelation of unconscious fears about the world we may be creating and the world we may already have lost. We *know* what kind of catastrophe is already a possibility but can only *think* about it in our dreams: a black hole of no-thinking warns us of a death of the imagination, a heart of darkness. But dream images are multi-layered. There can be no ultimate, 'true' interpretations of images and motifs which recur. What else might holes stand for in the symbolic language of these dreams?

Some of the various holes in the dreams appeared to be locations of extinction, dissolution and death, unspeakable orifices requiring barriers to avoid a sudden disappearance. Twice we glimpsed the oblique image of a black man, once diving, once obliterated. Our hypothesis is not simply that holes symbolize the end—the black-out—but that they represent the dark 'other' part of ourselves which we so clearly dread—the black man, the stranger, the shadow—the otherness of potential wisdom and strength which inhabits this void, if only we dare to look into it.

> Holes are a symbol of the threshold of the unknown through which one steps into the beyond or into the hidden (Otherworld in relation to the visible world) ... a passage through which ideas naturally come to birth ... holes may be seen as a symbol of all potentialities. In this respect they are related to fertility symbols on the biological plane and to those of spiritualization on the psychological.

(Chevalier & Gheerbrant, 1982)

As James Baldwin put it, "If you insist on being white, then I'll have to be black". In this context the hole equals whole. It is the thing we avoid which gives us aliveness, makes us complete. If we see our life as a work in progress, then it is this sequestered, hidden part of our mind which we need to find and make friends with, before it is too late.

> We shall not cease from exploration
> And the end of all our exploring will be
> To arrive where we started and know the place for the first time

(T.S. Eliot, 1942)

Finally, we will examine the two other motifs which reoccurred in this three-day matrix at Hay-on-Wye: namely sexual difference and the profusion of water.

* * * *

### Sexual difference

One of the associations emanating from the 'teddy bear and clitoris box' dream was to a woman called Cherry who had tragically died while being detained by the immigration service. This was a racial and gendered reference—this person was black as well as female. The ensuing conversation about racial conflict led on to a notion of sexual difference. One member of the matrix remembered the book "Sexing the Cherry" by Jeanette Winterson. Whilst the matrix did not dwell on this reference, we want to examine it in more detail in order to reflect on the subject of sexual difference occurring repeatedly in the dreams. Winterson's book is a cross-gender story of an outcast boy called Jordan with a huge dog-woman during the English Revolution. It is an attempt to give a history of how *patriarchal* forces shaped the lives of these characters. (Winterson, 1992) Winterson exposes the contingency of supposedly universal values, including the naturalness of heterosexuality and the father's authority in a patriarchal culture. While her view privileges lesbianism—replacing the patriarchal order with a new order—it does perceptively describe the linear nature of history as a masculine form of conceptualising. In other words, history is *man*-made, shaped by masculine methodologies with narratives of objective, verifiable, 'scientific' facts in chronological order going back in time. This patriarchal hegemony—of history's being connected to linear temporality—has been challenged by feminists such as Winterson and Angela Carter, who do not see the feminine as linear in time. Perhaps, they imply, female identity remains un-representable in historical forms traditionally associated with men. However the danger here is that in utterly rejecting linear time we create an inverted form of sexism, no better than the patriarchy it replaces. History is not exclusively feminine any more than it is masculine.

At this stage the work of Bulgarian-French psychoanalyst Julia Kristeva is helpful. (Kristeva, 1993) She identified three waves of feminism, each challenging the ideologies of histories written by men. The first-wave feminists, while seeking equality, identified with the very power structures previously identified as oppressive. The second-wave feminists refused to identify with these male power structures by creating a different narrative time in which to express repressed feminine histories. Winterson is one such author, celebrating lesbian desire and rejecting the patriarchal. But the problem here is of discarding the masculine. Kristeva described an emerging third wave which combined the first two by refusing to identify with male power but simultaneously refusing to reify a female counter-society. She avoids homogenizing or essentializing "woman" and insists on the recognition of sexual difference. Thus she rejects the dichotomy man/woman as an opposition between two rival entities. As opposed to conventional (masculine) notions of time, she sees female subjectivity as linked to both cyclical time (menstruation, pregnancy, repetition) and to monumental time in terms of eternity. To break out of contemporary codes we need a different discourse closer to the body and to the emotions, a third form of expression in place of the symbolic order of men (language, law, history, culture) or the adoption of masculine forms of femininity.

Kristeva believed in the idea of multiple sexual identities rather than the separate code of a unified "feminine" language. It was a feature of several of the matrixes described in this book that people—both men and women—dreamt of the need for new codes of thought which hinted at the imaginary narrative time of the maternal order. Indeed, it is interesting to compare this paradigm of femininity to the dream resolution which emerged in the post 9/11 matrix in Hampstead (see Chapter Four).

## Being and the female element

The work of the psychoanalyst, Donald Winnicott, gives meticulous attention to the role of the mother in shaping experience. For Winnicott the female element is the primary source of our sense of self. In the infant's development, the relationship with the mother establishes the basis for all future experience, the experience of *being*. Essentially, this starts with the mother but can be expressed by men too.

> *In the growth of the human baby, as the ego begins to organize, this that I am calling the object-relating of the pure female element establishes what is perhaps the simplest of all experiences, the experience of being. Here one finds a true continuity of generations, being which is passed on from one generation to another, via the female element of men and women ... It is a matter of the female elements in both males and females.* (Winnicott, 1971, p. 80)

Winnicott places 'doing' with the male element and 'being' with the female. "After being—being and being done to. But first being". (Winnicott, ibid p. 85) At the beginning the baby cannot differentiate between mother and self: the baby becomes the breast, the object is the subject. This subjective object (baby fused with mother) is thence the basis for any sense of self. It is this primary identification with the female (mother) which is the first vital experience before 'being-at-one-with' is possible.

If the initial capacity to 'be' comes from the maternal, this is why male (and female) envy of women is linked to a fear of women because of the fact that we were all once wholly dependent on a woman. Many of the dreams are suggestive of men's insecurity—weakness, uncertainty, fear, incompetence—in the face of this forgotten dependence. Perhaps this repressed fear of women is why so many societies have been misogynistic.

The dreams in this matrix laid bare the frailty of male authority, the failure of traditional political strategies, a passivity and fragility in male stances, the absence of fathers in the family, the apparent redundancy of the male in modern society, both biologically and symbolically. Synonymous with this is the anxiety of dereliction, of who is in charge, of whom we can turn to. There is unease about the political bankruptcy of old ideologies both communist and capitalist, about the problems of how to be a man.

However, we need to look behind the manifest content of the dreams. As we have seen, many of them reveal despair at the breakdown in sexual relations and ergo in all other relationships of difference, especially racial. Many of the associations were to the politics of race and religion. Behind the impossibility of sex lay a fear that racial harmony could be beyond reach and that politico-religious differences may end in apocalypse. The sexual dreams constantly led back to differences between black and white, rich and poor worlds, fundamentalists and agnostics, men and women, children and adults. People sensed the urgency of this metaphor as it signalled a breakdown in communication in a world of globalisation, ethnic cleansing, fundamentalist terrorism, the aids epidemic and mass starvation. It spoke of the need for action before it is too late.

* * * *

## Water

The profusion of dreams about water was impressive, combining hope, birth, joy and creativity, sometimes accompanied by loss and in particular the loss of loved ones. We saw the clear water of hope, rivers of playfulness and creativity; dreams of movement and fluidity. Water in these dreams seemed to represent the flowing passage of life, the ebb and flow of change, the potential to lose control and swim around in our dream life, our potential self. We have already mentioned water as a source of purification, as the founding myth in different civilisations, of the Flood as a recreation of the world, the boundless amniotic fluid from which we emerge at birth. Water has a strong symbolical dimension with which to build our relationship with nature and with other beings. It has a variety of mythological and anthropological meanings:

1. *Water is a symbol of fertility and growth*, endlessly changing shape and transforming itself as a formless container giving life and nourishment. As a clear liquid entity of fluidity, movement, and creativity, it symbolizes emotion and psychic energy.

2. *Water is a symbol of birth.* There is a variety of anthropological evidence on symbolism in dreams demonstrating the connection between water and the womb. Both child-birth and water were associated among the Kwakiutal Indians where a dream of a mother advising her pregnant daughter of purification rituals would lead the dreamer to go straight into water. Amongst the Tikopia of Polynesia if a woman dreams of entering a stream and filling her water bottles, this indicates she will bear a girl-child. (Lincoln, 1935, pp. 121–3) *In the Interpretation of Dreams,* Freud notes that dreams of being in water often evoke inter-uterine fantasies, memories of the womb. "In dreams, as in mythology, the delivery of the child from the uterine waters is commonly presented by the distortion of the entry of the child into water." (Freud, 1900, p. 526) He gives the example of a young woman whose dream of diving into dark water expressed a desire to be reborn (where diving back into the womb is an inversion of being born again). He emphasises the importance of unconscious thoughts about life in the womb, of the maternal body, of déjà vu and claustrophobia. Such dreams, "… afford the deepest unconscious basis for the belief in survival after death which merely represents a projection into the future of this uncanny life before birth." (ibid, p. 525) As a case of déjà vu (memory of the mother's genitals) it always implies a sense that one had been there before; and of course one definitely has. The fear of death and the desire to live again is common in dreams from many cultures. A memorable association here came from one dreamer at the Hay Festival. He remembered a quote from Dylan Thomas, which was of the poet's desire for "a womb with a view." (Perhaps this is an insight into how the Welsh bard actually lived his creative yet drunken life, always retaining the desire to return to the amniotic space within.)

3. *Water is also a symbol of femininity.* Gestation in the maternal waters of the womb is the primary experience of life. Held in a watery container, the innermost membrane encloses and sustains the embryo before the 'waters break' and birth ensues. Here too, there is much anthropological material on the association of water with the feminine, from the universal mythology of mermaids, to the feminine rites of water temples in Bali, the women's control of water supply in Melanesia and the female water deities of

the Huichal in Mexico. In Hindu cultures the sea represents the feminine elements and in most parts of the world ships are seen as female—the all-powerful mother, womb-like and protective or the enchantress of the sea of whom men are never certain. When a ship is launched, the moment it hits the water it becomes female, a living, feminine, anthropomorphic being; a buoyant life-saving container in a vulnerable environment.

4. As a symbol of the maternal containing environment, *water is also a symbol of the unconscious*, the deep ocean, the great river, the dark pool, the salty sea.; the formless void of our inner resources and hidden depths. It is, "the symbol of unconscious energy, the formless powers of the soul, of hidden and unrecognized motivation," (Chevalier & Gheerbrant, 1982) Water is simultaneously a motif for our dream life where we swim around in a different medium, below the surface and oblivious to the world above.

What is the significance in all of this for the dreams recounted at the Hay festival? Is it that dreams of water represent the life-giving force of our beleaguered selves—the sense of 'being' we are in danger of losing in a world of consumer robots, virtual reality and the utopian glow of cyber capital? This is important because it gets to the very core of what life is all about. *Being* is at the centre of any real experience of life. As Jan Abram puts it, "... if the individual has not had the opportunity to simply *be*, his future does not augur well in terms of the emotional quality of his life. The likelihood is that this individual will feel empty." (Abram, 1996, p. 66)

The dreams of water represented the creative, maternal, nurturing unconscious, the desire for new ideas to be born, the playfulness of letting-go in order to swim and float. Ultimately this enables the idea of a self with an internal space in which to think and reflect, *to be*. In other words such dreams are crucial for our psychic survival. If we lose them we lose a vital part of ourselves. At the same time, these dreams contained loss, dread and disharmony. The water is contaminated, sexual intercourse breaks down. In this way they give us invaluable clues as to what might be going wrong in the social world and in our personal lives, and what we could do to reverse this.

\* \* \* \*

## Conclusion

### Disconnection and knowledge

The sense of disconnection was a consistent theme over this three-day matrix. The first day's dreams suggested a lack of connection in a world where there is an inhibition to share dreams and to talk openly together. The activity is felt to be dangerous, there is a perceived risk in seeing clearly. The enemy is the formless, nondescript 'other', the shadow part of our self which we deny. With the 'end of the dance' we see the dissolution of the dream, where something vital and alive being lost. Between the idea and the reality, the imaginative space is avoided, turned away from. Dreaming is so easy, doing something about it so hard.

This position is compounded on day two, where the dreams indicate obfuscation and subterfuge. There is no body, obscure holes are fenced off, mindless authority predominates. We find a scenario of 'golden bollocks', sexual confusion, a man who could not listen. There is a big hole into which the previous day's alarming matrix has disappeared. In a sense these dreams *were* 'a load of bollocks', an inauthentic wild goose-chase to put us off the scent. Perhaps, even asleep, people will do anything to avoid learning from experience.

By day three this disconnection is being dreamed with clarity. We witness the apparent *impossibility of sex*. There is a disparate sexual union between a middle-aged woman and an adolescent. Then a man contaminates the act of love by urinating, pushing the woman away, apparently incapable of seeing what he's doing. In a later dream of female treachery, the sex act is not completed, an agreement is broken while the man remains passive. On a manifest level this reveals the difficulty in contemporary society for people to literally have straightforward sexual intercourse, physical intimacy, the warmth of loving closeness. In a paranoid world of grown-up polymorphous perversity, brief and furtive sexual encounters appear to be connected to hate and unhappiness. Sex becomes a temporary way of triumphing over anxiety and loneliness. In a world where anything is acceptable—telephone sex, virtual cybersex, intimacy on chat lines with 'friends' you never meet, speed dating, internet pornography—then ordinary sexual intimacy can become mundane, unexciting, even impossible. The meeting of bodies has to be either avoided or overlaid with pain and transgression. Then, going beyond this literal reading of such dreams, we find the metaphorical starkness of disconnection, loneliness and alienation in a world where it is increasingly perilous to get close to others. And this applies on the socio-political level as well as the personal. It can be seen in the many novels and motion pictures of the last twenty years which describe unauthentic lives in emotionless relationships, with ironic violence and trauma, all within the hegemony of the consumer market. Even though some of these themes may be directly intended to point up the remoteness of modern relationships, the effect is the same. The viewer is left with a cold, shallow and cynical view of friendship and marriage, of families where children routinely experience a gulf between men and women and consequently the division within the self: the remoteness of relationship.

And yet despite this theme of disconnection in the matrix, the last three dreams insisted on pointing to this process of denial. A kind of thinking—of taking responsibility—begins to take shape. At the end of day two, a living body, a precious little boy slips away like a good idea with a life ahead of it; a helpless crab warns of the danger if we metamorphose into passive creatures, unable to converse and share our dreams and nightmares. Finally we catch a glimpse of a boy with shells on his spine. The jewels of knowledge that could give us backbone and strength come into view. This hopeful image resurfaces in the final matrix with dreams of playing in the river, the pleasure of the collective, the value of play. There is laughter and enjoyment in diversity and difference, a nightingale sings with a hundred tongues. In this atmosphere of play, people began to work together, thinking seriously about authenticity and equality in human relations as worthwhile goals. Only the final dream of holes and a difficult place, brought forth associations of madness and annihilation, reminding us of the precarious reality which we face in the 21st Century.

* * * *

## ADDENDUM

What follows is a memory of Social Dreaming at the Hay-on-Wye Festival described in the last chapter.

*Reflections of a dreamer*

Jane Storr

Just simply being referred to as 'one of the dreamers' evoked a feeling of pleasure—and that's three years after the experience. From my earliest memories dreaming has been a source of wonder and fascination so the idea of social dreaming was always going to be intriguing. The sense of utter paradox—after all aren't dreams private and intensely personal so don't you only really share them with close, friends, lovers and therapists? How can you enter into a space where dreaming becomes a social experience and what can that possibly be like? I wondered if this sharing of our unconscious thoughts would be a sort of psychological collaboration—the middle-aged equivalent of the 'personal is political' slogan of our youth.

I approached the first morning of social dreaming with a sense of real curiosity and the pleasurable feeling of excitement you get when you feel you are taking just a bit of a risk. I had had a powerful narrative dream the night before and felt that it was a good omen and my unconscious was up for it, whatever 'it' was. The only thing I remember about any ground rules was that we were to listen, not interrupt, and not try to interpret or interrogate the dreams or the dreamers and that we only revealed or shared what we chose. If there were more rules, I don't remember them. The chairs were set out at random. No circle and no rows: no front and no back. We also weren't required to introduce ourselves in any way—not even by name.

I can't really begin to explain the power and significance of all this. It was as if by the flick of a conjurer's hand all egos had vanished and left a reflective community of dreamers. The combination of anonymity and intimacy produced in me a sense of personal freedom that I have never felt before in a group of strangers and that emotional state enabled me to feel particularly alert and alive. I loved the way people contributed through making connections and allowing collaborative ideas to emerge and grow organically rather than trying to impose meanings and order. I wasn't aware of any competitiveness and there was only one occasion when an over enthusiastic 'dreamer' wanted to start a dialogue with another dreamer and was gently reminded of the 'rules'.

The intensity with which people appeared to listen and the silence for reflection that followed each contribution created an unexpected sense of communion. I recognise that I have spent far too much of my adult life in meetings—which are 'chaired' and which follow a strict agenda where people seat themselves according to where they can exert the maximum power and where introductions are often an opportunity to display/assert seniority, expertise and intellectual prowess. I have often felt inhibited and powerless by this style of meeting and I have also actively used the structure to drive through my own agenda. It is intensely frustrating and irritating when an idea or contribution seems valid but doesn't fit neatly into the predetermined structure. Such meetings are often stymied by an emotional, unspoken agenda that never gets properly aired.

Social dreaming also made me realise how relatively inhibited I had become in some aspects of my social life. Since the experience I don't censor myself so much when I communicate and I have been much more adventurous in conversation, particularly with strangers. This is not a dramatic change but a subtle and significant shift that has been important for me. Being a social dreamer revealed to me a wholly different set of possibilities about how we might make sense of the world and how we relate to each other. It also made me re connect with that feeling of being much younger when new experiences and ideas are exciting and challenging.

Even after three years I can recall individual dreams and the distinct feeling that our dreams were talking to each other. Or were we talking to each other through our dreams and therefore having a much more creative conversation than we would normally have? A dream of the Pied Piper uncovered a memory from another dreamer's childhood when she was lifted onto her father's shoulders in order to get a better view of a festival. Whilst up on his shoulders her legs had become numb and 'fallen asleep'. So when the father put her down her legs buckled and she couldn't stand. Her father shouted at her to stop being silly but she was little and didn't understand what had happened to her legs and couldn't describe to her father what the problem was. This dream stood out as a rich metaphor for all sorts of the other themes that were emerging through our dreams in relation to the Iraq war; authoritarianism in the East and the West; the confusion around the role and responsibility of fathers and the way children, their needs, voices and creativity are systematically repressed in most cultures.

Being a social dreamer was stimulating and serious but mainly it was a playful experience. Playful as in those great moments as children when we are creative and spontaneous and we make it up as we go along weaving our fantasies and fears into a seamless shared adventure. An enduring image of this playfulness was one dreamer who showed us how her hot flushes 'made love' to her. Her hands undulated sensually over her body as she described how this feeling of warmth embraced her from her feet to her face. For me—fearing a hot, sweaty embarrassing menopause was around the corner—this woman was an inspiration.

Exploring the connections through the theatre of each other's dreams and streams of consciousness was a reminder of how much we need communication, imagination and creativity to address both the big global issues of our times and the anxieties of the everyday. The experience was a powerful reminder to me of my own and other people's creativity. The challenge has since become what to do with that insight.

Jane Storr—a dreamer
March 2008


## Note

1. The reference here of is to the nursery rhyme 'Sing a song of Sixpence' where the blackbird eventually got revenge by snapping off the maid's nose. However originally this nursery rhyme developed as a coded message, used by Blackbeard the pirate, to recruit crewmembers, who then hid in waiting, to rob and plunder passing ships. 'Blackbirds' were Blackbeard's men, concealed and about to pounce, like bad thoughts, sinister terrorists, or drunken hooligans.

*CHAPTER SIX*

# We are all slaves to babble–land: A mass dreaming experiment

> 'It is spring, moonless night in the small-town, star-less and bible black...and all the people of the lulled and dumbfound town are sleeping now...from where you are you can hear their dreams.'
>
> —Dylan Thomas, Under Milk Wood, p. 1

If 30,000 spectators at a premier league football match wrote down their dream of the night before, what would it tell us about the world? Perhaps many of them would have had the same dream. Perhaps we would be amazed at internal scenarios of which people rarely speak. The present chapter came out of a conversation with Gordon Lawrence about the possibilities of capturing the dreams of many people at one time, in one place—the idea of mass dreaming.

After the earlier social dreaming projects at the Hay on Wye Literary Festival, described in Chapter Five, we decided to ask people to take part, during the festival, in a mass dreaming experiment. We wanted to take a snapshot of what individuals in the same place at the same time might be dreaming about. Thus in 2005 we approached the Festival organizers for help in the project and were very grateful when they agreed to provide publicity for our 'Invitation to Dream'. We circulated a flyer, which was repeated on huge screens in the auditoria and marquees of the main events. Our aim was to collect as many dreams as possible in the week of the festival. As we wrote in the flyer, the idea was to gather many anonymous dreams 'in an attempt to understand the mood or spirit of the times, which is largely inaccessible to our conscious waking thoughts.'

The response was fascinating. Some people were suspicious; dismissive both of our project and of their own dreams, others were cynical about such an idea, what was the point? What could you get from remembering and telling your dreams? But on the whole, festival goers were curious, responsive and in some cases enthusiastic to give us their dreams there and then. We provided an address in the town to which dreams were posted, e-mailed, dropped through the door or in some cases spoken out loud while we wrote them down. In the house we were staying at there was a painting exhibition, thus there was a space' available for those who wished to deliver their dreams in person. What surprised us was the urgency with which people reported the dreams. They expressed a desire to tell, to understand, to wonder, to worry or laugh—but above all there was an urge to speak the dream to another and be listened to. Clearly this was qualitatively different from those written dreams, which were sent anonymously by letter and formed the main part of the material. However even in the latter correspondence there was often a request for more information, for feedback and sometimes writers added personal details as if to aid our understanding. There seemed to be an unformed desire in the very transmission of the dreams to us whether by note, letter, e-mail or in person. People wanted to talk about their dreams and seemed relieved that there was somewhere to 'put' them, something to be done with them. Participants seemed to want to find out how these night images could be used, rather than wasted and forgotten about.

This sense came through most forcefully with those who told their dreams in person, especially when describing disturbing dreams and in some cases the real-life trauma they evoked. Recurring dreams were reported. They wanted feedback, 'results', to see what the dreams might be saying about themselves and the world. After initial scepticism, some dreamers were surprised they had actually had a dream and were intrigued that they were then able to remember, report and reflect on their dream. What was noticeable was:

- the importance of being 'heard',
- the significance of being taken seriously
- the enjoyment and interest in the conversation, which developed as they told us and/or their companions of their inexplicable night-thoughts.

Clearly, there was a potential for these encounters to become counselling sessions, in that visiting respondents might understandably expect a therapeutic outcome. We were careful to explain that this was an academic piece of research for a book, which they would be able to read, and that if they wanted further exploration of their dreams one option was to consult a psychotherapist. Nevertheless, the therapeutic motivation of such respondents was a significant and poignant aspect of this mass dreaming project. Loneliness in adversity is common. Many people have difficulties but have nowhere to take them. When someone is listened to carefully without judgement or sentimentality, some kind of therapeutic rapport is inevitable and may even have stirred some dreamers to take this further. Under such circumstances it helps if the dream-takers themselves have some experience of psychotherapy.

However, the bulk of the dreams were written and then sent anonymously. All were written in English, for the most part legibly, coherently and in some cases eloquently. There is something in the telling of the dream, which liberates the writer/speaker from hyperbole. The process is surprisingly free from self-consciousness or pretension. The dream 'comes from another place' and just seems to write itself. It does not matter how logically or grammatically it is expressed as long as it retains the authentic 'language' of the dream. And since dreams are almost entirely visual, what the writer does is to describe images and the sensation, which go with them. The dream engenders a free form of expression unencumbered by the need to make sense, to be clever, well-read, or admired. A dream is just a dream. There are no cash prizes, no marks out of ten, no certificates for good dreaming are awarded. There is no hierarchy of dreaming, the inventiveness of the unconscious is available to all.

As we were compiling this extraordinary list of dreams from ten days at a festival we started to read a rich, creative and dense narrative. It was the multitude of stories in myriad unconscious minds at one time in May/June 2005. At first it read like a surrealist manifesto, a jumble of apparently unconnected images—riffs and arpeggios, from simple tunes to busy concerti. However, as we sifted through the material—marvelling at the imagery, baffled by the emotional syntax—patterns began to emerge, as similar subjects arose repeatedly in different guises. Whereas social dreaming involves a matrix of people collectively and consciously dreaming together over time, this was a disparate heterogenous mix of several hundred people who were mostly temporary citizens of a town at festival time. Thus the sense at first was of a multiplicity of different minds, a collage of separate intelligences each with its own biography and cultural hue, its own internal and external perceptions. In this kaleidoscope of self-images, there came a glimpse of each person's unique individual identity. At the same time as a dream acts as a conduit for the dreamer's idiomatic being or sense of self, it also provides an emotional barometer of the times we inhabit. Dreams provide a picture of the atmosphere of our social world, which, we would suggest, gets closer to the reality of experience than more 'objective' measurements of academic discourse. Dreams have the emotional immediacy of music, art or poetry. Like a good novel, they tell us what the world 'feels like'.

## Dreams of ambivalence

There were very few 'good' dreams of bliss, joy, satisfaction or tranquillity. Typically, when such 'positive' dreams did emerge they were accompanied by sinister or 'negative' features. Contradictory elements sat side by side, often creating an anxiety of ambivalence. The first three dreams are examples of this ambiguity, of the ordinary co-existing with the macabre:

> It's a flat grey light and mood. A small group of dark suited people are standing around casually talking. There is some kind of project or task or festival going on and it is related to anxiety. I have got something to do with a cylindrical object—like a bomb but not a bomb—with the letter 'N' on the side which is the start of a word which is going to be put on it. The cylinder is shining steel and has condensation on it.

*I turn to the side and say, "Is this what it is?" There's a very boring, 60's type suburban house, which has music playing from the breakfast room. 'The Darkness' are playing a song from their new album. It is very ordinary and 'middle of the road'.*

This first dream sets the theme. At a festival of anxiety there is a bomb, which is not a bomb, a suburban house with the 'darkness' present. Ordinariness and danger live together. There is uncertainty, darkness and boredom. The second dream continues this ambiguity:

*Two big red socks in a field of long grass. One is red, the other pink with stripes. They were retrieved with a long fishing-type pole and a crowd gathered to inspect them as if they were evidence in a murder drama. And yet the two big squashy socks were comforting and not related to nastiness.*

Again there is an uneasy juxtaposition of the soft and the nasty, placing cosiness and comfort side by side with murder.

Similarly with dream number three, reported by a young woman:

*I was lying on my side propped up on my left arm, which was in a puddle of my own blood. I was swirling shapes with my index finger of the right hand, in the puddle. Although I knew the blood was my own I was not at all disturbed by the experience. Instead I was at peace.*

Blood is all around. When surrounded by the sinister the dreamer feels at peace with the world. Perhaps the right hand does not know what the left hand has been doing. All three of these dreams express oblivion or passivity in the presence of danger. The dreamers are noticing this darker side but seem lacking in curiosity. It is as though their minds have come to a full stop. The woman is bleeding but using her index finger to make swirls in the blood as though she is playing. But what she is playing with is her own blood—her life. There is an obliviousness to this as it happens. An index is a pointer or a sign as well as a list of contents. It offers a way of finding something. The dreamer seems to be connecting with danger (blood), which has come from within. She does not recognize what she has found. There is no connection but it is still going on. We are in the presence of a group of ideas, which suggest that we do not know how to own, or respond to, a feeling of danger.

Could this ambivalence be an echo of the outside world where mass murder—in Rwanda, Kosovo, Sierra Leone, New York, Darfur, Iraq—co-exists with the comfortable consumerism of Western capitalism? A world where weapons of mass destruction—surely still a cause for huge anxiety—have become ordinary and 'middle of the road'. Those of us alive in the 60's will recall the huge anxiety felt at the development of the H-bomb, whereas today such realities appear to be a 'normal' part of the political landscape. Noam Chomsky is a lone voice at present warning of the inevitability of nuclear conflagration in the near future. The first dream describes a project which has been started beginning with the letter 'N'—could it stand for 'nuclear'?

Another dream puts blood right in front of us:

> In my car and the windscreen wipers are going and blood was going down the window. The blood was coming from the squirters,. Wipers were cleaning the blood away.

Other dreams reiterate this theme of ambiguity, of passivity in the face of horror, where danger cohabits with the mundane:

> I was so troubled that no one seemed remotely ill...
> The 'essence' always speaks wordlessly and seems to be telling me that it's all okay and not to worry, the people are meant to be dying.
> Watching a film where all my friends were being stalked and killed but I was waiting so I could not help them.

Blood is blurring the clear vision but the dreamer is 'mechanically' wiping the blood away. A robotic part of the psyche wipes out what we know, even though one of the dreams points out the contradiction, i.e., 'being troubled that no one is remotely ill'. There is an impassive stillness, a remoteness. In the last dream this is represented by the film, which creates a distancing from what is happening—his friends are being killed. Something is being denied, 'wiped away'. Again there is a sense of disconnection.

Are we now destined to live in a world where we are helpless in the face of atrocities? So that when reports of earthquakes in Pakistan, the aids epidemic in Africa, mass starvation, civil war, casual murder on the street, all become so commonplace on our television screens that we dismiss them as intractable. Apathy is all-pervasive. Disaster has become such a staple fixture on the periphery of our lives that the anxiety connected to it becomes taken for granted. For this writer such tension began in the 60's at the time of the Bay of Pigs. Perhaps the fear for many of us, forty years ago of nuclear war, never actually went away: we just learned to live with it as something felt but not thought about. When anxiety on a societal level becomes ordinary and has to be rationalized to be bearable, then the world becomes a much more dangerous place. But how do people cope with this anxiety?

The defence mechanisms of denial, which are activated to deal with such fear, create additional problems for the individual and society. A late 20th Century T-shirt slogan tells us that, *When the going gets tough, the tough go shopping*. And yet compulsive consumption, spending money to' cheer yourself up', does not seem to make us feel better. Shopping as self-assertion, drug and alcohol abuse, overeating, anorexia—each comes at a price. The body becomes a 'solution' for anxiety, both internal and external. Some of the dreams we received articulated this disease with a sensibility largely unavailable to waking consciousness. This is the expression of dread and impotence as rubrics of existence in the late capitalist world. The dilemma these dreams reveal is the relationship between our innate need to look after ourselves and the reluctance to take risks in the absence of any real or profound collective symbol of humanity. We seem to know about this, as we have to wipe the blood from our collective vision in order to avoid knowing what it is. Many of the dreams, however, offered solutions to this dichotomy, which we will come to shortly.

## Dreams of disaster

We were struck by the bleak atmosphere of many dreams in this mass dreaming project. A recent survey by the search engine Google revealed the depth of boredom reported by people and the huge number of individuals who typed into their computers, 'I am lonely'. We found a similar sense of disconnection, a concern with loneliness and dislocation, an inability to articulate the preoccupation people had with who they were. They struggled to define themselves. There was a sense of hopelessness and futility in their view of the world. Religion and violence were predominant themes with ideas that belief systems have become depressing, intent on killing each other, lacking mercy and compassion, no longer concerned with community. There was a feeling that in a world without God, there can be no greater understanding, just darkness, blood and murder. Bombs, assault, mayhem and panic pervaded the atmosphere of the dreams with a sense of nihilism and uncertainty. In one dream the sun was setting with a lack of clarity as to whether we are waiting for something to start or to end. No single dream represents this chronic sense of doom, rather it was an emotional climate in much of the dream imagery. Over and above all was a sense of insecurity and powerlessness.

Typically such dreams focused on the failure of masculine authority with images of delinquent teenage boys, of men getting out of control, branches breaking off, men needing support, a wife's breasts being fondled while her husband stood passively by. Two different women's dreams featured images of castration:

- *I dreamt I was in a hotel room and Nicholas Roeg was in the next room. He asked me to sleep with him—I felt angered—'woke up' and there on the bedside chair was a severed penis and I had something chewy in my mouth. A panic came over me—my reputation, the harm I had done and the newspapers etc.*
- *Dream about ex-husband—making love to him—at one point his body turned into a woman's body—very smooth—no pubic hair—genitals very different from mine. I had a sense the body belonged to his current partner. Later his erection needed to be hidden from onlookers—we covered it in a blanket as people passed by. Also realized I had pieces of his penis broken in my hand.*

The imagery is explicit, portraying the failure and fragility of the masculine at the end of the of 20th Century, with the cut-up, dream-like technique of Nicolas Roeg who made *Don't Look Now*, a foreboding film about an architect (the thinking, constructive man who could not save his daughter). We see the fragmentation of the phallus, women's conspicuous anger with men, the disintegration and emasculation of husbands.

Another (male) respondent dreamed of:

- *Being in an impossible situation when put into the cockpit of a plane and being asked to manoeuvre it backwards. The scene changed to a computer screen where images of accidents were to be accessed. The exercise is difficult, recovery of the images being very slow, the picture being faint, the sound blurred. I experienced powerful feelings of irritation, frustration and anxiety and woke up feeling that I was in the build-up to a nocturnal emission, which was forestalled.*

This is one of several dreams, which convey the complicated demands of being a man in a world where old values of manhood have been turned back to front. The conjunction of tension and anxiety with sexual arousal—*which was forestalled*—is striking, perhaps suggesting that sex and anger are closely connected in contemporary life.

Many dreams portrayed disaster, scenes of violence or a sense of impending doom. There were several references to the end of the world:

- *I am attending drama lessons with my daughter. We stand on the doorstep but the teachers—both men—say we must go elsewhere taking all the props with us. I go and get in one little car but there is no room and my daughter sits in the back. So I go to the other little car driven by a man I do not trust but it is too full of objects and I can't get in. Both cars are old and little and it is as if we have returned to the early 20th Century. At last we set off, me in one car and my daughter in the other. Somewhere behind a wall a funeral is taking place. I wonder if this is the end of the world*
- *I lay outside a shop waiting to go in. I had to eat black capsules like little bombs. Then I began to cough up brown bile. I thought 'This is the end'—then I woke up*
- *I dreamt that a dead hedge hog appeared as a sign of the end of the world.*

Another respondent had a 'ghastly' dream but with a safe ending:

- *Driving past my place of birth with one of my wife's friend's parents in my car and my wife in another. We went past a place that used to be a lunatic asylum near where I was born. My wife got lost. I needed to go back and find her. Then I met a man with two guns. I ripped them out of his hands and rushed to get my wife. She'd not just broken down. It was a bad crash. However I did reach her.*

This what Freud would have described as a 'typical dream' with its fear of losing a loved one and a return to the past. Of course, had this dream come from a patient during psychoanalysis, the hidden meaning of 'not just broken down' or the sexual symbolism of 'a man with two guns' could be explored within the context of the treatment. Such interpretation is not within our remit in this chapter. Our interest is rather to look at what the dreams tell us about the social context. Most of us at some time in our lives have experienced a trauma. In some way, we all carry around inside us fear of loss, of violence, break downs and 'bad crashes' which we dream of but maybe unable to think about when awake. Many of the disaster dreams were about survival fear. They suggested that forces beyond our control were determining our lives and threatening our existence. As if people felt powerless in the face of overwhelming events which threatened their very being. In the last dream however this loss of the feminine—our sense of being—gives urgency to the dreamer. It offers a solution amidst the madness. He 'needs to go back' to what is important and save her. When he needs to connect with her—i.e., get the male and female elements together—he finds hope and possibility. He is spurned into action and the man with two guns can be disarmed. The dreamer needed to connect with the intuitive self preserving part of himself (the female) in order to overcome the two-gun mentality, which represents an unthinking violence of confrontation and showdowns.

Clearly, these anxieties may also spring from external, as well as internal events, in an increasingly volatile and uncertain world of terrorism, nuclear threat and global warming. We may be sharing these concerns unconsciously as a dreaming civilization. What is more they may in turn impinge on that external political world as projections of inner states, which are entirely unrelated to the political situation in question. The death of Princess Diana and the hysterical mourning, which followed her tragic death, is a case in point. In America the neo-conservatives' intemperate, international search for a perpetrator after 9/11 is perhaps another.

## The dream as solution

However, these disaster dreams are useful. They can help us to understand our anxiety and cope with this dread of something unnameable, in both the outside, and our own internal, world. Firstly, there is much evidence to show that dreaming about trauma is a necessary and healing response to our experience of loss and the horror of disaster. Soldiers suffering from battle shock have been found to have recurring dreams and nightmares about the carnage and bereavement experienced in battle. In the disturbing dream or nightmare there can be a useful reliving of horror (accompanied by the rapid eye movement of deep sleep), which serves to process the unbearable event. Trauma literally means a wound, a shock which is 'too much' to bear. Something, which has been too much for us, may be impossible to access in conscious thought and so dreaming helps to come to terms with the unthinkable in ways that are curative.

Secondly, if we are able to access unthinkable reality in our nightly images, then the political, social and economic dangers which threaten our world can be thought about, talked about and maybe even acted upon. As Freud said, what cannot be remembered will have to be repeated. Most of us know much more than we are able to consciously think about. When history has to be forgotten, or even worse denied, then the result can be witch hunts, racism, ethnic cleansing and genocide. A careful reading of the dreams in this project suggested that people were not only dreaming of disaster. They were also searching for answers, trying to fill a gap, identifying what is missing that can be used to make sense of our complex world and how we live our lives in it. Some dreams even posed their own questions and problems to be solved. Our hypothesis is that these 'solution' dreams were attempts to understand both the inside and the outside world. Such dreams are a vital resource because they:

a. identify significant areas of difficulty, in both the personal and the political spheres
b. highlight missing elements of the self and the social world
c. provide tools with which to think and act, both personally and publicly.

All of this is made possible by the remembering and retelling of the dream, the key to our unthinkable knowledge. We will look now at several of these solution dreams with the above hypotheses in mind, each followed by an analysis of their 'solutions'.

## The dream within a dream

> I had a' dream within a dream'. In this dream I had arrived at a big
> event with lots of people—but where I was there were some men who
> were kicking a young boy around, kicking him over the rocks and grass
> as if he was a football, hurting him badly. They said they were doing
> it to show the existence of God, by showing him what pain was. I was
> terribly angry to see this happening. I was consumed with anger. Then
> I woke from my 'dream within a dream' still dreaming and knew I should
> report my dream to the dream collector. So I went to see her and I was
> telling her about the dream. I was crying because the dream had been so
> distressing but half the time she spoke to me in Spanish, which I didn't
> understand. And she took calls on her mobile phone while listening to
> me about how upsetting my dream was. I cried profusely.

a.  The 'dream within a dream' structure suggests a need for *self reflection*. The objectivity and 'thinking' component of the dream is heightened by this configuration, where one part of the dreaming self reflects on the other part. There is a container within a container. A traumatic event can be looked at in a safe space, a dream within a dream.

b.  The problem identified is of *masculine violence* against the innocent in the name of God. Whether perpetrated by suicide bombers or American imperialism, this is punishment in the name of ideology. Rather than religion's standing for care and compassion, it is increasingly about killing the unbeliever. People are angry that this is happening.

c.  Above all this dream highlights the objectivity of dreaming as an unused thinking tool. The dream within the dream is taken somewhere else. Here the dream needs reporting to a collector who is female i.e., *dreams need to be taken seriously*, especially with *the feminine part of the mind*. A part, which, we would suggest, refers to an unused and neglected part of our psyche: non-violent, caring, closer to the maternal body and less intellectual. In the language of Wifred Bion (see Chapter 1) this enables reverie rather than projection. When the mother is able to listen to and contain the baby's upset then the feelings can be processed gradually. This provides 'containment' of confused emotions from which thinking becomes possible.

d. The idea of a dream collector implies that social dreaming, *the process of sharing our dreams as a collective* and thinking about them, might be a useful idea in a violent world which is frequently not conducive to thought.

## The flock of birds dream

> *I am standing watching a massive flock of birds, maybe thousands flocking in the sunset. They perform incredible aerial patterns with such skill. But they are not starlings they are blue tits! And in one of their displays in the centre of the flock they make an exact image of a single blue tit, yet the edges of the shape are still random and moving.*

This evocative dream reads like a physical embodiment of the social potential if we dare to share our dreams, suggesting the communal patterns of communication in *some* pre-industrial societies—intuitive, harmonious and co-operative yet still able to flow and move.[1] In many ways this is the world we have lost. This evocative dream also suggests what we can learn from the animal kingdom, working together as a group, with a knowledge beyond our ken. (There is still no explanation, for example, of the long-range navigation/migration/communication/flying-while-sleeping capacities of birds.)

A 'single blue tit,' yet again could be seen as a reference to the wholesome maternal breast, to the mother figure, caring and nourishing, and representing bodily 'knowing' rather than logic, intellect and control which are possibly so over-valued in modern life.

Many of the dreams of course were more prosaic. Literal or *concrete* solution dreams are quite common. There were numerous examples in our study of these insistent or *palpable* forms of unconscious communication. Typical is the dream of the competent parent, emphasizing the capacity to think, not lose control, stay calm and be protective—the qualities needed to cope with life:

> *I dreamt about the wok incident where disaster struck in the kitchen and the meal being cooked was spilt whilst the tense adults talked in the next room. It could have been a disaster but dad's quick, calm thinking saved the day.*

Other forms of direct literal communication in dreams emerged with the appearance of words/sentences as questions, admonishments or puzzles. As already outlined, the appearance of words or speech in dreams is relatively rare and it can therefore have a force, which carries significance over and above the ambiguity of the images described. Phrases stop us in our tracks with wonderment as to how or why our mind would conjure up such stark expressions. After a complex and colourful dream, came the following:

> *Everything went black. All I could see was an old map with an island sketched onto it…a man's voice said out of nowhere, it begins with 'B'. I answered, "'B' is for Bourgeoisie".*

Similarly, in the first dream in this chapter, as well as the word 'darkness', we hear of a bomb with the letter 'N' written on its side and the question, "Is this what it is?"

Another dream had the gentle admonishment, "Relax or get hurt".

At a dream of the roadside a sign read, "No cats Eyes".

In another man's dream his son asks, "So are you going to stop being a sarcastic bastard?".

Elsewhere, in a dream a beautiful woman was swimming in dirty water, when she was warned of the danger she looked up and said, "You have no idea of the properties of this."

These dreams cause the subject to pause and question what the literal phrase is getting at. This brings to mind the work of Morton Schatzman on problem solving in dream work in which he gave participants complex mathematical problems to work out. Some dreamers were amazed when they were able to dream the correct answers despite having little conscious aptitude for maths. Perhaps the most famous case of such problem solving was that of Mandeleyev who dreamed the Periodic table and wrote it down when he woke up. The gaps he left have since been filled by new elements of which he was aware at the time of his original dream. Similarly, Kekule's dream of whirling snakes led him to the structure of Benzene. These inventors needed to swim around in the muddy unconscious to allow the hidden 'properties' to bring illumination to their thinking. As Jung put it, "We dream of our questions, our difficulties…Our dreams are most peculiarly independent of our consciousness and exceedingly valuable as they cannot cheat." (Jung, op cit p. 4)

More typical, however, are dreams, which present complex, whole, dense and visionary narratives with many layers of meaning.

These are what Jung called 'great dreams' of sweeping imagery and powerful feelings, where vision becomes possible through an intense aliveness.[2] The labyrinthine textures of these often subtle night-thoughts may stay with us for days, haunting us with their enigmatic emotional depth. Pregnant with meaning and carrying truths, which are difficult to access, these dreams, *if discarded*, represent an extraordinary waste of psychic work performed at night by active minds preoccupied with the strangeness of being alive. Unconsciously artists may paint them, musicians perform them and poets recite these jewels of consciousness, while countless 'ordinary' people discard them as they wake each morning. Our hypothesis is that such weighty dreams ask questions and provide answers that are vital to our survival, both psychically and as a species. The dream that follows is representative of these big narrative dreams of which there were several in this research. Each contained solutions to problems, which greatly preoccupied the dreamer.

## 'A can for every country' dream

I stood outside a tall high-rise. My sister ran past me and through a door to the side of the building. I ran after her. She carried on up a winding staircase and I followed. At the top of the stairs she opened up a door and threw a can she was holding inside before quickly slamming the door shut and running back downstairs. Outside again, I asked her what she was doing. She explained to me that she was doing her job. She had to deliver a can to every country in the flat. Every door in the flat led to another country so all she had to do was find the door of the country corresponding to the label on each can. She walked onto a field where hundreds of silver cans with different coloured labels lay scattered around. Dad was sitting on a bench nearby. I sat next to him and told him what my sister was doing. He said he was waiting for a bus. It was really dark out. The sky was grey and cloudy and the sun glowed orange in the sky, either it was just rising or just setting. I don't know which.

My sister who had left a minute or so ago came running back. She sat down on the ground by the bench and said she gave up. I asked what she meant. She said that as she got up to the second floor, near to where she was supposed to be, 'they' (whoever 'they' were, I don't know) wouldn't let her come any further and pushed her down the stairs.

*'Aaron' said Dad, 'go and get me one of those cans'.*

*I grabbed one from the field and handed it to him. He unscrewed the top and inside were three jelly sweets wrapped in plastic. He gave one to each of us and we all ate. After which I took the can my sister was holding and said I would deliver it myself. No one said anything.*

*I ran off through the door, up the steps, up some more steps; I didn't know where I was going and so stopped to check the label and noticed Dad standing right behind me. He had a stern, meaningless face and still no one said anything. We walked forwards across the second story landing and through a door straight in front. Inside it was my sister's bedroom. It looked like she'd been collecting things from the wood because there were leaves and twigs everywhere. There was a ring of braided sticks hanging on the door handle so that when I took hold of it to shut the door they fell and it took me a while longer to put them back together.*

*I ran up another flight of stairs and walked through another door straight in front. I opened it to a small closet like room. It was stuffy and hot. There was one window in front and on the carpeted floor sat three African natives; a skinny old woman, wearing only a short girdle made of what looked like bamboo shoots sat cross legged and playing with her toes, a fat women with rings pierced all over her body sat cross-legged, spitting into her hands and rubbing them together, a young boy also sat cross-legged, banging the floor with the palms of his hands and from time to time looking at the woman and the old man. There was no furniture in the room. A picture hung low down on the wall in front of them but not one of them seemed to pay any attention to it. Dad and I pointed it out to them and they looked up at us and then to the picture.*

*It was an impressionist painting—blurred with large brush strokes, of a river running through a cluster of trees and some African people wading through it. There was a teenage boy pictured at one end—an old man had hit him and he spilt a jug of water from his hands. The man looked upset and angry. The boy looked surprised and distressed. There was also a woman, on the left side of the picture, scooping water into a jug with her hands.*

*The three natives seemed to be so pleased with the picture that they cried out in joy (in the same way I think I'd have done to have won a six million pound jackpot in a lottery). The last thing I remember was that I was floating in a surrounding pale orange and I said, 'well we're all slaves to babble-land'.*

*PS; I didn't realise until I'd told Dad the dream that I must have*
*meant 'we're all slaves to Babylon' without ever knowing that there*
*was such a saying.*

Reading this extraordinary dream, what comes to mind? What sense
can we make of a block of flats with a country behind each door,
three jelly sweets, an African room on the top floor, an impressionist
painting of spilt water and rage, the reference to babble-land? What
is the personal difficulty being identified for each of us, what is the
world problem confronting us in this dream?

This story in this dream has an archetypal quality. The dreamer's
sister is being followed, a woman is leading the way with father and
brother coming up behind. A 'can' could contain liquid for nourishment, pleasure or intoxication. But the word 'can' also comes from
the verb 'to be able', standing for capability, potential, permission.
Thus it may also symbolize the positive, the art of the possible, the
opposite of the negative and the statement of what 'can' be achieved.
The 'can' is the reverse of the 'cannot' and represents the silencing
of the obsessional, negative darkness of inequality in a world which
has created plenty but where millions starve. The sister in the dream
seems to stand for the idea of the possible, of hope and creativity in
an often bleak world. The cans were delivered to a building of many
different countries (the United Nations?) and one, which contained
countries of different colours. However next we see the girl being
pushed away, rebuffed in her efforts. But then the father asked for a
can (the positive idea) and they ate the three sweets. Next the dreamer
himself took up the positive object and on the third floor encountered
three people (the recurring number three) from the poorest continent
on earth. All this time a father remains in the picture. The Impressionist (European) painting depicts a river and an angry man hit-
ting a boy, while precious water is spilt. So we see flowing water,
the symbol of life, with violence of man to man but there is also a
woman scooping up the water—the feminine attempt to repair. The
three natives cried out in joy.

'We are all slaves to Babylon'; the excesses of capitalism have
enslaved us all, including those from the rich 'developed' nations of
the world. There is something which CAN be done but which conventional (masculine, violent, acquisitive) forms of authority have
failed to achieve. This precedes Barak Obama's affirmative "Yes,

we can". Now a different approach is needed. But the language of Babble-land, where no one speaks the same language, is an ill form of communication. (The Tower of Babel was built in an attempt to reach heaven which God frustrated by confusing the language of its builders so that no one could understand each other.) (Genesis 11: 1–9)

Such a subtle dream brings forth an ingenious panoply of connotations:

- The incorporation of female authority,
- the prioritising of three (the oedipal trio, a child, a mother, a father, the essential threesome of a basic family, the reinstatement of the father, the 'third' way),
- the balancing of sexual politics,
- the huge responsibility of the capitalist world for the world's poor,
- the untapped potential of European culture and the sophistry of Babylon—the city, the symbol of capitalism.

Each of these elements can be found in this deep and complex dream. In a social dreaming context they would be available for playful elaboration leading to further dreams and associations. In a community of ideas—a school, university, hospital, factory, parish hall—they enable the communication of otherwise inaccessible ideas, leading to that most rare and valuable commodity, thinking. Indeed, someone wondered in a recent social dreaming matrix, what would happen if Gordon Brown's cabinet decided to take their dreams seriously.

But perhaps women do not need to lead the way; maybe the delivery of cans has other significance, babble-land is baby talk and babbling brooks, or Africa stands for dignified suffering, or female sexuality. The associations are endless. This is the symbolic in full flow where the infinite can be felt. There will never be just one fixed interpretation of a dream, one ultimate truth to be arrived at. The meaning of one dream is always another dream. The question is, when such compelling poetic images emerge in our waking thoughts, are we going to take any notice of them? What can we make of these powerful associations, which emerge, so insistently from such heavy-laden dreams? It is not a matter of whether a single truth can be established but of what we do with the latent thoughts, which lie concealed in the dreams. This is a matter of choice; and when we ignore the subtle contents of our dreams we choose not-knowing. As James Sully put it over a hundred years ago:

"Dreams are not the utter nonsense they are said to be…the chaotic aggregations of our night-fancy have a significance and communicate new knowledge. Like some letter in a cipher, the dream inscription when scrutinized closely, loses its first look of balderdash and takes on the aspect of a serious, intelligible message…it discloses beneath its worthless surface character traces of an old and previous communication." (Sully quoted in Freud. 1900. p. 216)

At that moment, when we disregard a dream, our lack of curiosity puts us at a disadvantage. Arrogance and ignorance are dangerous partners. The knowledge gleaned in the aftermath of our dreams may be the key to our survival individually and as a group. If this is felt to be overstating the case, then it is worth turning to the work of Charlotte Beradt. In *The Third Reich of Dreams* she catalogued hundreds of dreams, which she had courageously collected in Nazi Germany from 1933–39. Early dreams envisioned death camps and other horrors, which were to come 5 years later. People knew unconsciously what would be their fate. Totalitarian fear invaded people's minds as they unconsciously prepared for what was to come. In these "diaries of the night" she witnessed the inner world of fear and confusion which people felt, as their personal integrity disintegrated and their lives fell apart. From the very beginning, those from all walks of life were dreaming about the aims and principles of fascism. In the dreams they could foresee its consequences. Her work reveals just how potent dreams are as ways of studying troubled societies. The problem, especially for the Jewish population, was that few if any took their dreams seriously enough to share them with others and so be able to realistically contemplate their appalling fate. (Beradt op cit)

## Dreams of animals

Despite the insecurity and dread outlined above, some dreams indicated a quest to define the self. In a sense, all dreams are an attempt in some way to tell us who we are, reveal our desire, uncover our insecurities. As Freud suggests, even distressing anxiety dreams can be wish-fulfilments. All the dreams collected here could be seen as attempts to define some aspect of self experience, an intricate aesthetic unique to the dreamer, the myriad glimpses of self which make up a personality. We have seen in Chapter One that the idea of unified self is problematic and that dreams are a useful key to the mystery of who we actually are. Every dream will make up a tiny part of this ever changing, fluid phenomenon, which preoccupies and escapes us in waking life. One aspect of this ontological puzzle is touched on via the number of dreams about nature and in particular about animals, which appeared so frequently in the material of this research. It seemed that respondents dreamed more of the animal world than they might discuss, or be conscious of, in waking life. Interestingly there is no reference to animals in Freud's index of dream-content, although we know that animals featured significantly in the unconscious thoughts of several of his patients (cf Little Hans and the horse's widdler, the Wolf Man's famous dream). In the current project there were dreams of many creatures—hedge-hogs, hens, vultures, horses, foxes, kittens, flies, ants, hornets, swans, crows, snakes, starlings, whales, dogs, frogs, chickens, bears, herons, sea-horses, turkeys and fish. The following excerpts show the immense variety of contexts for these;

> A cat was scratching out the eyes of my kitten. I was very worried at this and wanted to stop it. Then I saw a sign at the roadside saying 'No cat's eyes.'
>
> I was walking along a beach and suddenly felt very disturbed because a black sea-horse was bouncing up and down on a stone. This created black smoke until I could no longer see.
>
> I dreamt I was in the sea and whales surrounded me and talked but I can't remember what they said. Then I was on a road with a cat and two horses who were strapped to either end with their legs flailing. They too talked to me and then one leapt off as if revived by something.
>
> I dreamt of a flying fox
>
> My son was worried by a scuttling noise behind the eaves in the attic. I opened it and was shocked to see that the roof had fallen in and some kind of bird of prey was about to eat a mouse.
>
> On my left a stream of cattle and horses walk along the side of the house. I can't understand why they are in the garden. The animals are

*going through the fence and some are getting caught in the wire as they go through.*

*A snake charmer has piped up an enormous snake as high as the house. Next to him is a large bird of prey. He catches it and puts it under a transparent tent-like cover where it sits spluttering and preening like a great brown turkey.*

*I am like a crow: a spooky cartoon-like Dracula figure.*

*I was looking after kittens, going from room to room, small spaces, a room full of flies. There were different species, in swarms crawling over my skin. I was aware I must find lost kittens and dead carcasses (perhaps dropped by the cat) and clean. I rushed off to find fly spray!*

*I dreamt of small dangerous brown/black hornets, which will kill me in the outhouse. They cannot be squashed but just go underground*

*A goat/man is being mistreated as someone's creature.*

*I dream of a primitive brown dog, dangerous and wild but it loves it when I cuddle and hold it tight.*

Clearly there is no consistent theme in the multifarious appearances of living creatures in these dreams but it seems reasonable to surmise that animals are much more important to us than we realize. Closer examination of the material gave rise to the following hypotheses:

1. People are acutely aware *unconsciously* of the potential danger of the extinction of species (to the human, as well as the animal, population). For example, despite dreaming such images, some dreamers reported rarely giving much thought to animals in their waking thoughts.
2. There is a latent fear of losing personal contact with nature, as wild animals, as beasts of burden, as companions and as food.
3. Unconsciously we know that we are, ourselves, animals and that we are heading for disaster if we lose touch with the animal part of ourselves. Symbolically, this is connected to the olfactory function. Sense of smell is our most primitive faculty with connections to intuitive knowledge and 'knowing' with our bodies. Significantly very few animals died in the Tsunami. They sensed what was coming and escaped to places of safety.
4. The animal world symbolizes our own tragedy in the world— i.e., loss of power and of joy and exhilaration at being alive— ultimately our own possible extinction.

5. Some of these dreams highlight the essential value of compassion towards all living things, not only instrumentally to serve our own ends but as a way of being—as in the Buddhist ideal.
6. When we dream of animals we dream about who we are. Animals can represent our own personalities. We dream of our own natures when we conjure up the ruthless cruelty of the crow, identify with the vulnerability of the whale, or wish our brilliant selves to fly like a bird of prey.
7. To fly like a fox is a poetic image of free-form expression, the sense of relief if we could just let ourselves go.

Perhaps these dreams tell us what we are really like. The poet, Ted Hughes, leaves us in no doubt as to the animal nature of man, the seething cauldron of the id, the dark violent pleasure of ruthlessness from which emanates guilt and self doubt. His poems in *Crow* confront the starkness of existence. As in a lost and ancient dream world, he brings us down to earth and challenges the sentimental humanist view that posits a world free of hate, where reason rules all. Rather than the Enlightenment's idea of progress, he underlines the eternal repetitive animal nature of existence:

*Crow's first lesson*

God tried to teach Crow how to talk
'Love', said God, 'Say, Love.'
Crow gaped, and the white shark crashed into the sea
And went rolling downwards, discovering its own depth.

'No, no,' said God. 'Say Love. Now try it. LOVE.'
Crow gaped, and a blue fly, a tsetse, a mosquito
Zoomed out and down
To their sundry flesh-pots.

'A final try,' said God. 'Now, LOVE.'
Crow convulsed, gaped, retched and
Man's bodiless, prodigious head
Bulbed out onto the earth, with swivelling eyes,
Jabbering protest –

*And crow retched again, before God could stop him.*
*And woman's vulva dropped over man's neck and tightened.*
*The two struggled together on the grass.*
*God struggled to part them, cursed, wept –*

*Crow flew guiltily off.*

(Hughes, 1970, p. 92)

Hughes's view may seem bleak but it provides a reality check on what we are actually capable of in our animal selves. Poetry, like our dreams, gets closer to existential truth than rationality or science. Hughes's world view is far from cynical, however, and he also tells us, through closely observed nature, what letting-go can mean:

From *Skylarks*

*And maybe the whole agony was for this*
*The plummeting dead drop*
*With long cutting screams buckling like razors*
*But just before they plunge into the earth*
*They flare and glide off low over the grass, then up*
*To land on a wall-top, crest up,*
*Weightless,*
*Paid-up,*
*Alert,*
*Conscience perfect*

(Hughes, 1970, p. 82)

## The natural world

Dreams too can have the quality of poetry with a beauty and inten-sity of emotion, expressed through the rhythm and juxtaposition of images. One particular dream from the Hay experiment stays in the mind as an emotional picture of human frailty and strength. of man's need for a healthy natural world and the interdependence between the two.

## The Crying Trees Dream

> *The trees were walking.*
> *They were sad,*
> *their leaves were wilting*
> *A man held on to the branches*  ,
> *like a father holding*
> *the hands of his child*
> *The trees came towards me –*
> *they opened a mouth and*
> *bled water profusely.*
> *It was a gush.*
> *I panicked.*
> *I knew they would die after they wept.*

> I woke soaked.

The tree is a sine qua non of life. In this remarkable dream we see the interdependence of father and child echoing the profound importance of the natural world to our human sense of well-being. It is full of feeling, sadness and loss, where pain at the inevitability of death is incorporated into the tree of knowledge, the tree of life. You do not need to be bright and clever to relate to this dream: you just 'know' it, as it speaks of the many-layers of care and need so vital to survival in a fragmented universe. It is our observation, during a decade of dream research that people are dreaming increasingly about a world, which we are in danger of losing. The centrality of nature and animal life to our existence was expressed in the dreams in a great variety of forms—as wild creatures, as animals hunted and bred, as meat on the butchers slab, as aids to work—and quintessentially as symbols of our own lot in life.

## Dreams of race and colour

The colour of things appeared in the dreams, often apparently denoting affect or mood—as with the black sea horse, bright red trees glowing like embers, brown as the colour of diplomats suits providing safety and immunity—and there were numerous references to people's skin colour, including scenes of racial violence, racial tension and racial oppression. It is difficult to interpret the possible unconscious meanings of colour in this anonymous sample of dreamers and we are unaware of the ethnic or racial origins of most respondents. A relatively small percentage of visitors to the festival came from ethnic minorities but *brown* was the colour occurring in people's night thoughts more than any other, often with a benign connotation:

> *They could get away with anything could the people with brown suits. This was the diplomats' colour and it gave you immunity. Wearing brown would make you safe.*
>
> *I lay with my head on the chests of three people. A mixed race woman from Sri Lanka, a friend with a red face and a man with a brown complexion.*
>
> *I dreamt my family ran a restaurant but they were not good cooks. A rough unshaven man came in and wanted peas with his meat. All I had in the pan was little brown slices of a root vegetable like small Jerusalem artichokes. He refused them not knowing how healthy they were.*

Brown is probably the predominant colour of the future. Maybe it will 'make us safe.' Perhaps in an increasingly multi-cultural society there is a growing awareness that eventually most people in the world will be varying shades of brown and that the preoccupation with skin colour is an unnecessary and primitive fixation of no real significance. This would mean that people of colour or difference would no longer have to play the role of betes noires, or *alien others*, for white society. If dreams entail the fulfilment of a wish, the following dream may stand for the hopes of many on the question of colour as a desire for unification and wholeness:

> *I dreamt that there were more black people at the festival.*

Last but not least:

The Compassionate Dream
> *A man called Arthur turned up in my art therapy group. He called me to one side and asked for advice about paying his fee. He explained he had very little money and was struggling to support his family.*

*Very few words were spoken but emotionally he was deeply sincere*
*and desperate for my help. I felt a great responsibility to him and a*
*huge amount of compassion. I knew I had the power to help him and*
*must use it wisely.*

This was the last dream we received in this project and the person
wrote, "Hope this hasn't arrived too late!" In fact it was very appropriate. Its final statement was the last word on the simple but profound value of *listening* to our dreams. The dreamer knew he had
the power to help and must use it wisely. Perhaps most of us are
rarely as kind as we would like to be.

This mass experiment reveals a subliminal landscape of many
minds full of imaginative possibilities. It is a resource, which is per-
manently available to us a human community. Though we are limited
in our perspective, we have such untapped potential for creativity
battling with our avaricious need to be right as a group, a church
or a state. The dreams imply that we do not realize what is good for
us. Real change is difficult—maybe for some the task is too much.
The archetypal dreams about the can and the tree stand as beacons
to our collective dilemma as we struggle to think about nature and
the maternal. There are also tears pointing to our mortality and the
inevitability of loss.

\* \* \* \*

## Notes

1. After a trip to Africa in 1928, Jung wrote "African primitives now
   depend on the English to guide them, no longer on the medicine
   man's dream. The general opinion is that the medicine man or chief
   has no such dreams since the English have been in the country. They
   said the commissioner *knew everything* now…this shows that the
   dream had formerly a social and political function, the leader…guid-
   ing his people directly from the unconscious." (Jung, 1958, p. 5)
2. Jung suggested primitive people believed in two different types of
   dream: the great dream which is visionary, big, meaningful and of
   collective importance and the ordinary small dream. Great dreams
   tended to point more to the collective and small dreams more to the
   individual.

# CHAPTER SEVEN

# Dreaming in the inner city

*A one-day matrix at a counselling centre for adolescents in North London*

> "Adolescence is a crisis—a madness one could say—because the adolescent is trying to work out whether life is worth living."
>
> —Phillips, 2005, p. 148

In July 2004 we were invited to host a day-long matrix with the staff of a drop-in counselling centre for adolescents, on a large multi-cultural housing estate in north London. The project manager, whom I will call Barbara, had been instrumental in seeking outside help to improve communication and try to ascertain what was wrong with the service. Morale was low and communication within the work teams was poor. They worked in a run-down urban environment. The social context was one of poverty, deprivation, drug abuse and family breakdown. It involved demanding work, often at crisis level with vulnerable people under cramped and underfunded conditions. In addition to the difficulties in their work with young people, the counsellors and office staff had already expressed a variety of other concerns:

- there was a state of uncertainty with the impending retirement of their project manager
- a lack of consultation over the move to another location,
- a feeling that they were unheard and powerless in the face of an unresponsive management,
- anxiety at unresolved personal tensions within their team.

The matrix took place on a rainy day in July in the offices of the primary care trust. Unlike most of the other case studies in this book, the task here was to use social dreaming as a tool to highlight unknown areas of conflict and resentment, after other forms of dialogue had failed. The staff was made up of sessional workers, who were counsellors and therapists, and core workers who were administrators and health advisors. The day's schedule was seen as out-of-hours work (it was a Saturday). Staff were encouraged to participate by management and were paid for attending. This point is mentioned because not all participants were happy to be there and, while most of the counsellors were interested in the project, some other members were sceptical and resistant to the idea of 'talking about dreams'. This, combined with vague and unspoken interpersonal hostility within the organization, made for an uneasy day with several flash-points of frustration, tears and anger, including one sudden walk-out by a participant when she recalled the death of a child. It by no means fitted the 'lightness of being' atmosphere described elsewhere in this book. However, the dreams *were* forthcoming and—although one person did not speak publicly throughout the eight hour session—the day yielded some profound if uneasy revelations. (This is by no means a criticism. The fact that this individual stayed throughout the day meant that they definitely had a presence and presumably heard what was spoken by others.)

## Working with adolescents

This was a service for young people. Constantly in the background of the matrix was the subject of their job—daily one-to-one work giving advice and counselling to adolescents. These were dedicated and sensitive workers who clearly cared about their clients and felt the full weight and responsibility of their daily encounters with often troubled young people. The estate had an ethnically mixed population, with a high proportion of people from the Asian subcontinent and many East European and African immigrants. Young clients came for sexual and employment advice and for help with a wide range of personal difficulties. They were usually offered ten sessions of counselling. There were problems of abuse—both sexual and physical—bullying and racism at school, drug and alcohol excesses and family breakdown. Communication via the use of English was complicated by the confusion of tongues amidst many different languages in the centre's intake.

Adolescents are, by definition, immature. The only 'cure' for this is the passage of time. Waiting and listening results in the growth of the adult person and this process should not be hurried or slowed. As Winnicott, (1986) puts it in his definitive paper, *Home is Where We Start From*, adolescents should not be given responsibility too soon. Irresponsibility is the adolescent's most sacred element. It lasts for a few years and is the necessary cost for maturity to be reached. False maturity deprives young people of their greatest asset—the freedom to have ideas and act on impulse. It is inevitable that therapists and others who are drawn to work with teenagers have to confront this sometimes anti-social tendency—not just in teenagers but also in themselves. They can be outspoken. They can also be painfully inhibited. And yet the spontaneous gesture is an essential achievement in the formation of each new generation. For adults, the paradox is that, in order to be true to themselves, an essential act may still be the unwavering, forceful, even aggressive statement of an idea, which they fear is too dangerous to voice. Other people must be protected from their 'real' feelings, difficult things must never be said out loud. It was this compliance and inhibition which was gradually exposed, painfully and not without anguish, in the course of the following matrix. Session workers and core workers, throughout a day of social dreaming, found their voices. They were more able to confront one another and put into words things they had hitherto thought were unsayable.

For adolescents, growing up is inevitably aggressive, as it entails 'getting rid of' adults, of taking their place. Parents with teenage children discover that sometimes they can do little more than survive the rages and tantrums and remain available. In the therapeutic encounter confrontation is needed. Confrontation, which is firm, containing and non-retaliatory. For this to happen the presence of a thinking adult who will be honest and non-manipulative is essential. In the fraught environment of this group of youth workers, there was a reflection of the adolescent scenario in their own work-day situation. This became apparent as the day unfolded. As they themselves put it, there was:

- a mother figure leaving and a sense that she was being 'killed off',
- a lack of responsible authority from management,
- the upheaval of 'leaving home' when they moved to new premises,
- a feeling that the session workers were misunderstood by the core workers

* * * *

## The dreams

The ongoing dream narrative of the day revealed the intense pressure these dedicated employee's felt under. They dreamed themselves into reality, coming face to face with what really troubled them. All this came via a relatively small number of short dreams, which revealed a tangled web of frustration and entrapment, fear, resentment and contempt. One dispute uncovered another, one inequality masked another, until hitherto unmentionable images were confronted. Participants began to see that clues lay hidden in the dreams. In particular there was a taboo on the expression of critical ideas; a helplessness in the face of complicated emotions, a desire for 'concrete' solutions. They wanted some one else to 'tell them what to do' but the emphasis was on 'protecting' others by never telling them what you thought. The question arose, "Who is going to save us?" There was an unspoken plea that we had arrived and would rescue them with something called 'social dreaming', which of course was not in anyway our purpose. However, this hope for a saviour gradually changed into the possibility of autonomy if each group took responsibility for the issues, which the dreams uncovered. Only they could help themselves; but this would involve the last thing most of them wanted to do—to talk about their dreams and how they felt inside. The dreams were stark, staccato statements which provided a clear list of problem areas and organizational difficulties. At first participants were tentative and cautious. Silences had an uneasy edge to them. It was difficult to speak. Thoughts and associations arose sporadically—in some cases several hours after the original dream images occurred. Given the inhibition and resistance felt by some, it was impressive that so much work was eventually achieved through the dreams. They burst out laughing when they suddenly realized that the dreams were precisely about the work situation.

The dreams will be presented in sequence—with dreamers' associations and my own comments (in brackets) where appropriate—followed by a discussion of the subjects, which arose in conversation during the day-long matrix. Where possible I will quote directly from comments made by members of the matrix.

## Dream 1

> *My daughter is not living in my house. Do I live here mother? South Africa. Do I live here?*

(Where do we belong, where is home?)

## Dream 2

> *A blind man. He jumped into a car, put his foot down and zoomed off. How does he manage to do this? Worried about pedestrians. He swerves. How do you manage to drive when you are blind? Perfectly safely it seems but he does not answer. It was a blue car.*

(Precarious, dangerous but showing great skill)

## Dream 3

> *Singing*

The association to this was 'Sinking'

## Dream 4

> *I am climbing up the outside of a building, like a school or college. I feel I cannot go any further. I need to get from one area to another but cannot get across as there is a gap.*

(High up, precarious, feeling stuck: something is missing)

## Dream 5

*I am with my younger brother who seems to be a little child even though I know he is an adult.*

(The need to grow up, act one's age)

## Dream 6

*I am in therapy but keeping falling asleep. It is not that I am trying to avoid anything it is just that I am tired.*

(Something is being avoided)

## Dream 7

*I am with an old boyfriend and watching him but I ask myself why am I trying to understand him. Utilize don't analyse!*

(Some resistance to understanding things)

"The blind driver dream felt very upsetting. It's about feelings of trust. Trusting yourself. It means a lot."

## Dream 8

*I have a friend who is in a wheelchair who is suddenly walking*

(Empowerment, standing on one's own two feet)

At this stage dreamers wondered if these dreams were 'part of a message'. The blind black man was an ambiguous figure associated with danger, strength, talent and vulnerability. Vision, they felt, is an obvious form of communication. There are other ways of being available for people. Blind drivers—how do they communicate? There was an idea of a poor father, a 'Nothing Dad'. Stevie Wonder emerged as a blind black man who was strong and talented, a good role model or leader—but who wrote a song about a naïve black youth arriving in the city, singing, "New York, New York—Just like I pictured it" just before being arrested by the police. This was an idea of a man with high hopes in the city but who was then disillusioned—a very hard place to be. Ray Charles was another blind black man who had suffered but worked hard and succeeded. A photograph of Ray Charles sitting behind a Cadillac. Many of the associations came from the only black male present, a young enthusiastic Afro-Caribbean counsellor who was inspired by the matrix and wanted to communicate his view of the 'black experience.'

Next came associations of trust, intuition and skill, "like the counselling situation at work each day. You have a child in front of you struggling to become an adult. They have their own ideas and thoughts about their experience."

"Yes, these young adults are so inexperienced—they show love and appreciation for the other person. But there's a real need for them to look after themselves."

"When people have died as children one cannot think of them as an adult. My brother died when he was 7. What would he have been like as an adult?"

"When I wake up from dreams I feel quite calm, nice and safe. I dream a lot about looking after babies and children."

## Dream 9

> I dream of looking after babies. Seeing a really young child—cushions—
> a baby who smears poo all over himself—was I supposed to be with him
> in the mess. I must clean him up—no I mustn't—just be with him.

Feeling restricted—really hard—very personal.

(Teenagers are such a mess; the work situation is a mess)

## Dream 10

> I had a dream about shit and having to clean it up. My shit.

Associations: Driving a car when you are blind. Finding out things you don't know. We are constantly dealing with a shitty mess—other people's mess. In this work you just have to trust the space. You're driving past schools and expecting to see them in their youth. It's good to be growing up but the end result is that you die and it's painful. You leave or are left. In this job we are in a constant state of being left. Year 11 is a painful year—I want to halt it. When you meet people 10 years later they seem to be the same age as when you last saw them. The body is ageing but the child within is evocative. I still feel like a child. It comes up with adolescents. Sometimes you can feel right back there.

> "Adolescents come and shit all over the place. We want to be messy and adolescent but can't be. We are having to be grown up as if it has all gone for us. A mourning of that loss. The blind man suggests disappointment."

### Dream 11

> *My dad was alive and it felt very vivid—then I woke up and realised he wasn't alive.*

(Desire for a father)

Associations were to a 'daddy by your side', fathers who feature in the work of counsellors. One member stated, "Dad's are absent in my work". At this point a female participant said she was finding it very difficult. She stood up and left the room in a state of distress. The project manager, Barbara, left to comfort her. The dialogue turned to dying and losing people. The loss of parents: of a father figure. "Barbara is leaving the organisation and that is like losing a parent."
"The changes will be unclear. It is very difficult to talk about."
"We are sure as adults but unsure as adolescents. We say to young people, 'Can I help'? but can we deal with anything in 10 weeks?"
At this stage Barbara returned to the room. Someone noted the pot was' hotting up.' There was anger and disagreement over her immanent departure from the job. (Possibly this anger was also because she had left the room and was felt to have been over-protective.) Someone said it was difficult knowing she was going to go. Others were unhappy about the timing and the announcement of her retirement. A woman, who had so far been silent, now left the room apparently in difficulty over the growing climate of disagreement.

### Dream 12

> *I dreamt that my son died. I was carrying him as a 30 year old man on my arms. He died suddenly, it was not a progression. I did not see him grow.*

(several people had mentioned that the counselling service was 30 years old)

The atmosphere was uneasy. Things now felt 'prickly'—"things can just happen." There was reference to the dangers of stirring the pot. They remarked on awareness that they could laugh and tell jokes and tell funny dreams, in order to avoid difficult material.

## Dream 13

> I am driving a red car with two friends on a motorway—a dual carriageway. It's J's car and I am not used to it. The other two are looking the opposite way. There is a horse and carriage on the road coming towards us and I hit it and kill the horse. Then we are sitting in front of a coal fire. I am going to lose my licence—or we are.

(A horse and carriage may represent two parts of the work force—the session and the core workers, or the workers and the project manager)

*Ass*: There were references to other dreams about people who had left. A pantomime horse—this would be one inside which people were not face to face: i.e., unlike the one-to-one relationship in the counselling situation. Barbara was again referred to as the parent who was leaving. "Parents help you to cope whatever."

## Dream 14

> I am taking pictures of young people without permission. 'P' came in and said she knew that the place would fall apart after I had left. (This was the manager's dream)

At this stage the matrix came alive and members began to use the wealth of material held in the dreams so far. They recognized themselves as the 'children', the subjects of the unconscious material: uncertain, in the dark but with hope and optimism:

But will it fall apart when Barbara leaves? The Pantomime horse was 'not real', not face to face. (Perhaps they did not want to face this reality.) Barbara leaving is like losing a trusted parent. This is about helping a young person to cope. We do have the facilities and faculties to deal with this. Sudden things can happen and there is no one there to hold it together. Sitting in the unknown has always felt like that. As if we can't make decisions. Can we keep it together? Will we make a mess? 5 months off was horrendous we were in survival mode. Actually leaving—just about clinging on—surviving. We've got attached to the building and this project. Can we be okay when Barbara leaves? It's like a family—she knows most people—can we cope with a new parent? The moving of building and parent makes me very anxious, moving into a different area, wondering, "Do I want to go there?" Change could be interesting and exciting. We could get a good person. The building is an old horse and cart. We are just so comfortable with the crap. Massive change can be good—you can see that with adolescents. Driving blind things can be okay. We need strong beliefs rather than pessimism. But I fear the blind driver will crash. We won't feel positive and optimistic but dragged like being dragged to school. We are talking about both crap and good things.

This searching discussion about change continued and somebody said:

"But there are no dreams about this organization."

"What about the dead horse?"

Laughter!

"What is so funny?"

It was clear to people at this point that the laughter was because they realized that most of the dreams had been about the organization and their hopes and fears inside it.

*Dream 15*

> *I also had a dream about a horse. I am walking through a building with Barbara who is taking me to a door. Outside is sunny and green and there is a big two tone brown and tan horse on the grass. It rears up and I am frightened but Barbara takes me out and then back. I couldn't get outside without her.*

(Two shades of brown)

Associations to this dream were:

- a fear of being responsible. There was a recognition that although they worked with young people these workers needed to be grown-up and take adult decisions. As they put it:
- "We need to come out and tame that horse—get control of the organizational issues—or knock it down. Or maybe we can

utilize it—the horse is very powerful. We are an organisation with lots of people running it. It will carry on and it will develop.

* being able to let go—"When is the best time to let go? Adolescence. We can block it as parents. When do you let clients go? Not being good at short term work means not being good at letting them go.
* question—who makes the decisions here? Answer—people who don't know much about what we actually do.
* the lack of men in the work. "How many youngsters don't have fathers? We have to be both mother and father in this job. There are very few black men in the counselling world in general. It feels as if we are the children left behind to tame a horse. We are reaching crisis point. There are so many young black men who need counselling from black men. It is a serious problem. Most of the teachers in school are female too."

(Now important subjects are being broached. The difficulties of black youth, the problems caused by fatherless families, the need to be responsible. Could it be that the horse, which reared up, was the problem posed by young black men? Or was it a more general fear that things could get out of control)

\* \* \* \*

*No space to think*

There was now a break for lunch after the strain and effort of the morning session. It was still raining. We then began the afternoon with a thinking space, a time to reflect. Participants were clearly very affected by the experience and began to look back on the morning of dream telling. They felt that impending change would be difficult but needed to prove they could do it. Now they were moving to a new stage. However people also felt powerless: "Decisions are being made top down: as usual we do not have a say." They agreed that there was a shared anxiety, which was not actually made specific.

"We are an organization full of women and need more men."

There was much focus, they noticed, on the dream about a blind black man and they felt this had been both "a catalyst and cataclysmic" implying it had moved things on but was dangerous territory. One woman said: "I feel as if my ears were affected, as if there's an obstacle. How much don't we want to hear?" And another, "I've got a fearful feeling inside, butterflies in my stomach. We've got a focus and yet we've got a blind dream."

Perhaps something connected to race and colour was falling on deaf ears. Nevertheless it was a useful chance to take stock of the day so far. They now ran through a litany of all the problems at work:

- too much to do, too little time
- chaos in the organization
- a sense of foreboding, waiting to move to new premises
- ten sessions of counselling was not enough with each client
- posts were being restructured
- there was a fear they'd be competing with each other for new posts

The phrase used more than once to sum it up was, "We've just no space to think".

"Where we are moving to is pleasant, overlooking a park. Things can be brought together with a combination of a drop-in and a counselling service. But we need to go into a bigger thinking space."

"It'd be more grown up—and the same with our clients. They've nowhere else to go. They are on their own and need a space just like we do. There is no physical and mental space out there."

This was a significant realization—about themselves, about their adolescent clients and also about the world we all live in. Their current workspace was comprised of two portacabins—small, temporary and makeshift. It was as if they could be moved at any time. But secondly they were recognizing the lack of internal capacity for thought, the need for mental space to reflect and take stock. We inhabit a society where people live lives so busy they do not even have time to think nor the mental space in which to process thought.

In the middle of this animated discussion there was reference to a boy from Iran who had had changed his identity and taken an English name ... Someone commented, "You can take the boy out of Iran but you cannot take Iran out of the boy." After this the Orient (a football club) was mentioned and someone said, "Where are the people from the East?" At the time this comment was not picked up but the dialogue, which followed, was perhaps significant—about waiting anxiously for something unknown, full of potential meaning.

"It's very chop, chop, chop—spaces, intrusions, cross-overs. Spaces you need but they need to be separated out. We have no vision of the building we are going to. I have a feeling of foreboding. We are in waiting. What will it be like? Just like adolescents we were not consulted, there's no information. Little bits are being said and nothing is out in the open. Things are being done which create internal divisions. One group can't keep the other in mind. There are complaints behind people's backs."

Social dreaming may alert us to horrific events to come. People unconsciously know things about institutions, which they work in. Some of these uncomfortable issues were coming out in the matrix— splits, resentments, mindless bureaucracy, racial tension. Some other things may be too painful, too dangerous to even think. At this point the conversation moved away from this difficult terrain to the emollient of the weather:

"It's stopped raining, the sun is coming out. This has been constructive. It's about allowing differences, having respect for difference."

"Having the appetite does not mean one can digest what one wants to eat. Maybe it's true you should be careful what you wish for or dream about."

"You have to be careful if you are climbing—you can't just go into the enjoyable."

* * * *

## Who do I help?

We now began the last matrix of the day.

### Dream 16

> I am flying upright not really high but just above the houses. I communicate with people down below. Not like Supergirl, as I am only at lamp post height.

Association was, "Angels are always that way up."

(An image of a powerful female with an overview)

## Dream 17

> *There is a great expanse of river. There is a bridge and several white people*
> *are going across it. We were in a hot air balloon, which was rising up.*
> *'I don't want to get too high—I don't know what is below'. So I start releas-*
> *ing myself. In the water with boys and black men—a shark is coming.*
> *Who do I help, boys or men? On the bridge were all the white people.*

This striking dream came from the young male therapist. Associations to it were immediate and intense:

"There is an urgent need for help for black kids. There could be so many different interpretations.

"It makes me think of '*Many Rivers to Cross*' by Jimmy Cliff."

"Yes, or '*Too High*' by Stevie Wonder, a black man who is creative and optimistic."

"Young black men need good fathers."

"This is so full of associations from lunch time and this morning. High up flying makes me think of communication with people down below. Adolescents have their heads in the clouds. They are either very low or too high—arrogant and difficult to be grounded."

"In each dream, you do not soar you're elevated and get a different perspective. If I continue to float I would get lost and detached. I must be involved down there. The profession is dominated by white people and women but the organisation deals with groups."

"We are the adults in the organisation: Where are we at? There's a hierarchy, above and below. There has to be a limit to what we respond to. Become more contained. What way the service goes and making decisions about it."

"My most consistent work is with young people. It grounded me and is worth a lot. But ten sessions is pretty thin. Even two years is pretty thin."

"The reality is that organisations don't do what they are supposed to do. Blair's government offers hope v delivery. There is too much need, too many needy groups everywhere. What is it about us that makes us choose the work? You can't be Superwoman. You can't save the world."

"But it does make a difference to people. 30 years means something—managing poor, poverty-stricken people. We just should be able to do more."

"Flying made me think of flights and how they always tell you in case of emergency you are supposed to put on your own oxygen mask before the children, even though instinctively you would save children first. But the instruction is look after yourself first so you can look after the children."

This pivotal association provides an answer to the question posed in the last dream—'who do I help?' The priority, if we are to be responsible for others, is to take care of ourselves. The dream had helped members of the matrix to think about how to be more adult, more decisive, and more realistic. The dream also has a social dimension. The idea of self empowerment can apply to poor people, black people and minority groups as well. There is a hierarchy of needs. The dream offers a view of different levels. Being up high, looking down, gives perspective. There is hot air rising. Poor people who feel dispossessed and powerless may have a choice. They may, as the dream puts it, 'start releasing themselves' and helping themselves and their children. They may rise up. In the dream, the white people are on one level, the black people are down in the water but what is the shark, which moves so dangerously beneath the surface of the water?

## There is a fence

Now the conversation returned to the difficulties at work and whether or not counselling really made any difference. In response to the assertion that, "this anxiety is because we cannot stand our diversity," another member said, "This is not specific enough, what are these criticisms you imply?"

The reply was immediate: "It's hard to work in a place where counsellors are criticised and we have to continually justify our own way of working."

"Yes. And maybe this is the unspeakable referred to earlier."

For some there was irritation that 'counselling has no practical application.' Quickly the mood shifted to an argument over the value of therapy. It was' just a lot of hot air.' One woman felt denigrated, working in the organisation when she did not have a counselling background.

"Is thinking useful or not? I feel patronised. It feels pretentious and not accessible—you counsellors are up your own arses; it's as if the red carpet should have been rolled out for you. We just have to fit in. There is a fence!"

Suddenly, after hours of preamble, a central issue was being confronted. There was a huge gap—a 'fence'—between the sessional and the core workers. The former (the counsellors) were felt to be not in the real world, while they themselves felt devalued and always on the defensive. Each group appeared to feel inferior and disadvantaged. Counselling was described as like 'floating off to the moon, floating off the ground as in the last two dreams.' One administrator said she was glad this was now in the open. A therapist described the core team as being like a legless chicken. When the outgoing manager attempted to smooth things over and looked at expectations for the roles of administrative staff, people became angry with her. It was suggested she had always taken on too much and had then 'had to have a nervous breakdown for the organization'.

"And now you leave us just at the point when we are moving."

It was a moment of intense emotion. Now she was able to say,

"I need to look after myself. You did murder me. It's so frustrating. We are always at one another's throats."

This cathartic exchange seemed to create calm, as people began to talk about the value of being honest with each other, the importance of mourning the loss of Barbara, the need for collaboration, the need for more communication. It then emerged that this was the first time some members of each team had met one another! Thus the introduction of the issue of racial inequality—which had subsequently been eclipsed—lead on to the feelings of inequality between different work groups. This, in turn, almost certainly stood for basic social class differences between these groups—in terms of older traditional working class values of the admin staff being usurped by these 'pretentious' counsellors who were 'up their own arses' and wanted the 'red carpet' put out. But there was another inequality lying dormant in the matrix.

It was suggested by one of the facilitators that the brown and tan colour of the dead horse may symbolize people of colour and the existence of racial prejudice. There was indignity from some older white staff members. They felt affronted—there was no prejudice, how could it possibly mean skin colour? However, this comment did ring true with others and now an Asian female worker—who had said very little throughout the day—said that she could hold her tongue no longer. Suffused with anger she said she too felt like walking out because there was an issue of brown-skinned people. Why, she wanted to know, had there been no mention all day of the Muslim population living on this estate, with their myriad problems especially among women? She felt that their voices had been excluded from this workshop; did we not remember what happened on 9th September 2001? Why were there so few referrals to the service from this group? Did no one stop to think where they fitted in to the hierarchy of this discussion? This was expressed with a sense of injustice and exasperation.

These were good questions. Where were the people from the East? Where were the brown and tan people from Pakistan, North Africa and the Middle East? They seemed to be left out of the picture although many of them lived on the nearby housing estate. Whether this resulted from their own unwillingness to participate or from discrimination on the part of others, they felt they were invisible, at the bottom of the hierarchy. People who are excluded and forgotten may carry deep grievances. This can, in extreme circumstances—when combined with religious fanaticism and alienation from Western capitalist values—create a terrifying shark in the waters of modern affluent societies. The London bombs the following July, which caused such death and devastation, could be seen, at least in part, as a grotesque manifestation of this sense of exclusion.

## Thinking together

Clearly this was a silence that had needed to be broken. People took notice and in no way dismissed this woman's powerful outcry. Now, after this vital and unexpected outburst, the final part of the day took on a thoughtful and cooperative mode. It served as an antidote to the tension and trauma of the previous seven hours. There was a poignancy in their urge to communicate honestly and constructively. This seemed to be facilitated by the fact that unmentionable issues had been broached. Now was a time for reflection and consolidation and they began to articulate a resumé of a hard day's work. Participants were exhausted and seemed surprised that they could get this far without further walkouts or anyone else being 'murdered'.

Nevertheless the interaction remained fragile with some people still harbouring scepticism about the usefulness of talking. They expressed guilt at having 'murdered' Barbara and being too difficult and too needy. They wondered if they could now allow themselves to be managed. When they expressed gratitude and appreciation to their retiring boss, she said,

"Gratitude? I am not sure I want to hear it. It's overwhelming. And I am excited about another job."

One woman said, "I want to protect you and you are buggering off! You bought us together today as a parting gift and I realize it is difficult for you to leave."

She replied, "But I fear that the practical will leave if you start talking about these things." Thus, at the eleventh hour it was still difficult for real feelings to be heard and considered in this overprotective environment.

Next the issue of 'colour' was again raised but from different perspectives. "This place is run by white middle class women. Now the jobs are going—that's the shark in the water, it's not fair. There is a race dimension in this place."

"I am white and convinced I will not get the job."

"There are feelings around these issues—core services are all white—who are we providing it to? This needs to change. We need to be more representative. Perhaps we need group counselling—it fits in with an African tradition .We also should encourage more refugees: and we need women to see women."

"Yes but what colour does one have to be to get a job here? It's not necessarily a good idea that a black client must see a black counsellor."

"There's a split between daytime and evening staff. There are all these ethnic groups but the core staff are white. We are not diverse enough to create a functional team. We employed six people in one year and they were all white women—there are serious implications here for new posts. Are people going to apply for these posts? It should represent diversity—this work helps you to work with anyone."

"Yes but we still need more men. I did not care if it was male or female when I had therapy. What the agency looks like is also an issue. We need someone who is Urdu speaking, Albanian speaking—our service should be need-orientated."

## Summary

### a. Growing up

It is noticeable that most of the dreams were about being with children and young people and of caring situations where people needed help. On one level, the dreams made clear, simple statements. They were preoccupied with growth from infancy to childhood, into adolescence and eventually to independence. We began with a daughter leaving home, an adult who remained a child, a boyfriend who needed understanding, someone in a wheelchair who is suddenly able to walk, children who needed nappies changing, the importance of fathers, a fear of going outside without 'mother', the need to rise up but finally not to get too high. Above all the need to be independent and think for ourselves.

### b. Autonomy

But this matrix explored the institution on different levels. Employees were able to think about unmentionable areas of conflict, which had lain dormant in an environment of dread and denial. The hysterical dimension, uncovered so eloquently in the dreams, was in their fear of their own power, their own capacity to be responsible, thinking adults rather than helpless babies who could not 'go outside' and be the mother and father of their own lives. It seemed this 'adolescent' crisis had been brought on by the fear of change, the loss of the project manager, lack of consultation from above and their dread of openly talking about their differences. Undoubtedly, lack of consultation and under-funding create an objective feeling of powerlessness. But this hysterical anxiety—the fear of growing-up—creates a subjective inner weakness, which becomes self-fulfilling and ultimately stultifying.

### c. The outside world

On a social level, the matrix pointed to the problems of perceived and actual racial prejudice in the workplace and the need for more honest dialogue. It also highlighted the gap created in our society by the absence of fathers, and in particular the lack of good male role models in the black community. Finally, it underlined the dangers when there is an excluded aggrieved minority—an 'invisible', unheard group who were not involved in the discourse until a late intervention by an exasperated worker. These are complex socio-political issues on which it would be inappropriate to elaborate in this context. What is noticeable is that they echo people's subliminal concerns expressed in images which are repeated throughout this book—the shark, the whale, the alligator, the horse—as the symbols of strength, weakness, dread and desire which we carry in our night thoughts.

* * * *

## Postscript

After this experience, the staff on the counselling service requested another training day. Social dreaming had helped to diagnose where they were as an organization. In a day entitled 'Working with Cultural Difference', the clinical staff embarked on a series of exercises to try and understand their own cultural pre-suppositions in their work with disadvantaged black and Asian youths. This exercise involved complex case studies in which clinical staff began to understand how they needed to be open to the 'stranger within themselves' in order to work with feelings of alienation encountered in their patients, in the organization and in the broader culture they were working in.

In the second training day, all the staff attended without the now departed manager. They spent a fruitful day considering the boundaries they were working within and defining what they actually did. In recognizing just how much work they had each day, they also began to see the extent to which this was defined by uncertainty, internal struggle and division within the organization. Through open discussion and clarification of roles, they were able to define new boundaries and responsibilities and to negotiate how to put them into practice. In this way the staff were able to 'own' the organization they were working in. They had become responsible adults, felt enlivened, excited and had a new feeling of potential in their work. They had come together as a team and had re-found why they were there in the first place and why this work was so important to them. They also learnt to treat their 'experience' as an important resource for future development. All of this became possible because, in sharing their dreams, they had located anxieties, which were unthinkable on a day to day level. Thus they developed a clear identity as a group of people engaged in a difficult task who had found a safe and creative way to communicate.

* * * *

CHAPTER EIGHT

# Too late! Social dreaming in the Haute Languedoc

## Introduction

In September of 2004 a group of people gathered in The Haute Languedoc in the South of France from across the globe. We were practised social dreamers, group relations practitioners, psychotherapists, psychoanalysts and artists. Whilst this is what we did professionally, we were also parents, refugees, academics, swimmers, snorers, drinkers and smokers. We met at the local airport and train station and were driven by mini bus away from the sea and into the country. We drove on a mountain road through ravines with the river either to our right or left. The landscape was dramatic, the driving fairly smooth and the conversation in the mini bus was varied. One of us was recounting how as a boy he had been allowed by his older brother to swim in a river which he later discovered had crocodiles in them. He was very angry and disappointed with his brother—perhaps the first steps in the loss of innocence. Other stories and free associations were told on this two-hour journey.

Finally we reached our destination; a tiered, almost deserted village perched on the side of the mountain with a grand view of the river and the green valley below. The mini bus drove steeply up to

153

the village and we walked to our various lodgings in village houses. The first social dreaming session took place that evening in the magnificent library of the house where we were to meet for the next five days. This session was for one hour. A social dreaming session always starts with one person stating the primary task which put simply is 'to bring dreams and free associations and any thinking which the matrix makes available. Then 'what is the first dream?' The sense of anticipation when we initially all sit together is always exciting. There is typically a silence of up to one minute before the first dream arrives and then the dreams come fast followed by associations and then more dreams and flashes of thinking.

The following matrix was unusual as we were confronted with social dreaming pointing to its 'own nature'. This will become clear as the reader goes on.

The weekend consisted of seven sessions with some activities in between. Each matrix had a number of dreams and associations. The weekend was concerned with understanding how social dreaming might be used in organisations. Such a topic is like a question being posed to the matrix. This was the only organising principle bringing this group of people together.

The following is a detailed exposition, which will quote the key dreams in each matrix and refer to other subsidiary dreams in italics, as well as associations, which were also part of the matrix but not mentioned verbatim in this exposition.

## How to read this chapter

For the reader it may be useful to read the dreams in terms of content, what the dream actually says, and in terms of process, that is, how the dreams follow each other thematically throughout the matrix. These themes also link dreams to associations made by the people in the matrix. An association can be a thought, an image, a story, a word or a feeling. It occurs freely to somebody in the gathering and is then voiced usually with the dream/s in mind. So a dream arrives and participants immediately think and speak of whatever comes into their minds. Thus a tapestry of images and thoughts is built up. The contents of the dreams call up another dream or association and this is the process of social dreaming. There are then themes, which are being elaborated through the content in the dreams and associations. By 'calling up'

I mean that something about a dream or an association may remind you of a dream you had forgotten about which is now being remembered. Another point which would be useful to keep in mind is once the process of dreams and associations starts, we become aware that we are in the presence of a number of created, shared or collective images made accessible by the unconscious minds of the individuals gathered in this matrix. Something larger is being discovered or found.

So I will often say 'the matrix points to this or that' which is a simple way of describing how the collective is being discovered or created in this matrix through the development of particular images and ways of thinking. The word matrix is linked to matter, or 'what matters', in other words, what ideas are embodied in the world. The matrix is concerned with a communal embodiment of our ideas and thinking. By embodied I mean how what one thinks is transmitted into action. We only discover the limitations and difficulties of what we imagine when we put it into practice. We also discover it 'in practice' which enables us to have new thoughts.

On the other hand, you may find it useful to just suspend your thinking and go with the flow. Imagine you are on a canoe going down a very challenging river. There are many surprises and sometimes you just want to give up but you hang on to get to the end. Only then will you start to know the immensity of the journey.

After the primary task was spoken, we barely had time to focus before three dreams arrived in quick succession.

## Too late!

### Dream 1

> I am asleep and wake up. The time is 7.10 am in the morning. I am late, as I should have woken up at 6.50. I can hear Gordon Brown running up the stairs. I have let him down and he is concerned. He may have to go without me. But who will keep the notes, as that is my job. I say to him its okay we still have time.

### Dream 2

> I am late to a matrix to meet Gordon. Appalling—pathetic. 'Get out of bed' Gordon tells me annoyed. It is 9.15. I run to where the matrix is supposed to be but there is nobody there

## Dream 3

*I am going over the primary task and feeling pretentious. A founder female colleague becomes a harridan and starts berating me. I was not sure whether this was a fantasy or a dream.*

## Commentary

In the first matrix the first two dreams are pointing to 'a lateness' or a 'not being on time' as though we may be too late. We are also being told off both about lateness and the about the nature of the task i.e., being berated. There is some anxiety about getting things right. The second dream takes us to where the matrix is 'supposed to be' but there is nobody there. This is then taken further in dream 3 where the dreamer is 'going over the primary task feeling pretentious' with an 'old' female colleague 'berating me'. The idea of 'pretentious' is linked to the primary task possibly of the weekend maybe linked to an idea of inflation as to what can be achieved. We are being pulled up by an 'older' feminine figure. This 'older' figure seems to represent a larger perspective connected also to the feminine i.e., nature and desire.

In the first dream the dreamer assures Gordon Brown the anxious one that we have plenty of time and dream 2 and 3 elaborate the anxious Gordon Brown figure who needs to nail time down maybe and not be late. The matrix is pointing to a tension in the task of infinite versus finite time and thinking. At this point a participant says 'the idea of 'moving' comes to mind'. Things are not where they are supposed to be—maybe they are moving around.

The theme of things not being where they are supposed to be is then illustrated by Dream 4:

'There are two ladies—one young and one old. I find myself waking up in a social dreaming session and Gordon is introducing these two ladies. I am horrified. There is a small baby in between these two ladies. They are kissing each other with their tongues. Where is the matrix'?

This scene of the forgotten baby and the kissing ladies feels 'horrendous' to the dreamer who has just 'woken up' in the dream and asks 'where is the matrix'? The coming together of the old and the new means that the creative is then overlooked or forgotten—i.e., the baby or the matrix. The bizarre part of this is that somehow the matrix through the dreams is noticing how it is being misused. The implication is that this is a metaphor for how we misuse in our civilization or our thinking. Something important is being overlooked. It is not apparently where we 'pretentiously' expect it to be as in dream 2. How do we deal with our limited and blinkered expectations? In the associations it is felt that Gordon Brown 'is too precise, one eyed therefore no perspective or half blind and a flawed or floored man like Frank Bruno who sleeps in his boxing ring in the garden when his wife leaves him'.

Gordon Brown apparently has 'breathing difficulties', is only barely alive and Frank Bruno was 'a brief champion'. The matrix is not about safe thinking and if you think it is you've missed it—it's too late. There is a question here about what the boxing ring represents as it is four sided and gives comfort to a boxer who has lost the feminine or nature in his life. It does not seem to be enough. The box can never replace what has been lost.

The theme of mismatching and old and new is then brilliantly illustrated by the next two dreams.

*Dream 5*

> *'I want to tune up my violin. When I open the case which has been stored for a while I find that my violin has turned into an alligator. How do I play an alligator? I put it below my chin and play it but think what a terrible thing to happen to an alligator to be closed up for years in a violin case.'*

*Dream 6*

> *'I have an alligator which will not fit into my case. It keeps growing.'*

In dream 5 the dreamer asks 'How do I play an alligator?' or as dream 6 puts it how do you fit an alligator into a box especially if it keeps growing? The dreamer does not realise what she has or had which seems dynamic and alive rather than static and kept hidden. The idea of 'growing' is antithetical to a type of thinking which requires 'boxing' or even a boxing 'ring'.

A member of the matrix then relates a story about an eco-feminist who despite warnings went and swam in the river and was taken down in a death role by an alligator. The alligators have not signed a social contract. The eco-feminist overestimated her 'rights' thinking and so violated herself. The violin like a particular type of thinking is a form of 'violence' and limitation trying to trap a particular 'you' which needs to grow and be on the 'move' rather than 'static' in a box. Somebody suggested that 'passivity' was being eaten up by 'activity' bottom up. This would suggest that passive or static thinking gets eaten or broken down by a thinking informed by practice and therefore able to move quickly with an eye on what goes on 'below' i.e., the unconscious.

A similar story led to a swimmer becoming one legged after being attacked by an alligator in a river—the alligator had shown him what he was, one eyed. The crocodile symbolically means 'death striking so life can be reborn' (Chevalier & Gheebrant, 1996, pp. 244–6) pointing to the importance of movement and change, death and rebirth to inform our thinking. Someone comments that we were talking about alligators and swimming on the journey here—as if the matrix had already begun a few hours earlier before we reached the village. A story was told on the journey of a thoughtless man sending his brother into a river awash with alligators without telling him. Is a lack of perspective being pointed to, an overrating of our own power or a need to face the alligator?

The mismatching theme is continued through dream 7 where the dreamer 'is to go to the theatre in the UK but find myself in France'. He is not where he is supposed to be and in the next dream 8 he 'misses the second act of a play' but the whole play is witnessed by a Taoist who says 'there was too much theatre in the event to be true'. He had seen the second act. For the Tao it is important to be 'true to oneself' and this then leads to a discussion in the matrix about how we sanitise our natures and reduce things to enable us to be comfortable. It is then remembered through the discussion how we celebrate sending our children to war at an airport like theatre and how we conveniently cut off our aggressive natures. We miss the second act—the brutality of war itself. The Taoist who sees the second act is 'shaken' and therefore 'true to myself'. To be shaken is to be 'disordered' and to experience 'the unpredictable'. How are we involved in what we witness? How responsible and close are we as the Tao points to what we do or do we prefer to miss the second act? We lie to ourselves, avoiding truth and watching rather than being responsible for our actions. We avoid being shaken.

Many stories and memories are now remembered by the participants. In one association a story of an Iranian woman is remembered who in response to the affect of the Islamic Revolution says 'this is all our fault'. She is making a 'judgement' which is very difficult to bear. Another association however is a story of a Jewish woman who marries a Nazi officer but when he returns from war and she is a working 'Judge' which he cannot bear and so the marriage breaks up. He lacked imagination and could not tolerate it and was trapped in a particular way of thinking which could not bear the feminine judge. Somehow a culpability or a lack is being recognised. A break in the rock of life is being impotently recognised by a woman who also sees the duplicity of this in making women, the feminine or nature as 'faulty'. Maybe, it is suggested, we have been eaten up by an 'alligator' we are now inside it and are being taken somewhere.

Somebody asks why is there such aggression in the world as if it is 'out there' and the response is 'you 'are' much closer to such aggression than you 'think'!' pointing to the lie that exists in a 'clean thinking' which sends young soldiers off to die. This type of thinking is 'brutal' as it imprisons and pins down and denies its 'transience' like Bruno the 'brief champion'. We have become separate from our natures and so lack 'judgement' which implicates us.

The theme of mismatching is continued in dream 9 where *'a seminar is being organised on how to fight where the necessary qualities for fighting are being taught'*. There is a realisation that you need to learn about 'what you can do' and 'what you can speak about' pointing to a gap in the difficulty of academically learning something which involves movement and being in. The issue of embodiment is pointed to here i.e., how one is in or practices what one imagines or thinks. The associations in the matrix point to how we try to sanitise violence or our natures continuing the violin theme. A story is told of an advertising agency thinking of re-positioning the army like Mr Kinsey's to some hilarity in the matrix. An association is that we say civilised things while creating mayhem.

The matrix ends with a dream about an African Bull:

## Dream 10

> *A huge bull is lying on the grass. An African bull. This bull has been dead for two days. There is a blur or mirage over the bull turning into war. I am with Clint Eastwood. I say I have never eaten a bull before. He does not believe it. I look at the bull and the tongue is moving. How do you eat a live animal? Clint says 'You know how you eat a live animal'.*

'Bulls arouse visions of irresistible strength and vitality ... a male impulsiveness.... whose free flowing sperm fertilised the world. In Greek mythology bulls symbolised the unleashing of uncontrolled violence' (Chevalier & Gheebrant, 1996, p. 131). The introduction of Clint Eastwood who represents a non-ambivalent masculinity points to the importance of the denial of the masculine, possibly a one eyed masculinity, where it is forgotten how you can eat and be nourished by the 'alive animal' within. In the associations it is suggested that we live in the era of the 'wounded dying bull'. A sacred father of the world is being destroyed through an 'unknowing violence'. This bull it seems is Africa. Africa is the father of man as DNA research points to the dawn of man being in North Africa. There are thoughts around George Bush and the Bear Market and how he is putting his country into difficulties by creating an atmosphere of primitiveness and violence with no perspective and no father. However the theme which is being developed is about how one type of thinking can do violence to the matrix which is dynamic and not static. This however is a multi-levelled statement as the matrix is also 'matter' or mother/ life so the violence we are doing is on a human level to civilisation.

## Conclusion to matrix 1

This matrix with two eyes to the title of the weekend responded with an idea of 'being late' or 'one eyed' and the importance of remembering how you cannot 'box' an 'alligator' which is constantly growing. 'How do you play an alligator?' asks a violinist who is used to being in control of her instrument. An intriguing relational challenge is put forward by the matrix. Is it possible to make use of something which constantly grows and moves and does not bow down to our need for control, power and pinned down thinking? This is re-emphasised in the idea of the wounded dying African bull or father and how we do not know how to use or eat the animal within in order to retain his two eyed rather than one eyed masculinity and crucially perspective. This matrix not only seems to be making a comment on our current 'one eyed' political world but also responding to the task of the weekend and re-phrasing and expanding the question. The question the matrix is now asking seems to be 'How is it possible to stay with a moving, growing and disordered or disorganised thinking in a place like an organisation, a group of people or a civilization requiring a 'boxing' thinking?'

## The sea is closed

At the end of this matrix we all went downstairs and had a marvellous dinner which we greatly enjoyed as we had all been travelling practically all day in more ways than one it seems. The conversation at dinner involved both the dreams and ideas in the matrix as well as other topics.

At this dinner an incident was remembered in Iran near the Caspian Sea. A group of cousins were sleeping in a villa when they were awoken by a tanoy from a Jeep driving up the seashore announcing very loudly 'THE SEA IS CLOSED! THE SEA IS CLOSED!' One of the cousins upstairs shouted back 'What do you mean the sea is closed? Do you want to change the water?' Perhaps there was a link between this story and the matrix pointing to how difficult it is for us as humans to conceive of the vastness and potential of the open sea confronted with our 'thinking' omnipotence like a regime who thinks they can close the sea. Maybe we constantly close the sea with our minds without realising it.

Next morning we woke up and went straight to the second matrix at 8am.

## The feminine guide

The second matrix starts with the following dream:

### Dream 1

> I am about to move into a new house. Before I view it I realise that it is owned by Terry Cromwell, an old school friend who was very

*primitive and violence was his only language. Shit I think I have got to get away. He realises it is me and that I am in flight mode and he comes after me. I am very frightened. There is an image of a finger/ penis encrusted with jewels around the tip. It starts decomposing as I wake up and there is an image of a random mutation.*

## Commentary

In the second matrix the idea of 'random mutation' in a new house or matrix is introduced in this first dream. We are in a new place as 'random' points to a lack of any definite plan or pre-arranged order. This house seems to be occupied by a violent and primitive man continuing the bull theme and it is difficult to stay with as the dreamer is in flight. There is an image of phallus encrusted with precious stones which feels like a random mutation or unpredictable. An association to this dream in the matrix points to the fragility of the primitive through a story of a cheetah whose brain reaches 104 centigrade when it is accelerating at full speed. However a small change in the environment could kill the cheetah. The brain can only take so much and you have to take some care with the primitive. In dream 2 there is confusion about '*a primitive painting which is black and white and 'could' have been a table but was a cat and was too big for the house it was in'.* Something is growing in this dream or house like the crocodile in the violin case. Can we contain it?

In dream 3 this new house is '*somehow bigger, darker and richer with more shadows'. A woman comes into the room and she is our caretaker and wearing a black swimming costume with long black hair and dark skin. She has two tiny breasts above her collar'*—Crocodile eyes someone suggests. She is obviously precious, as she needs to be protected in the outside world, as the dreamer is concerned to protect her in the streets against the car civilisation or a certain way of thinking. Are we now inside the dream being led by the crocodile or our random natures? By dream 4 it is clear that this random place in the matrix has now so many ingredients that '*a liquid is overflowing and becoming larger and larger'.*

An association which follows these four dreams is that the 'absurd' has entered the arena pointing to the mutation with examples of 'beards' representing wives of gay men. Some sort of transformation is taking place and by dream 5 the caretaker '*woman points to a huge square with a Cathedral* suggesting that a greater consciousness is at hand or just around the corner and we can only just glimpse it from our matrix *'in the back streets'*. In dream 6 after *'a perilous journey up these back streets where the travellers have to negotiate too many 'cars' the square'* is re-found where *'there is scaffolding and a playground and latticework over a large hole'*. There is a circus feeling about the place implying 'animals' and play and creativity. This is a busy place involving a lot of practical doing thinking i.e., in the scaffolding and lattice work. It is also difficult work as in the associations there are to two stories, one of a girl who fell down a hole and did not survive despite all efforts, and another where someone did survive.

The random space is elaborated in dream 7 about *'New York where I cannot get onto the major high ways but decide to go via the local streets* (or *'low'* ways) *and find that I am getting out of the city* (or his head) *quite quickly'*. Dream 8 continues the theme of the unexpected when the dreamer hitchhikes having got lost. *'There are two guys in the car and they are Palestinian. I suddenly become very frightened as they may kill me'*.

If you get lost you could discover some frightening things involving different spaces, languages and cultures. In the associations the 'confusion of tongues' and 'Alice in Wonderland' point to a new landscape where the expected rules are not present. We are being guided by the alligator. Social Dreaming requires you to be lost. This is brilliantly illustrated by the next dream 9 involving the shoal of fish.

## Dream 9

> *I am sitting at the bottom of a pond. There is a shoal of fish swimming towards me or in front of me. Deice—brilliant silver. They catch the light as they circle and there are small messages written on the fish. They however change shape and take off very fast. They change configuration. Quite beautiful to watch this movement. There is something about differential meaning. The meaning changes as they move. There is light coming into the pond refracting and it is quite a display.*

## Commentary

This dream illustrates where we are in the matrix and what type of thinking the matrix is showing us. We look to read the messages on the shoal of fish and then they move and change the configuration 'the meaning changes as they move'. The words 'differential meaning', 'refracting', 'displaced' are people's associations in the matrix and point to how our interest in the 'brilliant silver' means that we become the predator trying to reduce or eat up the message with our minds. In the associations it is asked what do dreams feed on and who eats them? It is hard to co-exist or be with dreams and not do some 'think' to them. It needs courage to stay with them. Transformation requires fear. It is suggested that the fish, a Christian symbol of a complex collective self, may carry the meaning. We have to just go with it. It has the meaning/s. We don't. We are too late. An association is that Alice did not get stuck she was in wonder.

The theme of transformation or movement is now followed in the latter dreams of the matrix when in dream 10 '*a woman is trying to find out how to make her husband understand but when he turns into a woman he still does not understand and she is doubly upset as she has also lost her husband*' pointing to transformation not being about 'sameness'. In the associations it is suggested that meaning is not fish or gender specific but in the relations between them so she needs the difference with her husband between masculine and feminine to discover meaning. An idea of movement and meaning is being played with rather than fixity and clarity. The themes of dark chocolate, shit and dark haired women with dark swim suits, following the caretaker woman in dream 3, are now present pointing to the shaded place the dreams are now in where clear light or thinking is not present.

In dream 11 the question '*of who is eating who*' is posed like the alligator and the feminist swimmer. The thought being played with is that anybody can eat anybody—creativity is fluid and can move in any direction and can feed off anything. It has many possibilities and directions. In the dream the man feels '*not big enough*' for the woman to eat and so he asks if he can eat her instead. He needs to make himself bigger and expand himself. In dream 12 '*the men are being given potions to make their feet gangrenous or greener and there is an Amish father—who decides that fish need to be put into the witch's cauldron to solve the problem of men being useless*'. (The Amish are generally a strict and disciplined sect who keep themselves separate from modern civilisation and wear traditional clothes and farm the land and do not use motorized vehicles or rely on the welfare services of the state (Bowker, 1997, p. 59).

There is a preoccupation with how to make masculinity more accepting of the feminine or a type of thinking more interested in playing and movement. In the associations it is suggested that transformation is not just big bang and drums, it could also be quite pedestrian. It is something you do not what you are. Forgetting is necessary for transformation—suspending who you think you are—your self-consciousness and need for power.

In dream 13 the dreamer is in a happy natural place and her companion says he *'transforms because he can see the dead. The dead want something from the blood of the wizard which is silver'*. The word silver in Christian symbolism stands for divine wisdom. It also stands for the feminine principle i.e., nature, where as gold stands for the masculine (Chevalier & Gheebrant, 1996, pp. 882–3). Magic and the wizard point to a struggle for understanding or being in a transformational space. The introduction of magical thinking in the last four dreams involving witches, wizards, potions and cauldrons is an attempt to find a more transformational type of thinking although it initially starts with showing the limits of wishful thinking like missing the second act. Magic, wizards and witches point to the irrational and darker contents of the unconscious which are incompatible with our egos and day world thinking (Chevalier & Gheebrant, 1996, pp. 1118–9). We need these types of thinking to inform our journey in the matrix.

## Conclusion—Matrix 2

In this matrix the new growing thinking space or house is being elaborated and described. The ingredients of this space are that we are to follow 'the alligator' or the caretaker woman and ensure she is not destroyed by the 'car civilisation'. We should not look for definite meanings as the central dream of the matrix the 'shoal of fish' dream clearly illustrates. It is a description of 'a process' of 'open thinking' shown through the content of the dream. The importance of 'wonder' and the task of somehow trying to find a way of making our one eyed thinking more two eyed, through making our feet more gangrenous or closer to earth, is being emphasised over and over again. The brilliance of the fish is both in their silver but also in their movement, not just one or the other. One needs to stay with the movement rather than trying to find out what the explicit meaning may be. This is why the dead, the cauldron, the darkness and shadows seem to be introduced to remind us of the value of non-brilliant or too much light thinking. Light also introduces a form of 'brief' thinking like the brief champion and the matrix is pointing to the profound density and importance in the shadows and moving meanings which introduce a creative randomness to our minds.

## Thinking sessions

After a short break two sessions followed devoted to trying to think about social dreaming and systemic thinking. The sessions though were it seems informed by 23 dreams and countless associations which had gone before in the previous two matrices. We had already been 'informed' by the matrix.

In this session the idea of bewilderment was introduced where 'everything is in everything else'. There is a waiting for 'a fit' to arrive. In these discussions social dreaming is seen to present us with a problem of 'are we seeing something or is it inside me?' Or is it both? Another question is how do we make order out of all these elements? Can they take many forms or are we discovering an order that already exists? Created or found? It is suggested that social dreaming requires 'a different way of being in the world'. We need to be released from thinking and allow wonder, awe and mystery to come in which is a non-analytic mode. An association is that this new way of being is one of 'movement'. If you try and understand you miss out the unconscious, which is the 'trap' of understanding. 'Social dreaming is about constant movement and being continuously created which is about transformation'.

The Senoia tribe used Social Dreaming to big effect in dealing with all aspects of their lives. They used the most ancient to help them with the most present and practical—they used their reptilian brains—the crocodile. An association to this is a story of someone walking down the street looking for a key to a house under a lamp and refusing to look for it in the darkness out there. The key is in the darkness not under the lamp. Social dreaming is a 'no goal' method. The idea of a goal requires a certain type of conscious focus and so something gets forced into a way of thinking like the violin case. A no-goal method poses us with the challenge of remaining 'unfocused' in order to discover a deeper movement of shapes which randomly liberates us from our obsessional need for control. The 'real' work is to use what we don't know to discover knowledge. We need to discover the new out of the old and like a mutation it is very fragile like the wondrous cheetah.

After these sessions there was lunch followed by a swim in the local river. It seemed that with all the alligators and water around in the dreams and associations a swim in the local river was the most obvious thing to do.

## Far shore thinking

The third Matrix started in the early evening before supper with the following dream:

### Dream 1

> 'A dream I had in Istanbul and had it every night and remembered the fourth night.' I was at the Bosphorus and jumped in the water. I started to swim. It was sensory and very real. I am swimming to the other shore. Europe to Asia. All the while as I am swimming I am looking at the other shore and seeing it. When I get one metre away from the shore my sight goes very blurred even though I carry on swimming but I do not know whether I touch the other shore or not. So I start again and do the same sequence over again several times. I was not swimming back but wanted to keep trying.

### Commentary

The theme of the informing but challenging 'no goal' reptilian task is continued in the next matrix with the first dream when a 'sensory real swim' from West to East seems like a very important thing to be doing over and over again. The far shore of comfort is never reached but always attempted and involves 'blurred' vision continuing a theme from the previous matrix to do with the shadows. The implication is that the main work is in the effort or the movement of the swim in the sensory unconscious and that 'thinking'—the shore— has an elusive quality which can never be tangible or too concrete and cannot be seen properly but needs to be strived towards. Thinking is always changing where as 'the real' is the unconscious.

In the associations a story is told of an English Lord going to his club. He is sitting in the library—a place of thinking—drinking hard, implying the difficulty of staying in this type of thinking place, when he falls asleep and dreams. In the dream he is going through a place of prostitutes and sees a wonderful woman. He wants to stay with her for a long time but the pimp disapproves and gives him a bang. The bang is the butler waking him up and telling him the club is about to close. An association to this is 'I don't want to be a member of a club which will have me as a member' in other words this Lord has met his 'wonder' or the caretaker woman alligator in the previous matrix and a club is too easy. You need to struggle to feel alive rather than sitting comfortably in a static thinking place.

A further association is of a group of Buddhist monks who in their haste to reach the summit of a mountain—somewhere very high—they neglect to bring a spade to build a fire to keep themselves warm and only a monk who is suffering from cancer has the 'presence' of mind amongst the arguments to go back and get it. Like the Tao in the second matrix, this monk has seen the second act through his suffering and pain and is moved and shaken to be self less. The theme of 'being in' the moving space of 'not knowing better' is being elaborated.

An association to this form of neglect, where in order to get somewhere 'high' we forget what we need most, is elaborated through an association to the Myth of Sisyphus 'whose punishment in the world of shades was to role a huge stone up a hill to the top. As it constantly rolled down again just as it reached the summit, his task was everlasting.' A reason given for this punishment of Sisyphus is that he imprisoned Thanatos 'so that no mortals could die' (Ayto, 2005, p. 996). If you cannot die you cannot transform or learn anything. This association repeats the first dream of the matrix about the far shore—that anything worth getting requires an everlasting movement and toil but it also involves an awareness of limitation and death.*('If Faust and Don Quixote are eminent creations of Art this is because of the immeasurable nobilities they point out to us with their earthly hands. Yet a moment always comes when the mind negates the truth that those hands can touch. A moment comes when the creation ceases to be taken tragically; it is merely taken seriously. Then man is concerned with hope. But this is not his business. His business is to turn away from subterfuge' (Camus, 1975, pp. 123–4).

The difficulty of this 'not easy mutating space' is then underlined by dream 2 where the dreamer goes '*into a room to pee but there are no obvious containers to pee in.* The dreamer cannot find relief as easily and when '*finally I find a cavity in the corner, which looks possible, and start to pee into it. Someone appears behind me. I feel ashamed and I stop and soil myself.* There is shame at being seen to be doing something primitive in such a restricted way. A restricted mindset cannot cope with too many possibilities like the violin case cannot hold a crocodile especially if it is growing. There is a violence going on. We need to be liberated from having to put things in specific places. This is associated in the next dream where an organisation is seen to be a trap impersonating itself and becoming imprisoned by its own rhetoric, becoming an impoverished place, rather than moving and becoming creative. ('A parody: a mimicking of another composer author, something so badly done as to seem an intentional mockery; travesty –dying, -died' (Mcleod, 1982, p. 822). A club is a very restricted civilised place and a trap for good behaviour. This is illustrated by the next dream.

## Dream 4

> *A place I was living in with chairs and corners in this room. There were cushions piled up in the middle of the room. A very large snake lived under there. I had meant to do something about it as I may be surprised by it but had forgotten. It suddenly emerged from under the cushions moving from one side of the room to the other and stood up with its teeth hissing. I was looking into its mouth. I call my mother and tell her that I am looking into the mouth of a snake. I realise that this is no use so I ring my husband. Meanwhile the snake crawls back under the cushions again.*

## Commentary

The dreamer had wanted to get rid of 'surprises' but had fortunately forgotten. But this civilised snake or surprise with teeth is living in a cushioned place and an association is of a 'lie' in the dream and self-deception and in the associations we are reminded of Walter Benjamin's gravestone 'the history of civilisation is the history of barbarism'. Something profound like the reptile has been sanitised in this dream like the army who are civilised barbarians—snakes with teeth. Also there is an idea like 'looking a gift horse in the mouth' something not realised when the dreamer looks in the snake's mouth. Something not comprehended means the snake goes back under pillows. It seems that we need to be open to surprises rather than closed to them. We need to keep the sea open.

An association from the matrix is 'What goes on in the pillow civilisation? The pillars of civilisation seem to be maybe two women kissing each other and dropping the baby'—a crude sameness where creativity and difference are ignored. The implication is that like the snake in the pillow dream the pillars of our civilization are based on self-deception.

In dream 5 the question of how we save our civilisation is posed where 'I am at the end of the world' and the dreamer is given 'a choice between the Bible which is boring and Alice in Wonderland which is the one I want'. The dreamer wonders whether it is really possible to save something given the choice between the static and the imaginative and the next dream gives a sort of answer to this question.

### Dream 6

> I am on a beach and some guys come out of the water dressed as gladiators. They go straight past me and up the beach. They are searching for this civilisation's orientation and how it values itself. They go to the church. Are they going to kidnap the vicar? No—they find a small grain of something and put it into a piece of equipment—a piece of modern technology where it starts growing fast. I start running. The power of this thing is making the Golden Gate bridge flap wildly while the whole street is shaking from the shock waves. I go into the church and dive down under one of the pews. Suddenly there is a knock, knock, knock and I wake up. 'I ask the person I am sharing the house with did you knock? No he says'.

### Commentary

It seems that the answer is yes as long as we realise that out of something very small like a dream a vast possibility can emerge. The gladiators who come out of the water like 'fish' are pointing to a 'grain' to discover possibility. A little piece of life with all of life in it.

Something which moves and grows. Our 'Golden Gate' thinking bridge is being made to flap in the presence of this 'knock, knock, knock!' In the associations there is a story of a woman who goes to a Buddha carrying a dead child and she is desperate and inconsolable. Can the Buddha bring the child back to life? He tells her to go to the house of a family who have not suffered such a loss and bring me a grain of mustard. The woman goes from village to village and hears many stories of suffering and loss and realises what the Buddha is telling her and comes back to bury her child.

We need to face the limitations in our thinking in order to open up and be creative and grow like a grain. Suffering and facing 'not easy' feelings within us is part of this opening up. In the associations someone says 'maybe we are at the end of civilisation' but the answer in a different association is that 'maybe it is important to dream about the end of the world. It would be more dangerous if we did not dream it. If you dream it you know you have something to be frightened about. Winnicott said that Vertigo is the fear of *not* being afraid. Maybe in our culture today the terrorist like the soldier captures all our most destructive dreams'.

The last three dreams of the matrix elaborate this theme of 'highness mindedness' where in one dream the dreamer who is being watched rather anxiously by his son and wife as he flies, wonders *'how close could I go before I am unable to come down'*? There is tremendous excitement about highness but in the next dream the dreamer becomes 'unwell' when he cannot maintain his speed and height and in the last dream a plane has crashed and the passenger is *having to walk to the shore which is 100 metres away.*

In the associations it is suggested that all you can do is come to the edge and not get beyond. If you go too far you end up in a cage— you lose touch—like Ezra Pound who returned to America and was imprisoned. There is an association about an updated version of Jacob's Ladder implying that rather than looking up as Jacob did to heaven in Genesis the dreamer has landed somewhere much more difficult on earth. It is a reversal from a high to a low mindedness. Like the dream about the high climbing Buddha's there is proposition being put forward about how to use social dreaming. It is not a 'high minded' place but something much more serious about being able to stay with, being in and exploring 'unwellness', an eternal and profoundly dynamic condition full of change and movement.

## Conclusion to Matrix 3

This matrix elaborates the difficulties of staying with a 'blurred vision' thinking and how we need to live in a pillow civilisation in a comfortable thinking space which is self-deceptive because it professes clarity. The civilised snake is of no use to us as we are unable to live with 'surprise'—we miss the second act. It is too much for us. We try and stay too high but end up feeling unwell. The proposition is that 'far shore thinking' is worthwhile without ever reaching the shore, reaching out without ever feeling certainty. East and West is an apt social dream about movement and uncertainty in the world today and the need to reach out rather than impose. Social Dreaming is pointing to a limitation in the matrix in our ways of thinking as well as the limitations we struggle with as a civilization determined to stay 'high' minded and therefore one eyed.

After this matrix we all went down for dinner. The next morning we started at 8.30 with the 4th matrix.

## The dropped child of civilisation

The theme of highness and lowness are now taken up in the first four dreams of the next matrix where the dropped child of civilisation or our neglected creative or synthetic thinking is being looked at for the first time. What is this unwell neglected place?

### Dream 1

> I am in a very yellow apartment in the shape of a sort of half cross. Very bright. There is a couple there with a baby they do not want. I am dressed in black, like something out of a Van Gogh painting and have a squished black bakers cap on. I can see myself from the back but not the front and find myself running around on tippy toes looking for the baby. I feel silly but realise it is necessary.

The half cross suggests something 'half' not complete. 'Like the square, the cross symbolises Earth, but it expresses aspects of intervention, dynamism and the rarefied. The cross in large part shares the same symbolism as the number four and in particular what relates to an interplay of relationships within the number four and the square. The cross is above all other symbols the one which creates a totality.' (Chevalier & Gheebrant, 1996, p. 248).

This dream sets the scene for our predicament represented by Van Gogh who was a tortured and emotionally vulnerable man who was at the same time extremely creative and needed his images in his paintings to give some meaning to his life. But Van Gogh was also a lonely man—an outsider or stranger—who ultimately committed suicide continuing the Sisythus theme and puzzle earlier in the matrix. The dream though points to a bakers cap—the bread maker—a very basic staple and to a needing to find a vision from the back rather than the front. Only if we find a way of seeing from the back is it possible then to be 'silly' and try and pick up this important neglected child. A view from the front it seems means that the child gets dropped like the women kissing each other in the earlier matrix. You have to change your view to something strange and unusual before you can realise what is 'necessary'.

Maybe the baby can only be found in this way rather than in a very bright yellow place where everything is visible and bright. In the next dream the baby has been found it seems but '*has red marks and small wounds and I find myself feeling very concerned even though the baby does not seem to be suffering. The wounds are like little holes and not deep*'. The dreamer though recognises that even though '*the baby is not my baby … it has to be cured*'. Something greater than individual possession is at stake here. There is a statement being made about not losing our ability to be with the wondrous which is also fragile. The baby is apparently not only wounded but in dream 3 is '*playing with impoverished toys*' which were very difficult to get. The theme of violence is also introduced in a dream where a family on a beach are somehow '*abused by a couple of thugs who leave saliva on their faces*' and this is elaborated in the next dream where the dreamer '*deliberately frightens the baby by sounding like a monster*' and the baby nearly goes under the car civilisation. There is an attempt to destroy something precious.

It seems clear that the matrix is pointing to a very young civilisation who has forgotten to look after itself and has neglected the creative Van Gogh child who is in danger of dying. In the associations it is suggested that the baby is Social Dreaming dropt on the first day and we are working with an 'impoverished psyche' and our creativity has been mugged by two thugs. Thugs are not mind 'ful' but mind 'less'. The matrix is pointing to how we have as a civilisation dropped our mindfulness.

However a further association to the word 'Gremlins' is pointed to and 'devil child' but a look at the dictionary reminds us that Gremlins were 'imaginary imps jokingly said to be responsible for mechanical troubles in aircraft especially during world war 2' or 'any mischievous troublemaker' (Mcleod, 1982, p. 490) which points to difficulty in remaining 'high' without thinking of the earth. Despite the attempts to live in a pillow civilisation we cannot manage to stay there for too long as the Gremlin metaphor points to. There is something greater at work than just our need for control and thinking. This is further elaborated by another association of a 'friend who married an already created family and adopted two Korean children and pasted together for herself a world where people loved her. She was recently widowed'. She had to face mortality. Death stalked her. Again the theme of pretending and pasting and not doing the real work of creating your own family points to how we can not notice our responsibilities to the 'dropped child of civilization' by needing to be in too yellow a room which is again a challenge to a particular type of thinking or perspective.

In dream 5 and 6 our magical thinking is somehow not enough.

*Dream 5*

> *I am in this friend of mine's apartment. She introduces me to a new type of car that can be redesigned and collapsed and we could house in the apartment and solve all our garaging problems.*

*Associations*: Collapsible and instant transformation car

*Dream 6*

> *I am in my car, which is a beetle. It has started to travel so fast that it is out of my control and I give up trying to control it. We reach a square and the trip seems like it has lasted for years. The square is like a Magritte painting. There is an intimation of an ancient temple. The time that has passed is represented by the turning leaves of a book in the wind. I had come to the end of my journey and decided that this was not quite it and so I folded my car and decided to go on foot—which felt more normal.*

*Association*: Things are getting smaller and smaller.

## Commentary

The matrix introduces the idea of the an instant transformation car so we can forget about our garaging problems—the unconscious or our difficulties but despite this mode of transport and the marvellous landscapes we can visit in our minds it becomes clear that 'this is not quite it' and it is necessary to be in a more 'normal' place. Social Dreaming is introducing us to the idea of connecting our imagination to our normal lives. This requires travelling on foot which means connecting to the ground. The implication rather like a Magritte painting is that we need to work harder i.e., look below the surface as there is an intimation of ancient temple, and a book's leaves being turned in the wind. Things are not as they seem and we need to slow down and ponder our blurred vision or just be in the 'blur' rather than the yellow. In the next dream–7, there is 'a concern that if there are too many children(dreams!) then we go higher and higher to get away from them'. Dreams frighten us. There is a paradox of needing to be high to avoid the ground yet needing the ground to feel normal.

In the associations 'yellow' is seen as a form of contamination, cowardice. Another association 'Yellow is the paint they put on the door of people who are dying of the plague'. Yet another association is 'so much in awe he dropped to the flaw—dead from awe'. It is suggested that 'far shore painting' should be the way we live by getting to the flaw or floor where awe and death are a new path to understanding. Somebody suggests that imitation and feigning like Halloween means we are not sure what is normal anymore. Yellow is also baby shit—who cries and shits and does not speak. The baby represents social dreaming. It cannot speak but like the baby it represents the creative and all of life. There is a story of a woman with a beard and a child with a Halloween mask at a supermarket and it is not clear who is more frightening the bearded woman or the Halloween mask. Both seem to represent 'lost souls' linked to Halloween. Somebody asks what is normal? Maybe we are tying to get to the new thinking via the old thinking. Maybe normal is not what we imagine.

The worry about the baby that cannot speak is now elaborated in the next two dreams and countless associations. In dream 8 there is a worry about it 'being slated so the life is taken out of it'(suicide) and in dream 9 there is a concern 'about two prominent group relations *consultants who need to evaluate or put value on the Social Dreaming project'.* There is a sense that all the good things will be devalued or as the dream puts it *'somebody had performed so well, their pay was to be reduced'.* In the associations this is illustrated by the idea of the 'clear skies initiative' or 'clean air act' which are seen as dangerous and brutal rather like sacking somebody by text it is suggested. There is a preoccupation with how the Social Dreaming project can be sacked and got rid of with ease. The enemy is clean thinking. Too much certainty will contaminate the matrix baby.

This dream seems related to a discussion where BT was being discussed—i.e., how do you introduce the idea of social dreaming to a large corporate company like BT. The discussion highlighted the difficulties in 'selling' or 'fitting' social dreaming into corporate thinking where things need to be evaluated. How do you introduce the infinite to the finite without it becoming incorporated and somehow lost. The matrix again is pointing to the title of the weekend and how easy it is to 'misuse' social dreaming in the modern world so it gets lost as it did for hundreds of years. Somebody suggests this is the second coming but in the next dream there is a fear expressed in a dream where a woman says *'she decided not have a baby'.* It is pointed out that there is a fear of the matrix baby like Rosemary's baby—the dreams are frightening. What do we do with them?

An association is that if you do not know how to respond, it can be very frightening to be with children or with social dreaming. Rather like the Van Gogh painting you have to look at it from a different angle. It is suggested that yellow is one united colour and it erases all other colours and so can make you blind which is a form of dehumanization. But people who become blind compensate by using their other senses and it need not be apocalyptic if only one can learn to use different senses or thinking.

In the next dream *'I dreamt of my mother dying. It was the end of her life and I was being made to feel accountable'* it is suggested that you only feel accountable and responsible when you start losing something important. There is an intimation that if the baby is not looked after then the mother or matrix also suffers or becomes impoverished. This immediately leads to a dream about *'Raiders of the lost Ark and the Temple of doom'* and an association to Nazi's. The matrix is pointing to an idea of a lost Ark, Social Dreaming, being raided i.e., overrun with thinking and turned into a temple where doom awaits or something is lost.

The puzzle about how to use Social dreaming in the world is then elaborated in a thinking session about the corporate sector. In this session the problems of the enormity of the challenge become clear as it is discussed in terms of how to 'fit' social dreaming into 'organisational thinking'. This however is a metaphor for how difficult it is to fit an alligator into a violin case especially if it is growing. There seems to be another meaning to this growing which may also be dangerous. Someone suggests that dreams are bits that move among us like atoms through pictures and images which gives us common information. But is it creative or dangerous like the atom bomb? The smaller and fragmented things get the more dangerous they become if we are not conscious of the bits and how they may be part of something larger and shared. This association is linked to dream 6 with the gladiators who come out of the water and are *'searching for this civilization's orientation and how it values itself'*. An unconscious collective is being intimated here. There is then an elaborate discussion about doing a social dreaming matrix in the West Bank and this somehow feels more appropriate and hopeful as presumably there is a sense of 'getting to the flaw' or giving shape to the bits.

## Conclusion to Matrix 4

It seems clear that there is a fear of the dreams. Maybe the reason we fear our dreams is that we are frightened of the enormity of what we may see. The fear is linked to being very uncomfortable and also having to think differently like Van Gogh. Social Dreaming challenges our civilisation as it reminds us of the ancient temple—the temple also being a part of the head and a structure for meditation and orientation of the divine or the infinite. We are living in impoverished times where speed and instant gratification and raiding are more important than 'doing things or thinks on foot' and having to really stay with our human un-wellness or mortality which is creative, interesting and very difficult.

## Losing our collective memory

In this matrix the theme of memory is elaborated. Having understood how the matrix is pointing to how civilisation is afraid of dreaming which is becoming more present in the matrix, the dreams and associations start pointing to how memory is lost and some of the consequences for us as human beings. If you lose your memory you may lose your collective mind.

The matrix starts with two dreams:

### Dream 1

> I was lying on the chez on the terrace where I am staying down below with a large book on my lap. The wind is turning the leaves of the book, which has white beautiful blank pages.

### Dream 2

> I was writing the history of Israel and as I was writing it the book became blank. Has the book a subject? I don't know.

### Commentary

In the first two dreams there are books with blank pages which sound alluring and romantic but in the associations one of us remembers seeing a beautiful white set of geese flying in the sky down the valley which turn out to be a jet plane formation. There is a mirage present. The mirage of beauty is based on a form of violence which casts out history.

The associations then turn to how this belies a terrible 'begging noise' which comes out of 'the wild' from owls or lost lambs or warthogs. There is a bellowing noise or a noise from 'below'. But noises are seen as ambivalent. Some associations see it as an enemy of sleep and therefore dreaming whereas another association is that if you snore it may help you sleep and dream. Perhaps this is to do with how far or close the noise is to 'you'. However it emerges that what may be going on is that the dreams are elaborating a place where 'we dream about having no dreams'. An association is 'I lost my girl to a dreamless sleep—a girl in a car crash' referring again to the car civilisation we live in. The White Book which is linked to Israel is seen as a thinking which is not dream based and so it evaporates or has no meaning because there is no deep memory. Dreams have a 'moving' memory and are not static. In the associations 'Dreams remind us that no matter what you do about trying to make things last something starts disappearing as you write it'. It is a dimension with different proportions in terms of time and memory.

There is a story told of a man and a woman who stop and look up at the sky. There is a bald eagle with white markings high up like a dot in the sky. Another couple stop and look even though it is now a spec and then disappears. The importance of longing—something disappears. An association is the eagle and the United States and baldness. The great eagle is almost extinct in the USA due to hunting. Symbolically the eagle is 'king of the birds and deputy of the highest godhead and the fire of heaven, the Sun, at which it alone dares stare without burning its eyes …. the eagle is also the primitive and collective symbol of the father and of all father-figures' (Chevalier & Gheebrant, 1996, p. 323).

The matrix again is pointing to important symbols like the father who stands for history and perspective disappearing. We are losing our collective memories. As dream 3 puts it the matrix is like an eternal *'trolley where things fall in and disappear'* but maybe it has a memory and this is elaborated in an association to do with witches who wrote in some kind of ink(dreams?) in order to transmit it for the future. However it could only be read if you looked at the page in a particular way. This particular way may be linked to a particular attitude which is linked to somehow 'being involved' or seduced by the feminine like dream 4

> *'There are witches dancing around me and it is very erotic and charged. My mother is very disapproving. I feel like Tony Blair frozen inside like a mountain deep inside I cannot move. It is not necessarily a problem though as a wizard is looking after things.'*

The witches are attempting to seduce her despite her frozen attitude. It is suggested in the associations that we are in touch with clear and present danger but the dreamer despite her inability to do anything feels comforted as she knows that there is a Wizard looking after things. The eternal trolley and the wizard have a secret knowledge beyond the frozen Tony Blair character in dream 4.

The memories which are lost are the uncomfortable ones which involve what really matters—the matrix—or matter. The issue of memory is relayed in the last dream of the matrix about a psychiatrist who sexually abuses a patient and is let off by the judge because the dreamer cannot remember her—a form of paralysis takes over.

## Dream 5

> There was a trial of a psychiatrist who sexually abused a patient and I was asked to evaluate her. I came to see her in court. She was a young blond beautiful patient. I was told this was my patient but I could not remember her. I suddenly became paralysed and found I could say nothing about her. The judge decided that the Psychiatrist was innocent and she was guilty. I go outside and a friend says to me, from now on document everything you do—ME TU YUM—for documenting and giving names.

This dream is like a parable of our situation and civilization where a disconnected type of thinking is the only form of memory we have. A woman in the dream—a feminine figure suggests that the dreamer needs to document everything and suggests a phrase *me tu yum* as the way forward.

In the associations me tu yum is rephrased me and you—yum! This is then discussed in terms of memory and desire. Another association is that lack of desire leads to lack of memory. Memory requires desires or a form of synthesis between conscious and unconscious. If you lose your memory you lose your 'mind' or we lose our collective minds. Someone says like the owl longing for food—the terrible sound from the wild—no food no owl. There is now a feeling that the matrix has lost some dreams and there is a need for them.

For something to be created we need sex or we need to bring things together. If not there is conflict. A white book needs responsible words which mean something which come out of this process. Not writing is also not sharing. There is a loss of faith in writing. My word is my bond did not work for the Palestinians and so words need to be responsible.

## Conclusion to Matrix 5

In this matrix there is a discussion of memory and its basis. How we remember things and what is worth remembering. What is necessary for useful memory and the place of writing and responsibility. Writing is only useful if it reflects a deep memory otherwise it is meaningless and has no 'bonding' in it. For something to bond requires an internal coming together otherwise it is forgotten. The matrix is also though touching on the broader issue or process present in the matrix and in civilization where we loose or forget our collective dreams and how there is a yearning for a renewal—a need to leap forward to a next step rather than stagnating in a deprived thinking place. There is a search for a bold eagle.

## Searching for the big dream

The theme and puzzle of having no dreams is now taken up by the next matrix.

### Dream 1

> I am at the top of a mountain. I ask myself what would I have to do not to dream? I decide that I need to walk down the mountain and let go of each thing as I descend. At the bottom of the mountain is a bridge and as I get close to it the alarm went off and I woke up.

*Associations*: A fear of dreaming a big dream. Managerialism in politics is about a fear of a real dream. Other side of a bridge. A big organ.

### Commentary

The first dream wonders how this is possible and in the associations it becomes clear that the no dream is the no 'big dream' which is being thought about. How do we go from our individual dreams to a 'big dream' without being terrified of the bridge we may have to cross. A big dream is like a big organ and frightening like the bull. Dream 2 then points to the type of big dream we may be in the presence of:

### Dream 2

> I had been in a house in Venice next to the water. There was feeling of vibrations and sound. (The room was like the one we are in now). I woke up and it was completely dark as a huge ship was going past in front of the house. It overshadowed the house hence the darkness.

*It was made of dark steel like a clash of stone and metal. Many vibrations. Part of the ship had huge windows in its body, which I could look through. I saw many people standing together tightly and then the whole thing (the people) moved and turned as if in elevators and were transferred into another part of the ship.*

We are in the presence of a vast modern dream represented by a large ship with canned or processed people on it presumably trapped on the ship rather than moving like a shoal of fish. This dream overshadows our view from the house in this temporary place called Venice which is sinking into the sea. We are dazzled by something which does not represent our situation or context. We are canned or conned rather than free or moving. But it is suggested that the bull is much more tenacious than we realise even though we are in the presence of canned thinking which was also responsible for the holocaust with its clean thinking.

In the next dream the idea of a key is introduced. '*I discovered I had the wrong keys for the wrong side of the parking lot. On this side there were poor people and this had something to do with them—a group*'. If we think in terms of group we have the wrong keys and we are on the wrong side of the car park. The answer *is not* in the impoverished group. In the associations it is suggested that a big iron key is to do with staying centred rather than fragmented. There is a need for a big centring dream where community rather than group is re-found. There is then a dream about '*Glenn Miller*' and the association is that he died in a great ship disaster and another dream about how the '*Campaign Director of Green Peace looks sad*' and in the associations it is suggested that Green Peace had a huge sense of identity and then lost their way. Dreams like Glenn Miller and Green Peace being lost in our modern big dream of canned ships and people. Glenn Miller was known for his 'big band' and Green Peace is a big issue organisation to do with the planet. These 'big dreams' though seem to have been lost.

The idea of being lost is associated to in a memory of the film Raiders of the Lost Ark where the two protagonists only survive at the end if they keep their eyes closed whilst the Nazis look greedily into the Ark of the Covenant. Someone suggests that maybe we will only survive if we keep our eyes closed. The unconscious like 'spirit' in the film cannot be looked at directly and used in this way like the church using religion. Another movie remembered is Minority Report where three woman are suspended in water and used by a bureaucracy for their psychic abilities. They are kept semi-drugged in order to be useful to the machine. We live in a semi-drugged state. In the next dream the idea of semi-consciousness is elaborated in a dream where somewhere *'very posh has a yearning for hot dogs which are felt to be more real'*. In the associations someone says that Roosevelt gave the King and Queen of England hot dogs when they visited. A hot dog is a dog who is alive to his deep intuitive self—man's best friend.

The idea of grandness and ordinariness is now discussed in the associations where our grand ideas are discussed in terms of our limits both in the West Bank and in terms of organisations with their consultants and thought controllers. Anything man made like Venice eventually sinks into the sea. Even Ghandi in attempting to get independence for India led to the partition of India and Pakistan. Our attempts to change things with our minds is a myth. Things and life move on like the Fish and our ideas are left behind.

In the final two dreams of the matrix the idea of what is real and of value is discussed in terms of land. In the first dream a man says *'he has enough without having to buy land around an oilfield'* and in the second dream the *'idea of buying land in a desert is seen to be absurd'*. An association is that in Columbia the locals saw the introduction of a labour system as the work of the devil. Acquisitiveness did not operate in this place. There was a misuse present and it did not have value to the Columbians but did to the acquisitive Westerners. How do we use things—for what purpose?

## Conclusion to Matrix 6

There are a number of thoughts which are emerging in this matrix but the main point seems to be in relation to how we treat each other in the world as a 'group' or as a 'community'? How do we use or misuse what is available? How do we write on a blank page and how do we read it? Have we become blank pages because we have lost access to our collective dreams? Has whiteness and yellowness i.e., clarity a sort of imperialism of thinking—taken over in the name of materialism and rationalism. Are we now ruled by the men in coats who need to can or kill the fish or the creative? Is the nature of judgement fixed or moving?

After these sessions there was a drawing session and then a plenary of all the three days so far. The drawing session was dominated by images of the dropped baby of civilization as well as crocodiles and serpents.

The plenary though continued the main topic of use and misuse in relation to the matrix. There was a degree of strife and difficulty between some who felt that the integrity of the matrix was being compromised and others who felt that some members were playing out a group dynamic. Issues of power and a fight for the truth and meaning were very present in this plenary. An enduring image was of a dream in which the dreamer *'having buried a child has to return because he feels the child is still alive'*. The thought was that something gets prematurely buried or rationalised or pinned down and lost and in this process we miss the process and forget our civilisations future. Social dreaming was the baby re-found.

## The no-goal matrix

At the beginning of the last matrix three members of the group had left. However the significance of this matrix is that it happened almost as an afterthought on the morning of our last breakfast before everybody else left at around lunchtime. The actual weekend conference had ended the evening before with a plenary. So this matrix was outside the title of the weekend which had been concluded. The response of the matrix was that it was suddenly freed up.

### Dream 1

> *I have been lying on a bed on my back—straight—in a big room. Another man had been lying on the bed next to me naked. The room has high ceilings with a balcony and two men are looking down. A naked woman is sitting on me and we are trying to get our genitals as close as possible so we can touch better. Suddenly my ex-wife appears on the balcony and shouts 'why don't you take Frieda (?) instead of this woman?' The women on top of me suddenly becomes crazy, jumps on to the naked man next to me and then back on to me. She does this several times.*

### Dream 2

> *I get back home from this social dreaming weekend in the South of France. I go into the bedroom and wife is naked and has shaved off all*

*her pubic hairs. I am astonished at this and make passionate love to*
*her, which lasts a long time.*

## Commentary

The first two dreams point to this freeing experience. The men and the women are trying to get their genitals as close together as possible and there is an exciting synthesis between masculine and feminine. As the associations to the second dream puts it 'the beards' have left and this 'astonishment' can lead to wild and passionate lovemaking. Once the 'covers' or the 'thought police' have left then it is possible for synthesis to begin. The 'thing' that has left is 'the task', or the men in coats type of thinking.

This is discussed in terms of how difficult it is to be free like Palestine when one is open to the power of Israel to do what they please. As someone says 'it is not so simple to make love in this situation' again pointing to how difficult to is to be creative when a particular type of gaze or thinking is present. The next dream points to how somehow we are now in '*the back of a car which is driving backwards and we are riding the driver'*. Everything has been reversed and the driver is now being ridden like a horse. We are where we should be being guided by the unconscious which we ride rather than determine with our thinking.

In the next dream '*the head explodes where there is a ceremony going on involving a lot of people'*. The head needs to explode for things to move on. The next dream though somehow reverses the metaphor for the weekend i.e., being too late:

> '*I am asleep and dreaming of the matrix and the people in it…. I am in this vehicle and think I must get up because the matrix is earlier. I wake up and see the time and it is very early. I look out the window and it is nighttime with beautiful stars. I did not know there were so many stars.'*

The dreamer is in wonder as he had not realised how many stars there were in the night. Something had been forgotten but something has also been understood i.e., that we are facing something vast and it is not in the 'vehicle' but out there in the night. It requires a different attitude something earlier than we had imagined—something unplanned. To not plan means you are not too late.

In the next dream *'there are only three cards or dreams visible out of possible nine'* and in the associations this limitation imposed on Social Dreaming is being discussed—how we had forgotten the other dreams which have now become present. How we indulge in a form of incomplete sex if we imagine we are the driver going forwards. Something has now become possible. This is elaborated in the next dream where a deck of cards having been thrown in the air *'contrary to all expectations they do not disperse'*. There is a need for the cards to disperse rather than remaining one monolithic deck like the ship with canned people. The cards rather like the Shoal of fish dream need to disperse for movement and wonder to be present. In the associations three images of the serpent are remembered in the paintings emerging out of glass, stomach and a fish's head. The serpent in this context points to the idea of a larger knowledge inside that needs to grow rather like the alligator in the violin case.

There is then a dream about *'stomach cramp on the right side'* and in the associations there is a reference to the aqueduct in the painting session and the idea of the tether i.e., how Social Dreaming requires one to 'hold a pulling' sensation and not to feel the relief of no pain. In the next dream the fragile-ness of holding on to the old and the new i.e., the tether is emphasised where *'something plastic or synthetic'* can lose this connection *'by accidentally severing the link'*. In the associations someone says that the paintings had already been dreamt and so could not be played with—it was already there and all we have to do is notice rather like the old and the new in the previous dream and the stars.

The synthetic can damage our thinking side. A way of seeing 'flounders' and then we lose the fish which becomes flat with two eyes. The last dream of the matrix however is very important. The dream is as follows:

## Dream 10

> I was back at the Tavistock building. A woman who I knew says to me *'Paddy is saying terrible things about you.'* Some idea about reneging on first contract. This woman did the first Social Dreaming with me. I knew something about this contract but had no evidence.

In the associations to the 'absence of the beginning' something crucial is felt to be forgotten. In the associations someone says the contract though is 'with the dream' not the dreamer. In the dream the dreamer says *'I knew something about this contract but had no evidence'*. This key statement in the dream points to forgetting somehow that one knows something because it cannot be held onto in the conventional empirical way—but the dreamer knows it is there. Perhaps this is Bion's 'O' or Lacan's 'The Real' or Jung's 'the archetypal'. Something taken for granted or just 'present'.

Ultimately this last dreams points to a social contract not being observed in the project of the Social Dreaming weekend, in the thought police in our civilisation and culture and the ultimately our blinkered thinking where evidence based thinking—daylight thinking closes many doors and the wonder of the stars are lost. If however we adopt a moving thinking like this last session we are immediately in the presence of the infinite, the democratic and the creative. *It is only when you finish what you think you are doing that something becomes possible and you are on time and not too late.*

## Conclusion

This Social Dreaming Matrix was pointing to its own nature which is one of wonder and expansiveness. It also points to a different type of awareness which, like the shoal of fish dream and the Van Gough dream, faces us with an oblique experience which cannot be pinned down. If you try and analyse it you have missed it—you are too late. It just exists and will then expand within us like the grain of sand and enrich us in ways we cannot know. Social dreaming is not about solving anything. It is merely a bedrock of our collective consciousness which we ignore in our day world. We need to return to this collective knowingness to regenerate ourselves and find new perspectives— moving perspectives rather than static truths. Our thinking needs to sit like the student learning from the task-less master.

Social dreaming engenders a no-goal attitude, which is open: a constant un-wellness where the struggle for life becomes tangible and new thoughts become incorporated in the participants' daily lives. At the beginning of this chapter I pointed to the idea of a 'pure' experience. Pure Social Dreaming is task-less and creates possibilities of creative thinking on many levels from the human to the cultural, the organisational to the family. Every social dreaming matrix taps into deep collective possibilities which can be discovered in that moment with that group of people on many levels. The possibilities expand our minds in unpredictable ways. It does not face us with anxiety but enables every individual to experience, momentarily, the collective. In this way relating to one another is made more possible, unfettered by a pre-occupation with individual selves and more open to a space where our humanity is shared and our worries are collectively faced.

# CHAPTER NINE

# Conclusion

T his research took in dreams from a wide variety of people and places—amongst psychotherapists in London, cultural thinkers in the south of France, counsellors on a sink estate in the inner city, visitors to a literary festival, members of a small community and various others who were simply interested in what could be done with their dreams. The recurrent themes of our research suggested that Social Dreaming:

- reflects psychic processes in wider contemporary society.
- reveals our resistance to knowledge.
- is experiential.
- is problem solving.
- creates an aesthetic space of the imagination.

## What the Dreams tell us about the world

Some dreams are born privately for dialogue in psychoanalysis but, as Gordon Lawrence discovered, when you join the matrix you make contact with something 'out there'. If individuals share their dreams the focus shifts to the social world.

Our findings were complex and diverse but clear patterns did emerge. There was an underlying sense of powerlessness and desire for benign authority: the sense of something ominous happening in the world and at the same time a need for human solidarity. Our impression is that the West is suffering from a sort of mass depression, an 'anomie' of the mind. In crucial ways modern life has become meaningless, dominated by consumerism and devoid of a fundamental sense of what might be good for us. People 'know' that every day, oppressed people are being subjugated and destroyed in the name of progress, globalisation, religion or some other ideology. Our personal lives are increasingly privatised with the disappearance of traditional forms of work and the subsequent breakdown of communities. People are fearful of crime, overprotective of their children and intensely anxious about terrorism. Sociologists tell us we have the most depressed young people in the Western world. The dream material in this book indicates that this knowledge creates a combination of guilt, despair and helplessness which has to be hidden from our daily consciousness. This is a depression which mostly cannot be thought but is frequently dreamed. More hopefully, we found that people seem to be trying to dream solutions to these problems, searching for new thoughts in order to create a different form of moral authority, in racial understanding, sexual relationships and political situations. People dreamed specifically of the need for another language, closer to the maternal order, for a more creative kind of conversation. Concerns for ecology and the natural world were repeated themes. One dreamer suggested that perhaps "it is not a matter of changing the world but of whether we can stop being who we are."

## Fear of change

A repeated theme was of metamorphosis, a Kafka-esque fear of rapid change where something quintessentially human is lost. Age-old modes of communication have vanished, largely in the service of speed. As one participant said, life can feel like a slickly made documentary, all manipulation and no affective content. If our life is a 'work in progress' how can we make sense of it in a fast-changing technological society of quick-fixes, fast forward, cyber-net, channel-hopping, 'virtual' life on the run? Despite the ease of communication by mobile phone or the internet, people describe lonely lives with heightened anxiety—especially when their phone call is not immediately answered. Dreams implied that dreamers experienced what we could call the 'death of the personal' where people are no longer seen as sacred, a diminishing of what Karen Armstrong calls 'internal holiness'.

## Helplessness

The sense of *helplessness* appeared in every matrix. Several dreams featured the loss of the body and separation from the mind. This suggestion that a schizoid otherness—where a part of our selves is cut off and observes us from a distance—has become predominant and entails overdue emphasis on the intellectual and the scientific. This is synonymous with a moving away from the soft substance of female intuition, from care and 'smell' as a form of knowledge. Many dreams warned of danger if we move too far from the imaginary to the symbolic order, away from the containing body of the mother to the colder law of the father. As long as we yearn for certainty, for facts, for measurable truths, we miss the point. Always the real, that 'other' part of ourselves will be unreachable while ordinary not knowing—in the dance, the dream, the symphony, the play—may come closer to reality than scientific truth. Poetry can have a subtle clarity to reveal the ineffable. Music may tell us more about how loneliness feels than any social survey. Just as the dream mixes up experience to convey the complexity of our personal worlds, other kinds of emotional and aesthetic sensibility convey a reality which is otherwise inexpressible in rational forms. We are helpless as long as we rely solely on rational/humanistic forms of communication. We are losing touch with unconscious or poetic ways of being.

## The impossibility of sex

Many dreams described the breakdown in sexual relations between men and women. This was seen to highlight key features of modern relationships—in particular a fear of difference, the crisis of masculine identity, a fear of the female and an increasing difficulty with intimacy (See Chapters Five and Eight). Furthermore, it was remarkable how frequently dreams of sexual difference were found to cover racial differences and vice versa, as if the two were interchangeable.

(See in particular Chapter Five). Repeatedly there was unease about racial difference, fear of racial/religious conflict and guilt about the plight of ethnic groups in war zones, famines and situations of colonialist exploitation. What shone through was that when this material came to light in the dreams, people were able to talk openly about an otherwise taboo subject. Thus the dreams helped individuals to discover what they actually thought with respect to these no-go areas of discourse.

## Knowledge

And yet encapsulated in these themes of helplessness, disconnection and fear was the potential for hope. Our difficulties need to be dreamed into view in order to be thought about, talked about and acted upon. First 'being' and then 'doing'. Amidst the subterfuge and evasion, the dreams repeatedly insisted on revealing our denial, resistance and hatred of taking responsibility. This made way for the possibility of new thoughts to take shape. In the Hay Festival matrix a precious little boy slips away with his whole life ahead of him, a helpless crab warns of the danger if we metamorphose into passive creatures, unable to converse and share our dreams. A boy with shells on his spine is sighted and we espy the sparkling emeralds of wisdom that could give us backbone and strength in an uncertain world. An adult man takes a risk but also shoulders his paternal responsibility. In Chapter Four the determined search for maternal wisdom gleans a source of sweet honey in the rock. Elsewhere, counsellors in the inner city faced pain and anguish in the brave pursuit of self-knowledge via their dreaming selves. Social dreamers in the mountains of the Haut Languedoc creatively dreamed themselves into confluence with the coming together of opposites, out of which wholeness and creativity is possible. Here, harmonious intercourse only becomes a reality with the mutual acceptance of difference. Throughout, there was evidence of the dream as a healing property, as a search for solutions to sociopolitical problems which greatly preoccupied members of the matrix.

## Social dreams reveal our resistance to 'knowing'

An underpinning theme which we observed was of *denial*, something being turned away from, avoided, obscured. The matrix reflects what is happening in the world. A tragedy is being ignored so that it cannot be thought about. Obfuscation is an inevitable facet of trauma because catastrophe cannot be held in consciousness for long. The crisis in Africa, nuclear stand-off, fundamentalist terror, ecological disaster, the transience of our own subjective lives, death in a godless world, the shallowness of the modern world—these are the dark chasms of our age. There are holes and poles but they do not meet, no intercourse seems possible. The precious jewels and real treasures of life disappear. Something of great value from the fully lived day is lost. While precious shells of wisdom are tantalisingly attached to a boy's spine, or to a crying tree or on a beautiful boat, there is some hope on the horizon. Meanwhile, however, the trauma of the dream material has to be split off, as if it is too much to think about. The importance of these findings lies in what they reveal about everyday life in the Western world. Something is being dreamed which we afraid to think. Even our dreams camouflage what we know.

Often we evade what really preoccupies us, politically, culturally and personally. In the matrix people constantly turned away from realities which were staring them in the face. When something ominous is happening in society it may be impossible to think about what it really means. Instead individuals will dream this knowledge, this "unthought known" (Bollas, 1989). This happens despite the body of evidence to suggest that dreams are vital part of our intuition, our creative intellect, our humane caring aesthetic, our bodily thinking, our psychic genera, and our innate self-knowledge.

In an increasingly *paranoid* world people are fearful and suspicious of each other. The dreams frequently revealed a crisis of confidence in the process of sharing and responding to dreams. Sometimes it was hard to trust each other and to return to the perilous subjects of the material. Synchronicity was notable. Dream after dream was about loss, something missing, stolen, avoided. It was as if the glittering sites of illumination were glimpsed and then obscured. An opportunity was being missed to confront the real issues of life, issues which we continually avoid in our fear of what we might find out. Could we be honest with one another? Could we look at what terrifies us? Do we dare to speak our dreams or must they be censored so that we never really get to the heart of things which preoccupy us?

When undesirable parts of ourselves have to be split off—unwanted and forgotten but free to haunt us with guilt or self loathing—the danger is that they are unconsciously projected into others (aliens, foreigners, different ethnic groups) who can be similarly persecuted. Many of the dreams were of outsiders. Perhaps if we want to know what a society is really like, we need to look at the people it rejects— in prisons, mental hospitals, care homes, refugee centres. Thus we witness what people fear inside themselves, the thing which has to be put out of sight and denied.

## Social dreaming is experiential

The experience of Social Dreaming can be an end in itself once the process is divested of the desire to 'get somewhere.' As noticed elsewhere:

> "The unrehearsed freedom of the matrix as a process can pro-
> mote a sense of human solidarity. Social dreaming is a buffer to
> anomie, an antidote to the emptiness and isolation inherent in
> narcissistic, consumerist societies. Lack of hierarchy and com-
> petition engenders a climate of democracy and the acceptance
> of difference. Extending and elaborating the self via dreams can
> create a sense of relatedness. Telling the dream leads to a mosaic
> of associations that connect us to others. We project ourselves
> into the future by trusting the dream and discovering how it
> relates to the social environment." (Clare, 2003, p. 57)

In the words of one member of the matrix:

"It could be empowering to converse in dreams. When I meet people in my dreams, seeing each other on another plane, I wonder if they are meeting me in theirs. Freud said that dreams are a residue of our shared life and history. But what strictly *is* a dream? Maybe it's the interaction between the self and the group."

The timeless nature of a dream overrides boundaries so that many different facets of our shared lives can work together. Perhaps this is why memory can seem so like a dream because past experiences are stored in the infinity of the unconscious and return unwittingly at the sound of a tune, the smell of a flower, or the slip of a tongue.

Thus dreams have the immediacy of a repressed memory and come from the same source. They are our creations but we do not know how or from whence they came. Social dreaming and speaking the ideas which spring from the dream-telling is a way of continuing the dream process; a way of keeping this playful and creative function of the psyche alive and busy, of holding on to this fluidity of thinking. As one participant put it, "This place is a luxury and yet is extraordinarily normal. The space is quiet, gives us time to think and so ideas can move. A thought can grow and there are places—dreams—for it to grow into." Thus, we begin to find this other, 'foreign' part of ourselves interesting. This in turn creates further dreams. We begin to think the unthinkable, the thing we know which could not be thought.

Social dreaming is primarily a process rather than a rational means to an obvious end. It is about what we do not know, there is no final resolution, no ultimate truth. The process — of sharing dreams with others and relating to those dreams — is an end in itself. It opens up infinite possibilities. The meaning of one dream is always another dream. To dream is to be dreamed. The dream contents are broken up and this in turn leads to more material. It involves the suspension of the moral frame, rationality is discarded, and truth can be discovered by abandoning the attempt to find it. This rejection of any rational attempt to create meaning or structure, other than through the dreams, makes for the possibility of new discoveries. By not trying to get anywhere, we do in fact arrive somewhere new. This is the 'creative leap' of Chapter Five, which emerged from a matrix at a literary festival.

In our research in London, Wales and France, we noticed that, even in the face of resistance from dreamers, the dreams insisted on outcomes which were indeed transformational. Furthermore, there was an enthusiasm for the dream forum. People had dreams but they did not know what to do with them. Many participants in the mass dreaming experiment expressed a desire to be involved in this ongoing venture. They wanted to know the results, they wanted to be connected, to know what to do next. The implication here was that there is in many communities an untapped desire to communicate. To express that creative yet private part of the self and to hear the dreams of others, people like them and yet different from them. It became increasingly clear that the criteria for doing social dreaming are not based on intellect, education, social class, religion or any other demarcation. Everyone has a creative unconscious. Everybody dreams and can tell their dreams to others if they choose to. No expertise is required. Indeed, experts who already 'know', inhibit the experience.

A monthly social dreaming matrix can be a meeting where nothing is decided, no one elected, nothing prohibited, no one marked out of ten or voted 'best dreamer', no product bought or sold, no one feared as an expert. People can share their dreams regardless of politics, race or religion. Our unconscious mind ignores such boundaries and so does the matrix. The results of this apparently subversive idea could be both liberating and surprising not just in the world of psychotherapy, group analysis or academia but in the village hall, the community centre, the theatre or the school. Dreams are not just junk mail to be dropped in the bin as soon as they come through the door. They are the stuff of life for the health and survival of self and society. As one dreamer said, "If the dreams are not just remnants, then we are more than the discards."

## Dreaming as problem solving

Dreams provided ways of thinking outside the confines of the orthodox or ideological—the theory which we already know—and enable us to resist the compliant stance of conforming to please others. Social dreaming enabled people to find out what they actually thought about subjects hitherto obscure or ignored and to speak it out loud. As we saw in the Mass Dreaming chapter, dreamers were searching for answers and trying to identify missing elements in the cultural world, so as to find new ways to think and act. They dreamed about what had failed and created devastation. The extraordinary 'Can for every Country' dream stood out as a prodigious piece of night-work from a dreamer who laid before us a detailed exposition of the art of the possible. Such dreams enable the communication of otherwise inaccessible ideas. Charlotte Beradt has demonstrated how different history might have been, had dreams in Nazi Germany been identified as accurate premonitions of the nightmare to come. (Beradt op cit).

*Social dreaming as a creative space for the imagination*

We saw in Chapter 1 the work of Winnicott and the origins of crea-tivity. Here cultural experience begins as play in a space between the interior self and outside world—initially between the baby and the mother. The matrix replicates this potential space with a shared reality that begins with the dream and then goes on to talking and listening. Thus is established an imaginative space where the individual's own aesthetic can be expressed poetically, comically, visually (through dream images) and with their own idiomatic sen-sibility. The dream is our own unique creation. Its recounting can be a poignant experience which moves the listener, as when we hear a Bach fugue or a Miles Davis ballad. *The Crying Tree* dream in Chap-ter 6 touches us in this way. The image of an alligator growing in a violin case (Chapter Eight) conveys the strangeness of experience with the intensity of a painting by Magritte or De Chirico. These dreams are aesthetic expressions of the shared imaginative space which has a potential to change and extend who we are. As one dreamer said, "Reality is more like the dream world. I am baffled by people who see things clearly because things are so complex and the dream world is closer to how reality actually is."

\* \* \* \*

# GLOSSARY

## Social dreaming

Social dreaming is an opportunity to share one's dream with others in a Matrix. The focus is on the dream and not the individual dreamer. The dreamer recounts his/her dream to others in the Matrix but the dream is not only his/her dream for it captures the social, political, institutional and spiritual aspects of the dreamers' social environment. The meaning of the dream develops through the use of free association and amplification to give form to echoes of thinking and thought that exist in the space between the minds of individuals and the shared social environment.

## The matrix

The Matrix is the web of feelings, emotions, thinking and thought that is present in every social relation but unattended and unacknowledged. The Matrix mirrors during the daytime the unconscious processes that create dreaming in the night. It provides a social container, or space, in which the potentialities of dreaming can be explored to apprehend the infinite.

## Associations

The ideas, memories, dreams or feelings which come to mind after someone else has reported a dream or spoken a thought.

# BIBLIOGRAPHY

Abram, J. (1996). *The Language of Winnicott*. London: Karnac Books.
Ayto, J. (ed) (2005). *Brewers Dictionary of Phrase and Fable*. London: Weidenfeld and Nicholson.
Bain, A. (2003). *Not Two and Not One* in W.G. Lawrence (ed) *Experiences in Social Dreaming*. (pp. 60–71). London: Karnac Books.
Baldwin, J. (1964). *The Fire Next Time*. Penguin: London.
Beck, J. (2002). *Lost in Thought: the Receptive Unconscious* in J, Scalia (ed) *The Vitality of Objects*. New York: Continuum.
Beckett, S. (1989). *Proust*. New York: Riverrun Press.
Benevenuto, R. & Kennedy, R. (1986). *The Works of Jacques Lacan*. London: Free Association.
Beradt, C. (1966). *The Third Reich of Dreams*. Chicago: Quadrangle.
Bettleheim, B. (1989). *Freud and Man's Soul*. London: Penguin.
Bion, W.R. (1961). *Experiences in Groups*. London: Tavistock Publications.
Bion, W. (1967). *Second Thoughts*. London: Karnac Books.
Bion, W. (1970). *Attention and Interpretation*. London: Karnac Books.
Bollas, C. (1987). *The Shadow of the Object*. New York: Columbia University Press/London: Free Association Books.

Bollas, C. (1989). *Forces of Destiny*. London: Free Association.

Bollas, C. (1992). *Being a Character*. London: Routledge.

Bollas, C. (1995). *Cracking Up: the Work of Unconscious Experience*. New York: Hill & Wang.

Bollas, C. (1999). *The Mystery of Things*. London: Routledge.

Bollas, C. (2002). *Free Association*. London: Icon.

Bowker, J. (ed) (1997). *Oxford Dictionary of World Religions*. Kent: Oxford University Press.

Bulkeley, K. (2002). *Bin Laden's Dreams and Ours*. www.Kellybulkeley. com

Camus, A. (1975). *The Myth of Sisyphus*. Middlesex: Penguin.

Clare, J. (2003). *Dreaming the Future* in W.G. Lawrence (ed) *Experiences in Social Dreaming*. London: Karnac.

Chevalier, A. and Gheerbrant, A. (eds) (1982). *Dictionary of Symbols*. London: Penguin.

Cohen, T. (1999). *Jokes: Philosophical Thoughts on Joking Matters*. Chicago: University University Press.

DeLillo, D. (2001). Guardian newspaper 22/12/01.

Eliot, T. (1942). *Little Gidding*. London: Faber & Faber.

Ehrenzweig, A. (1964). The undifferentiated matrix of artistic imagination. *Psychoanalytic Study of Society*, 3: 373–398.

Ehrenzweig, A. (2000). *The Hidden Order of Art*. London: Weidenfeld and Nicholson.

Frankel, C. (1989). *The Social History of the Unconscious*. London: Open Gate Press.

Frankl, G. (1989). *The Social History of the Unconscious*. London: Open Gate Press.

Freud, S. (1900a). *The Interpretation of Dreams*. London: Pelican. 1986.

Freud, S. (1913c). On Beginning the Treatment. London: Pelican S.E. 12.

Furedi, F. (2001). *Paranoid Parents*. London: Allen Lane.

Gray, J. (2002). *Straw Dogs*. London: Granta.

Hughes, T. (1970). *New Selected Poems. 1957–94*. London: Faber & Faber.

Jameson, F. (1996). *Postmodernism, or The Cultural Logic of Late Capitalism*. London: Verso.

Jung, C. (1923). *Psychological Types*. London: Routledge. 1989.

Jung, C. (1961). *Memories, Dreams, Reflections*. London: Fontana. 1995.

Jung, C. (1958). *Dream Analysis*. London: Routledge. 1995.

Kristeva, J. (1993). *New Maladies of the Soul*. New York: Columbia University Press.

Lawrence, W.G. (1991). *Won From the Void and Formless Infinite*. Free Associations 2. Part 2. No. 22.

Lawrence, W.G. (1998). *Social Dreaming @ Work*. London: Karnac Books.

Lawrence, W.G. (2000). *Tongued with Fire*. London: Karnac Books.

Lawrence, W.G. (2005). *Introduction to Social Dreaming*. London: Karnac.

Lawrence, W.G. (2007). *The Infinite Possibilities of Social Dreaming*. London: Karnac.

Lincoln, J.S. (1935). *The Dream in Primitive Cultures*. New York: Cresset.

MacMurray, J. (1935). *Reason and Emotion*. London: Faber & Faber.

Phillips, A. (2005). *Going Sane*. London: Penguin.

Plato (2007). *The Republic*. London: Penguin.

Richter, H. (1965). *Dada*. Cologne: Thames and Hudson.

Rieff, P. (1987). *The Triumph of the Therapeutic*. Chicago: University of Chicago Press.

Roth, P. (2002). *The Dying Animal*. London: Vantage.

Rorty, R. (1989). *Contingency, Irony and Solidarity*. Cambridge/ New York: Cambridge.

Samuels, A., Shorter, B., and Plant, F. (eds.) (1987). *A Critical Dictionary of Jungian Analysis*. London and New York: Routledge.

Thomas, D. (1954). *Under Milkwood*. London: New Directions.

Ullman and Zimmerman. (1979). *Working with Dreams*. New York: E. Friede Books.

Unamuno, M. de (1954). *The Tragic Sense of Life*. New York: Dover. 1954 University Press.

Weber, M. (1905). *The Growth of Capitalism and the Protestant Ethic*.

Weber, M. (1946) in Gerth and Mills (eds). *From Max Weber*. New York: Galaxy.

Winnicott, D. (1947). *Hate in the Countertransference* in *Collected papers: Through Paedriatrics to Psychoanalysis*. London: Tavistock. 1958.

Winnicott, D. (1964). *The Child, the Family, and the Outside World*. Harmondsworth: Penguin.

Winnicott, D. (1971). *Playing and Reality*. Harmondsworth: Penguin.

Winnicott, D. (1986). *Home is Where We Start From*. London: Penguin.

Winnicott, D. (1990). *The Maturational Processes and the Facilitating Environment*. London: Karnac Books.

Winterson, J. (1992). *Sexing the Cherry*. London: Bloomsbury.

Wolfe, T. (1999). *Radical Chic and Mau-Mauing the Flak Catchers*. New York: Bantam.

World Health Symposium on Race (1966).

Wright, L. (2006). *The Looming Tower: Al-Qaida's Road to 9/11*. London: Allen Lane.

Zarbafi, A., Clare, J. & Lawrence, W.G. (2007). 'Don't Explain, Just Go' in W.G. Lawrence *Infinite Possibilities of Social Dreaming*. London: Karnac Books.

Zizek, S. (2001). *Welcome to the Desert of the Real*. New York: Wooster Press.

# INDEX

205